# OXFORD THEOLOGY AND RELIGION MONOGRAPHS

T0355157

# OXFORD THEOLOGY AND RELIGION MONOGRAPHS

# Non-Identity Theodicy

*A Grace-Based Response to the
Problem of Evil*

VINCE R. VITALE

OXFORD
UNIVERSITY PRESS

## UNIVERSITY PRESS

Great Clarendon Street, Oxford, OX2 6DP,
United Kingdom

Oxford University Press is a department of the University of Oxford.
It furthers the University's objective of excellence in research, scholarship,
and education by publishing worldwide. Oxford is a registered trade mark of
Oxford University Press in the UK and in certain other countries.

First published 2020
First published in paperback 2023

Published in the United States of America by Oxford University Press
198 Madison Avenue, New York, NY 10016, United States of America

British Library Cataloguing in Publication Data
Data available

Library of Congress Cataloging in Publication Data
Data available

ISBN 978–0–19–886422–6 (Hbk.)
ISBN 978–0–19–284517–7 (Pbk.)

DOI: 10.1093/oso/9780198864226.001.0001

*For Luca—*

*our light who shines out of the darkness*

# Preface

In one of the first substantial conversations I had on the topic of suffering, my aunt Regina expressed to me how difficult it was to see her son, Charles, struggle with a profound disability. Putting the question before the questioner, I began spouting some of my abstract, philosophical ideas about why God might allow suffering. After listening very graciously, Aunt Regina turned to me and said, "But Vince, that doesn't speak to me *as a mother.*"

Since that conversation I have been convinced that questions as personal as those about suffering require a very personal response. But when as a graduate student I began to dig deeply into the literature on "the problem of evil," that is not generally what I found. I found many abstract discussions of greater goods, maximization of value, and best possible worlds. Sometimes these discussions were cashed out in terms of an economic model whereby costs are evaluated primarily for their instrumental use in increasing profit. Other times they leaned on aesthetic analogies—ugly brown blotches can make an impressionist painting more beautiful when viewed as a whole.

But while cost-benefit analyses may be useful in economics and ugly brown blotches may befit impressionist painting, it should unsettle our thinking when the costs and blotches are people's lives being torn apart. So as I approached the dissertation stage of my doctoral work, I was in search of a different type of response to the problem of evil. With Aunt Regina still in mind, I worried that the most popular theories depicted God as at best an impartial bureaucrat and at worst a utility fanatic, rather than as a loving parent concerned first and foremost for his children. My wife Jo and I recently had our first child—Raphael. The depth of our love for him is difficult to articulate fully because it is so particular to *him*. The question "Why do you love your child?" barely makes sense to us. "What do you mean *why* do we love him? He's our child; we made him; he's in our image; he has my nose!" That's enough to justify our love for him. That's more than enough.

Our love for Raphael is not conditional on how impressive he is, how good looking he is, or how productive he will be for society or for the family business; it is not even conditional on how good of a person he will grow up to be. None of that would affect the measure of my love for him or my desire for him to exist as my child. If I were offered a genetically enhanced superbaby in his stead (now only barely science fiction)—one who would accomplish more, suffer less, and make fewer mistakes—I would have no interest. No one could get me to make that trade. There is an intense particularity to the best forms of love. This is equally true of my marriage to Jo. "For better *or* for worse," I pledged. In other words, even if life were to be worse overall, I would rather be worse off with Jo than better-off with anyone else.

If God's parental love is particular and unconditional in this way, then there is something amiss about insisting that God ought to have created a *better* world. As a loving parent, God's primary creative desire would not have been for some general type of world. His primary desire would have been for particular individuals, created in his image, loved unconditionally and for their own sakes. I have come to believe that God created this world because he loves you and the people you love and every person you see walking down the street.

But why not create *us* better? Well, perhaps easier asked than done. In a moment of deep sadness, I might wish that God had created me as a happy little butterfly. But, of course, this is an incoherent complaint. *I* couldn't have been a butterfly. Likewise, in a moment of frustration with me, Raphael might one day wish that Jo had wound up with a different guy. But in his rashness to find a better dad, Raphael would be forgetting that any child produced by a different couple would not have been him. How much can our circumstances deviate and still result in *us*? Perhaps not as much as we sometimes assume.

This thought can be made even more concrete. A couple of years ago a dear friend of mine and Jo's, Naomi, suffered a miscarriage. Some people said, "You already have three beautiful children; you have so much to be thankful for." But that was not comforting. No amount of *other* children would have been comforting. There was a fierce particularity to Naomi's love; she had a Christ-like longing for the *one* who was lost.

Not long afterward Naomi became pregnant again, and she had a beautiful baby boy. Jo and I were honored to be present at his dedication, and just before he was dedicated Naomi spoke these words to her baby:

> [Son], you were longed for—an answer to a prayer and to more than a prayer. Standing by us right now is a weeping willow tree that lights up each night in remembrance of a little one I carried before you. Often now, as I stare at your face and memorize your features, I am reminded that you are this magnificent, beloved life that came from loss, because of loss. You were given to us in months when I would have still carried another, but for loss. We grieved, and will always grieve the one we did not meet. But nor can I imagine life without you. And so we live in that space that most often we don't have the awareness to know we stand in. But this time we do—the tension of bearing loss that remains while holding the beautiful life that is not in spite of it but through it. And what a treasure you are to my arms, my heart, my soul.

Often we wish we could take suffering out of our world while keeping everything else the same, but it doesn't work that way. What we love is intricately interwoven with the contingent features of the world we inhabit. Sometimes we very understandably wish that the world had been different. But, in doing so, we may be unwittingly wishing ourselves—and those we love—right out of existence.

Once we realize this, the complaint that God ought to have created a better world falls flat. God wasn't after a *better* world; he was after *you*. And you wouldn't have benefited from a better world because you wouldn't have been there to enjoy it. The problem of evil is thereby reframed in the form of a question: Could God have wronged us by creating a world in which we came to exist and are offered eternal life rather than creating a different world in which we never would have lived?

Some people would say that, because of the suffering caused by his disability, it would have been better if my cousin Charles had never existed. Then there would have been less suffering overall; the world would be better-off. I adamantly disagree. It is because I knew Charles intimately that his suffering was so frustrating, but it is also because I knew Charles intimately that I can understand why God loves him so deeply and why God would value a world that allowed for him to have life and to be offered eternal life.

Why didn't God create a very different world? When this world fell into ruin, why didn't God give up on it and start over? Well, it depends on what God values, and what if one of the things he values—greatly and individually and unconditionally—is every one of us?

These are some of the ideas that I explore philosophically and theologically, and much more rigorously, in what follows. My hope is to develop an explanation of suffering that depicts God not primarily as an impartial maximizer of goods, value, or worlds, but with parental love for particular individuals, including you and me and my cousin, Charles. My deeper hope is for the theoretical work done here to undergird a posture toward suffering that behooves the personal nature of the questions it raises, as well as responses to those questions that can be heard by my aunt, Regina, as a mother.

# Acknowledgments

So many people have supported this project far beyond their obligation and my desert. Among them are Max Baker-Hytch, Isaac Choi, Eric Gregory, Hans Halvorson, Allison Hamilton, Matthew Lee, Brian Leftow, Michael Lloyd, Tim Mawson, Michael Murray, Martin Noble, Ben Page, Derek Parfit, Randy Pistor, Alexander Pruss, Markcus Sandanraj, Jeffrey Stout, Eleonore Stump, Richard Swinburne, and Mark Wynn.

The generosity of mentorship and friendship extended to me by Marilyn and Bob Adams was extravagant beyond measure and stunningly selfless. Never before or since have I witnessed such intentionality and integrity of supervision. This book owes its existence to their grace.

This book also owes its existence to the exceptional Daniel M. Sachs whose suffering led to the establishment of the Daniel M. Sachs Class of 1960 Graduating Scholarship, which in turn enabled the initial development of some of this project's key ideas. With deep gratitude to Dan and to the Sachs community am I reminded of how dependent I am on the lives of others.

I appreciate so much that the Issachar Fund saw value in this project and through their generous support have made it more accessible to readers. I am also very thankful to the Editors of *Philosophia Christi* and *Mind*, respectively, for their permission to republish parts of my article "Non-Identity Theodicy" (which first appeared in *Philosophia Christi* 19 (2) 2017: 269–290, www.epsociety.org) and my review of Eleonore Stump's *Wandering in Darkness: Narrative and the Problem of Suffering* (which first appeared in *Mind* 122 (488) 2013: 1193–1201).

Thank you, Vincent and Carla, for longing to love me even before I existed. Thank you, Jo, for your commitment to love me even when existence is tough. Thank you, Raphael, for filling existence with joy. Thank you, God, for making existence possible and true life eternal.

# Contents

# PART I
# A FRAMEWORK FOR THEODICY

# 1

# Introduction

## The Problem of *Horrendous Evils*

There might be a God. If there is, he is—*ex hypothesi*—a being than which there can be no more perfect. Such a being would be—inter alia—omniscient, omnipotent, and ethically perfect. There are evils; an evil is understood as any bad state of affairs. Arguments from evil in contemporary analytical philosophy of religion, standardly termed *problems of evil*, are attempts to show that the existence of evils makes the existence of God either impossible or improbable.

One way to respond to problems of evil is to specify reasons God could have for allowing the relevant evils that are consistent with maintaining divine perfection. Attempts to specify such reasons range from those that purport to show the mere logical compatibility of God's existence with the existence of some stipulated evils—typically termed *defenses*—to those that purport to show that the probability of the existence of God is in no way diminished by the existence of the stipulated evils. This project is concerned with *theodicy*, where theodicy is understood as any attempt to specify possible divine reasons for allowing evils that would be supposed to be successful in rebutting arguments to the effect that the existence of evil leaves the existence of God with a very low probability.[1] As such, I won't be treating mere logical *defenses* at any length. That it is logically possible that you have an identical twin of whom there is no record, who lives on a deserted island, and who committed the crime you are charged with would not carry significant weight in a courtroom.

---

[1] "Theodicy" is used in a variety of ways in the literature. My use of "theodicy" differs from Alvin Plantinga's, for instance. Plantinga counts something as a theodicy only if it purports to give God's actual reasons for causing or permitting the evils in question. A theodicy in Plantinga's sense may or may not count as a theodicy in my sense. One might believe on the basis of revelation or tradition that God's actual reasons for allowing the suffering of this world have much to do with the sins of angels, but might not expect those who press problems of evil to take this line of thought seriously. In that case, one might offer a theodicy in my sense that is different from one's theodicy in Plantinga's sense. As I use the term, the theodicist does not need to claim to *know* that the reasons proposed by her theodicy are in fact among God's reasons. She only needs to claim that *for all we know* they are among God's reasons and that, if they are among God's reasons, they plausibly depict God as loving and morally perfect despite his allowance of evil and suffering. Cf. Alvin Plantinga, *God, Freedom, and Evil* (New York: Harper and Row, 1974), 10; Alvin Plantinga, "Self-Profile," in *Alvin Plantinga*, ed. James E. Tomberlin and Peter van Inwagen (Dordrecht: D. Reidel Publishing Company, 1985), 35.

*Non-Identity Theodicy: A Grace-Based Response to the Problem of Evil.* Vince R. Vitale, Oxford University Press (2020).
© Vince R. Vitale.
DOI: 10.1093/oso/9780198864226.003.0001

This project also leaves to one side the extent to which successful theodicy is necessary for the rationality of theism. This will depend, in part, on the prospects of *skeptical theism*—roughly, the position that not being able to imagine the reasons a God would have for allowing certain types of evil is not good reason to think a God would not have such reasons—and on whether there are positive arguments for the existence of God that provide more reason for believing God exists than problems of evil do for believing God does not exist. For my part, I am inclined to agree with Richard Swinburne that many will need a theodicy[2] and with Eleonore Stump that even the theist who in no way becomes anxious about the rationality of his belief in God may "still be weakened in his religious belief by the consideration that the deity in whom he is to place his *trust* seems to act in ways which are unintelligible to him at best and apparently evil at worst."[3]

## Successful Theodicy

For a theodicy to be successful, I hold it must meet at least three primary conditions. Firstly, it must depict God as meeting all of his moral obligations. I assume moral obligations exist only between persons, and that meeting all of one's moral obligations is coextensive with not wronging (i.e. violating the rights of) anyone. Unless otherwise noted, when I use terms such as *morality* and *moral*, I refer only to the part of ethics having to do with moral obligations.

Secondly, a successful theodicy must not only depict God as being within his rights, but also as having a flawless character. Robert Adams urges the distinction between this condition and the first:

> It might be claimed that even if no one would be wronged or treated unkindly by the creation of an inferior world, the creator's choice of an inferior world must manifest a defect of character...The perfectly good moral agent must not only be kind and refrain from violating the rights of others, but must also have other virtues. For instance, He must be noble, generous, high-minded, and free from envy. He must satisfy the moral ideal.[4]

Conversely, showing oneself to be ideally virtuous does not excuse one from the charge of having acted contrary to moral obligation. Evaluations of character

---

[2] Richard Swinburne, *Providence and the Problem of Evil* (Oxford: Oxford University Press, 1998), 17.

[3] Eleonore Stump, "The Problem of Evil," *Faith and Philosophy* 2 (1985): 395.

[4] Robert Merrihew Adams, "Must God Create the Best?," *The Philosophical Review* 81 (1972): 318, 323 (conflated). Another way of seeing this distinction is by conceiving of ethically deficient ways to spend a lifetime where you are the only sentient creature and you know it to be so, say, by spending all day everyday drinking intoxicants and wrecking the scenery.

depend significantly on the intentions of the agents in question, but some of the best-meaning people can do things seriously wrong. Ignorance or bad reasoning, for instance, may cause them to wrongly discern what they are obliged to do in any particular instance.

One note of the ethical ideal that I will emphasize in my consideration of divine character is that of being ideally loving. This emphasis is important for theodicy because harm does not clearly presuppose moral obligation and yet is *ceteris paribus* at odds with love. It is not obvious whether my nephew has any moral obligations to mice, for example. But if he harms them by cutting them open for fun, it is very reasonable to conclude that he doesn't love them.[5] Similarly, if God has harmed us or allowed us to be harmed, then—independently of whether he has wronged us—this calls into question whether he could be said to love us with the steadfast concern for our well-being that a perfect lover would have.

For a theodicy to be successful, I hold, it must depict God as ideally loving, and I further specify that God's ideal love must be not just a love for the world as a whole or for humanity in general, but a particular love for individual persons. An omnipotent, omniscient, ethically perfect being would not only satisfy any obligations of his but would reach out in love to each created person.

If a theodicy meets both of the first two criteria, I say that it is *structurally promising*—that is, *if* the story of divine creation and sustenance of the universe proposed by the theodicy were true, God would be ethically in the clear. Lastly, for a theodicy to be successful, it must be not otherwise implausible. Its claims, for instance, must not be at odds with what we know historically or scientifically, and any claims of metaphysical necessity must be not implausible.

## The Problem of Any Evil at All

This project is concerned with evaluating the prospects for successful theodicy in response to the problem of *horrendous evils* in particular. The rest of this introduction situates this problem amidst other problems of evil and suggests why it is particularly worthy of philosophical attention.

The canonical argument from evil—often referred to as the *logical problem of evil*—attempts to show that it is irrational to believe in the existence of both God and any evil at all because the coexistence of God and evil can be readily shown to be logically contradictory. According to the argument, there is a hidden contradiction between

---

[5] To take a second example, even if we do not violate the rights of a beggar as we pass by him without acknowledging him, it is fair to say we have not acted lovingly toward him.

(1) God exists and is omnipotent, omniscient, and ethically perfect.

and

(2) Evil exists.

that can be deduced by adding the further corollaries

(3) An ethically perfect being always tries to eliminate evil so far as it can.

and

(4) An omnipotent, omniscient being who tries to eliminate evil so far as it can, eliminates all evil.[6]

Now there is an inconsistent quadruplet. The truth of any three entails the denial of the fourth.

But offering a theodicy for this logical problem of some evil or other has proven practicable. The main approach is to question (3). As Nelson Pike has indicated, (3) is underdetermined because "as a general statement, a being who permits or brings about an instance of suffering might be perfectly good providing only that there is a morally sufficient reason for his action."[7] Moreover, it seems highly likely that a God would have morally sufficient reasons—like any caring parent—for bringing about or permitting at least *some* types of evils, for example a moderate amount of just punishment or certain evils intimately connected with character formation.


## The Problems of Actual Evil


Much more difficult to solve are the problems of the evil of the actual world.[8] Maybe a God would have morally sufficient reason for bringing about or allowing some evil or other, but is it possible for a God to create and sustain the degree and distribution of *all* extant evil? It is more difficult to justify the divine causation or permission of certain evils of the actual world than of others. Some of the hardest cases include seemingly pointless suffering, the sheer global quantity of evil, and unjust suffering. Even here, theodicists have offered some not implausible reasons why an ethically perfect, all-powerful, and all-knowledgeable being might allow such

---

[6] For a similar formulation of the argument, see J. L. Mackie, "Evil and Omnipotence," in *The Problem of Evil*, ed. Marilyn McCord Adams and Robert Merrihew Adams (New York: Oxford University Press, 1990), 25–6.

[7] Nelson Pike, "Hume on Evil," in *The Problem of Evil*, ed. Marilyn McCord Adams and Robert Merrihew Adams (New York: Oxford University Press, 1990), 41.

[8] Though they often are not, I think these problems should still be considered "logical" problems of evil. I refer to as logical any argument from evil to the impossibility of God's existence in the actual world. Most so-called "logical" and "evidential" arguments from evil satisfy this requirement. Paul Draper's probabilistic argument is a notable exception. See Paul Draper, "Pain and Pleasure: An Evidential Problem for Theists," in *The Evidential Argument from Evil*, ed. Daniel Howard-Snyder (Bloomington and Indianapolis: Indiana University Press, 1996), 12–29.

evils, many of which I will explore in Chapters 3 and 4. However, this method of beginning with any evil at all and working toward more problematic evils has tended to keep the very worst evils on only the horizons of most theodicies.[9]

## *Horrors* Defined

Marilyn Adams tries to capture the worst evils within the category of *horrendous evils* or *horrors*. She defines *horrors* as follows:

> H1: *Horrors* are evils the participation in which (that is, the doing or suffering of which) constitutes *prima facie* reason to believe that the participant's life (given their inclusion in it) cannot be a great good to him/her on the whole.[10]

While not explicit about this in her definition, Adams understands *horrors* to be suffered exclusively by persons, or, at least, by other animals only insofar as they approach the personal. This understanding is motivated by the thought that participation in grave evils is particularly bad for those who are meaning-makers— those with the potential to find, reflect on, and construct significant personal meaning in their lives. This focus on meaning-makers is reflected in Adams's common shorthand definition of *horrors*:

> H2: *Horrors* are *prima facie* life ruining evils, in the sense that they *prima facie* destroy the positive meaning of one's life.

Finally, Adams suggests that *horrors* find their measure in the fact that

> H3: *Horrors* are so bad that nothing within our power or within the scope of any package of merely created goods could balance-off or *defeat* them.[11]

---

[9] Marilyn Adams agrees: "In my judgment, excessive focus on the abstract logical problem has combined with the tendency to construe the difference between logical and evidential problems in terms of amounts, to distract philosophers from engaging the problems raised by evils of the very worst types" (Marilyn McCord Adams, "Afterword," in *Encountering Evil*, ed. Stephen T. Davis (Louisville and London: John Knox Press, 2001), 193).

[10] Marilyn McCord Adams, *Horrendous Evils and the Goodness of God* (Ithaca: Cornell University Press, 1999), 26.

[11] See, for instance, *Horrendous Evils and the Goodness of God*, 82, 205. A horror would be *defeated*, in Roderick Chisholm's technical sense that Adams references here, if it (or something as bad as it) were a logically indispensable constituent of some complex good state of affairs that is at least as good as the state of affairs obtained by replacing the *horror* with its neutral negation. The concept of *defeat* has a useful analogy in visual arts, where for example a painting can be more beautiful overall due to the inclusion of a portion that, when viewed in isolation, is ugly. Cf. Roderick Chisholm, "The Defeat of Good and Evil," in *The Problem of Evil*, eds. Marilyn McCord Adams and Robert Merrihew Adams (Oxford: Oxford University Press, 1990), 53–68. See also additional material in Chisholm's earlier version "The Defeat of Good and Evil," *Proceedings and Addresses of the American Philosophical Association* 42 (1969): 21–38.

The criterion is objective but relative to individuals.[12] It is person-relative in two senses. Firstly, people are endowed with different strengths, and therefore different evils will be *prima facie* life-ruining for different people. In Adams's concise phrasing, "one bears easily what crushes another."[13] Secondly, a person's own estimate of whether his life is worth living—though by no means incorrigible—is to be given serious weight in the overall objective judgment.

Paradigmatic examples of *horrors* include both individual and massive collective suffering: the rape of a woman and axing off of her arms, psycho-physical torture whose ultimate goal is the disintegration of personality, betrayal of one's deepest loyalties, child abuse, child pornography, parental incest, the accidental running over and killing of one's own child, the explosion of nuclear bombs over populated areas, slow death by starvation as a crowd of billions look on with indifference, et cetera.[14]

Adams's category of the *horrendous* could be understood to contain within it Simone Weil's category of *affliction*, which "deprives its victims of their personality and turns them into things…They will never find warmth again. They will never again believe that they are anyone."[15] *Horrors* give reasons to doubt whether one's life could be worth living because it is so difficult humanly to conceive how they could be overcome. Their destructive power reaches far beyond their concrete disvalue, destroying meaning-making capacities at the most fundamental levels, engulfing the positive values of human life, and thereby symbolically degrading their participants to sub-human status.[16] Participants in *horrors* are often left with strong reason to believe that their lives can never again be unified and integrated into wholes with positive meaning.[17]

## The Problem of *Horrendous Evils*

I affirm Adams's strategy of homing in on *horrendous evils*, which I take to be particularly threatening to the project of theodicy. *Horrors* are unique because not only do we know that they exist but also there is a widespread and strong intuition that there is an absolute (or near absolute) moral prohibition against the intentional causation of them. By contrast, causing human persons to suffer

---

[12] Adams, *Horrendous Evils and the Goodness of God*, 27. See also Marilyn McCord Adams, "Horrendous Evils and the Goodness of God," in *Philosophy of Religion: The Big Questions*, ed. Eleonore Stump and Michael J. Murray (Oxford: Blackwell Publishers Ltd, 1999), 252.

[13] Adams, *Horrendous Evils and the Goodness of God*, 27.

[14] Some but not all of these examples are taken from Marilyn Adams. See *Horrendous Evils and the Goodness of God*, 26.

[15] Simone Weil, "The Love of God and Affliction," in Simone Weil, *On Science, Necessity, and the Love of God*, ed. Richard Rees (London: Oxford University Press, 1968), 175.

[16] Adams, *Horrendous Evils and the Goodness of God*, 26–7.

[17] Adams, *Horrendous Evils and the Goodness of God*, 148.

pointless evils may be universally morally prohibited, but we don't know that any actual evils are pointless. We do know that painful evils exist, but their causation is not universally morally prohibited, for example when a dentist drills inside one's mouth to attain the greater good of healthy teeth. *Horror* perpetration is generally condemned regardless of its utility, as when a dictator ends a long war by publicly and severely torturing a few individuals, and *horrors* are thought by many to be too cruel and degrading to act as just punishments.[18] The intuitions at work where *horrors* are concerned call into question whether any being could have a morally sufficient reason for causing or permitting them. Thus, *horrors* threaten to reload the canonical problem of evil. Substitute "*horrors*" for "evil" and (3) becomes exceedingly more compelling.[19]

Any fully successful theodicy must account for *horrors*—even the worst *horrors*—but *horrors* appear immune to standard approaches.

## The Insufficiency of Greater Goods Solutions

Focus on *horrendous evils* generates a distinction between two dimensions of ethical perfection in relation to creation: "producer of global goods" and "goodness to or love of individual created persons."[20] Since *horrors prima facie* ruin individual lives, they call into question God's ethical perfection not merely in relation to the world as a whole but in relation to each created *horror*-participant. With Adams, I take divine love to include love of each and every created person. In a *horror*-laden world, then, the ways of God with respect to evil cannot be justified on the level of world-value alone.

Gottfried Leibniz, Nelson Pike, Alvin Plantinga, and other best-try theodicists claim that the world we have may be the result of God trying to make the best possible world he could, where the value of the world is judged according to the aggregate value of its features. For Leibniz and Pike, that would be the best-possible-world *simpliciter*; for Plantinga, the best world that it was in God's all-things-considered power to weakly actualize.[21] They reason—not

---

[18] Cf. Article 5 of the *Universal Declaration of Human Rights*, adopted by the United Nations General Assembly on December 10, 1948.

[19] Simone Weil takes a similar line: "The great enigma of human life is not suffering but affliction. It is not surprising that the innocent are killed, tortured, driven from their country, made destitute, or reduced to slavery, put in concentration camps or prison cells, since there are criminals to perform such actions. It is not surprising either that disease is the cause of long sufferings, which paralyze life and make it into an image of death, since nature is at the mercy of the blind play of mechanical necessities. But it *is* surprising that God should have given affliction the power to seize the very souls of the innocent and to possess them as sovereign master. At the very best, he who is branded by affliction will only keep half his soul" ("The Love of God and Affliction," 171–2).

[20] Adams, *Horrendous Evils and the Goodness of God*, 29.

[21] According to Plantinga, God's choice is constrained by Molinist truths. Molinism is the view that there is a true counterfactual corresponding to every possible situation in which a possible free creature is faced with a free decision, and that God knows the truth values of all of these counterfactuals.

implausibly—that it is possible that the best world God can get contains evils, even many and great evils, as logically indispensable constituents. To use Adams's analogy, they think the actual world is like an impressionist painting that is better on the whole for its inclusion of some ugly brown blotches.[22] But they then make the following assumption: An agent is always morally permitted to bring about the best state of affairs she can.[23]

Focusing on *horrendous evils* exposes the dubiousness of the assumption. As Adams puts it, "Where entrenched horrors are figured into the bargain … it is far from obvious that a perfectly good God would accept them as the price of a very good world with as favorable a balance of moral good over moral evil as God could weakly actualize."[24] It seems doubtful that divine moral perfection and love of each and every created person is compatible with God accepting the *prima facie* ruin of some of their lives for the sake of greater overall world value.[25]

Moreover, Chapters 2 and 3 will suggest that because human persons have interests other than and more specific than an interest in their all-things-told well-being, it is even doubtful that divine morality and love is compatible with God causing or permitting people to suffer *horrendous evils* for *their own* all-things-considered benefit. Greater goods approaches to theodicy in a *horror*-laden world threaten to depict God as a utility fanatic. Ugly brown blotches may be fine and good in impressionist painting, but we should think again when the ugly blotches are human lives being desecrated.

## The Impotence of Blame-Shifting Solutions

According to Adams, not only does focusing on *horrors* show the insufficiency of greater goods solutions to the problem of evil, but it also decisively undermines approaches that rely on shifting the blame for evil away from God. These classical fall-of-humanity approaches generally look to acquit God by shifting responsibility for evil onto new intervening agents in the first generation of human persons.

Adams thinks such approaches are *structurally unpromising* in a *horror*-ridden world because they vastly overestimate the competency of human agency relative to *horrendous evils*. This misestimation fails to recognize that *horror* perpetration

---

Such counterfactuals are allegedly contingent truths God has to work with when deciding whether and which universe to create. God's knowledge of the truth values of these counterfactuals is referred to as *middle knowledge*.

[22]   Cf. *Horrendous Evils and the Goodness of God*, 21.
[23]   Adams notes that "Plantinga explicitly hopes that the problem of horrendous evils can thus be solved without being squarely confronted" ("Horrendous Evils and the Goodness of God," 252). Cf. Plantinga, "Self-Profile," 38.
[24]   Adams, *Horrendous Evils and the Goodness of God*, 30.
[25]   Adams, *Horrendous Evils and the Goodness of God*, 149.

cannot be a simple function of human moral wrongdoing for at least two reasons. Firstly, we sometimes produce *horrors* "contrary to our fully conscientious efforts and intentions,"[26] like the father who accidentally and through no fault of his own runs over his child with a car. Secondly, the extent of one's responsibility for something depends on one's ability to conceive how bad it is, and it is not clear that anyone other than God could have conceptual abilities great enough to bear primary responsibility for *horrendous evils*. Where *horrors* are concerned, an individual human's capacity to produce suffering often exceeds his ability to experience it. Since we cannot adequately conceive what we cannot adequately experience, our powers to cause suffering also exceed our powers to conceive it.[27] Adams therefore concludes that "the *necessary* disproportion between human agency and horrendous evils makes it impossible for humans to bear full responsibility for their occurrence. For we cannot bear full responsibility for something to the extent that—through no fault of our own—'we know not what we do.'"[28]

Classical blame-shifting attempts to solve the problem of *horrors* seem analogous to blaming a young child for getting run over when his mother left him to play near a heavily-trafficked highway.[29] Just as the child is not competent enough to be solely to blame, even if he knew he shouldn't play in the street, human persons are not competent enough to take full responsibility where *horrors* are concerned. As Adams sees it, primary responsibility must rest with God, who created us and sustains us at every moment in an environment where we are radically prone to *horrors*.[30]

## Adams's Solution

Adams's contention is that "free fall approaches founder while soul-making theodicies at least teeter on the rock of horrendous evils."[31] In fact, she suggests that "how bad horrors are finds its epistemic measure in our inability to think of plausible candidates for sufficient reasons why."[32] If she is right, and if God is obliged to have sufficient reasons for his *horror*-producing actions, the prospects for theodicy—the project of offering plausible candidates for sufficient reasons why—are hopeless. Adams believes she can accept this conclusion, giving up on

---

[26] Adams, *Horrendous Evils and the Goodness of God*, 60.
[27] Adams, *Horrendous Evils and the Goodness of God*, 36.
[28] Adams, *Horrendous Evils and the Goodness of God*, 38. I pick up and further develop this line of argumentation in Chapter 5.
[29] For a related analogy, see Adams, *Horrendous Evils and the Goodness of God*, 39.
[30] Note that some of those who attempt to shift the blame to our primordial forebears attribute to them understanding and competence in action far beyond our own. This raises a number of interesting plausibility and structural questions that I will return to in Chapter 5.
[31] Adams, *Horrendous Evils and the Goodness of God*, 33.
[32] Adams, *Horrendous Evils and the Goodness of God*, 155.

what she calls "the futile search for sufficient reasons why,"[33] and yet frame a Christian response to the problem of *horrors* by first denying that God has any moral obligations to human persons.

She claims that God and human creatures are not "near enough" peers to be networked by mutual rights and obligations,[34] any more than human beings could have moral obligations to ladybugs or worms.[35] In emphasizing the " 'size-gap' between Divine and created personhood,"[36] Adams is not in bad company. She claims lineage with medieval, Reformation, and biblical philosophical theology in understanding God "to be of the wrong metaphysical category to have obligations to creatures" and in seeking "to resize Deity without sacrificing Divine thought and choice."[37] Her approach raises challenging questions about whether moral obligations presuppose a social context that cannot exist between finite and infinite beings.

## The View from a Few Steps Back

Still, Adams's denial of divine moral obligations is a minority report among contemporary philosophers of religion. My project affirms Adams's focus on *horrors* but reconfigures the challenges they pose for a God *with* moral obligations to human persons.

My methodology requires two other divergences from Adams as well. She claims that *horrors* find their "epistemic measure in our inability to think of plausible candidates for sufficient reasons why."[38] I disagree and contend that some of the cases considered in Chapter 2 and their divine analogues in Chapters 3 and 4 show that, even where *horrors* are concerned, it is possible to conceive of enough partial reasons why to get a theodicy off the ground. Moreover, in Part II, I develop reasons why that I take to have a reasonable claim to both *structural promise* and plausibility.

Secondly, I reject Adams's claim that no package of merely created goods could balance-off *horror* participation. She gives little support for this claim, and I believe it is under-motivated. There are *horrors* that Adams means to capture in her characterization that satisfy H1 and H2 without satisfying H3. The exemplary life of Helen Keller—who remarkably overcame the permanent deafness and

[33] Adams, *Horrendous Evils and the Goodness of God*, 156. See also 205.
[34] Adams, *Horrendous Evils and the Goodness of God*, 103.
[35] Adams, *Horrendous Evils and the Goodness of God*, 127, 95.
[36] Adams, *Horrendous Evils and the Goodness of God*, 49.
[37] Adams, *Horrendous Evils and the Goodness of God*, 64. See also 12, 69–70. Adams cites David Burrell and Katherine Tanner as contemporary philosophical allies in this project.
[38] Adams, *Horrendous Evils and the Goodness of God*, 155.

blindness resulting from a childhood illness—provides one notable counterexample to Adams's H3.

## Project Summary

Once we conceive of God as a moral agent with obligations to human persons, and of *horrendous evils* as capable of being balanced-off by earthly goods, there is a natural analogy between the ethics of human *horror*-inducement and the ethics of divine creation and sustenance. In Chapter 2, I exploit this analogy to develop an ethical framework for theodicy. I construct a taxonomy by sketching four cases of human action where *horrors* are either caused, permitted, or risked, either for pure benefit (i.e., a benefit that does not avert a still greater harm) or for harm avoidance.

Then, in Chapters 3 and 4, I bring the taxonomy and the ethical valuations confirmed by the casuistry of Chapter 2 to bear on the project of theodicy. I construct four analogous theodicy structures—one for each case—and identify examples of each structure in theodicies in contemporary philosophy of religion. I summarize each theodicy and evaluate whether it is *structurally promising* with respect to *horrendous evils*.

My initial conclusions impugn the dominant structural approach of depicting God as causing or permitting *horrors* in individual lives for the sake of some merely pure benefit. This approach is insensitive to relevant asymmetries in the justificatory demands made by *horrendous* and non-*horrendous evil* and in the justificatory work done by averting harm and bestowing pure benefit. When moral constraints on the causing and permitting of *horrors* are considered and the justificatory asymmetry of harm-averting and non-harm-averting benefits brought to bear, pure benefit will not do the justificatory work (on its own) of securing God the status of an ethically perfect being.

Chapter 5 argues that those theodicies identified as *structurally promising* in Chapter 4 face a number of challenges rooted in modern science and theological tradition and are implausible due to their overestimation of the extent to which finite human agents can bear primary responsibility for *horrendous evils*. The most influential contemporary theodicies fail either ethically or otherwise. The project of theodicy is in trouble.

Part II develops an approach to theodicy that falls outside the ethical framework constructed in Part I. Following a suggestion of Leibniz's, Robert Adams has argued that theodicy can be aided by the insight that almost all of the evil of the actual world is metaphysically necessary for the community of actual world inhabitants to be comprised of the specific individuals who comprise it. Beginning with this insight, I develop (what I term) Non-Identity Theodicy. It suggests that God allows the evil he does in order to create and love the specific individuals comprising the community of inhabitants of the actual world. This approach to theodicy is unique because the justifying good recommended is neither harm aversion nor pure benefit. It is not a good that *betters the lives* of individual human persons (for they wouldn't exist otherwise), but it is the individual human persons themselves.

In order to aim successfully at the creation of particular individuals, however, God would need a control of history so complete that it might be argued to be inconsistent with beliefs about human free will that are important to some theologies. I construct a second version of Non-Identity Theodicy designed to avoid this problem by considering whether God's justifying motivation for allowing the evil of this world could be his aiming for beings of our *type*, even if it could not be his aiming for particular individuals. I suggest that God would be interested in loving those he creates under various descriptions (e.g., biological, psychological, and narrative descriptions), and argue that a *horror*-prone environment is necessary for us to be the type of being we are under these descriptions.

In Chapter 6, I argue that both forms of Non-Identity Theodicy can plausibly resist objections to its depiction of divine character and to its plausibility. In Chapter 7, I consider the implications of Non-Identity Theodicy for divine morality. I argue (by way of criticism of Derek Parfit's *No-Difference View* and of some influential assumptions in the ethics of procreation literature) that the good of a worthwhile human life (lived by someone who otherwise would not have existed) has unique justificatory power, and further that the good of a *God-given* human life (lived by someone who otherwise would not have existed) has justificatory power great enough to plausibly depict God as not violating moral obligations to human persons by his policy of evil allowance.

These arguments are aided by an analogy between divine creation and human procreation. Reflection on the morality of human procreation implies, I suggest, that it is not always wrong to create people in an environment in which you know they will suffer seriously. I argue, further, that if you think voluntary human procreation is in general morally permissible, you have even more reason to think divine creation and sustenance is morally permissible; conversely, if you think it would be immoral for God to create and sustain our universe, then you have even more reason to think voluntary human procreation is in general immoral.

I conclude that Non-Identity Theodicy can reasonably be taken to be successful. In Chapter 8—the final chapter—I recap what I take to be the key areas of overemphasis and under-emphasis in contemporary theodicy, and I show that Non-Identity Theodicy corrects for these various misemphases by conceiving of God first and foremost not as a maximizer of value but as a lover of persons. I end by discussing how Non-Identity Theodicy can be combined with other theodicies in the formulation of a cumulative case theodicy.

# 2

# The Ethics of *Horror* Inducement

In addition to *horrendous evils*, the most important concepts for my taxonomy are harm and benefit, harm-averting and pure benefits, and causation, permission, and risk. I use this chapter to clarify these concepts and then to construct a framework for moral assessment out of them. In the following two chapters, I bring this framework to bear on the project of theodicy.

## Harm and Benefit

Very generally, problems of evil claim that the actual world contains bad states of affairs that cannot be morally justified by its good states of affairs. Theodicies claim that the bad states of affairs can be morally justified by the good states of affairs, and seek to explain how they can be. The bad states of affairs highlighted by problems of evil tend to be states of human persons (or other animals) being harmed. Many of the examples of *horrendous evils* I referenced in the last chapter, for instance, are plausibly taken to be cases of harm. (Hereafter, I will sometimes use *horrendous harm* to refer to *horrendous evil* that is also harm.) The justificatory goods offered by theodicies tend to be states of human persons (or other animals) being benefited. The concepts of harm and benefit are thus central to the assessment of theodicy.

## The Metaphysics of Harm

I'll begin with harm. The type of harm I am primarily concerned with is harm *to people*, to be contrasted with derivative senses of harm such as one's garden being harmed.[1] Matthew Hanser usefully delineates three of the most popular accounts of the metaphysics of personal harm: the counterfactual comparative account, the temporal comparative account, and the non-comparative account.[2] The first two of these are comparative in the sense that to be harmed "is to be put into a certain

---

[1] Cf. Joel Feinberg, *Harm to Others* (New York: Oxford University Press, 1984), 32.
[2] Matthew Hanser, "The Metaphysics of Harm," *Philosophy and Phenomenological Research* 77 (2008): 421–50.

*Non-Identity Theodicy: A Grace-Based Response to the Problem of Evil*. Vince R. Vitale, Oxford University Press (2020).
© Vince R. Vitale.
DOI: 10.1093/oso/9780198864226.003.0002

sort of *comparatively* bad state—a state that is *worse* for one than some relevant alternative state."[3]

Hanser and I are in agreement that the comparative accounts of harm are unsuccessful. I begin by presenting some of the reasons for affirming this conclusion. I next defend the non-comparative account of harm against Hanser's objections to it. After discussing why "non-comparative" is a misleading term for this account, I recommend a more precise formulation of the non-comparative account that I term the trans-comparative account.

## The Counterfactual Comparative Account of Harm

Roughly, the counterfactual comparative account claims that

> a person suffers harm if and only if there occurs an event *e* such that had *e* not occurred, he would have been better off in some respect for some interval of time.[4]

The qualification "in some respect" is necessary to account for the fact that a person can be harmed and benefited by a single event. This is often the case, for instance, when inflicting a lesser harm—the injection of a painful needle, say—is the only way to bestow a benefit—an immunization, perhaps. The immunized person is made worse off than he would have been with respect to one of his interests but better-off than he would have been with respect to another of his interests.

One result of this qualification is that a person can be harmed by the occurrence of an event even if there is never a point at which that event harms him more than it benefits him. If I drop a bag full of five million dollars on you from a low-flying plane, breaking your arm in the process, the negative consequence of your arm being broken may be immediately and at all times thereafter outweighed by the benefit of the five million dollars. Still, according to the counterfactual comparative account, the broken arm comes to you as a harm. You are made worse off in some respect even if better-off overall. This seems to me a useful linguistic result. It helps us account for why there can be strong reasons against certain actions due to their foreseeable effects on people even when those effects will raise the level of overall well-being of the relevant people in the short or even the long run.

The qualification "for some interval of time" is necessary to account for the fact that a person can be made "to suffer a short-term harm for the sake of bestowing

---

[3]  Hanser, "The Metaphysics of Harm," 421.
[4]  This definition is taken from Hanser, "The Metaphysics of Harm," 424.

upon him a longer-term benefit, where the harm and the benefit are both with respect to *the same aspect of the person's well-being*."[5] Think here of a painful needle used to inject a pain reliever. With respect to pain, the patient is made worse off than she would have been for a period of time for the sake of making her better-off than she would have been for a different—and hopefully longer—period of time.

The counterfactual comparative account has problems accounting for at least two common intuitions. Firstly, there are cases in which a person is made to be counterfactually worse off, but not badly off, and it is intuitive that at least some of these cases are not cases of harm. For example, consider former New York Yankees' captain Derek Jeter's annual salary increasing from 15 million dollars to 20 million, but not to the 25 million that was probable and expected. Here Jeter has become significantly better-off financially; by most standards he has received an enormous pay raise. Yet, because his pay raise makes him counterfactually worse off than the pay raise he was predicted to receive would have made him, the counterfactual comparative account yields the counterintuitive result that Jeter has been harmed.[6]

Cases of overdetermined (sometimes called preemptive) harm cause a second problem for the counterfactual comparative account. These are cases in which the harm in question preempts the occurrence of equivalent or worse harms in the same respect at the same (or nearly the same) time. As such, the subject is made to be badly off, though not counterfactually worse off.

Breaking a person's legs because he owes you money harms him, even if his legs would have been broken by someone else at the same time had this other person not been scared off by the sight of you approaching bat in hand. The counterfactual comparative account has trouble accommodating this intuition, however, because the victim in this example is not counterfactually worse off for your harming him. According to the counterfactual comparative account, people suffer no harm in such cases because the supposed harming event leaves the victim no worse off that he otherwise would have been.

At best, the counterfactual comparative account can say that the victim was harmed by both you and the other potential leg-breaker. The victim *is* worse off for the actions of the two of you, taken together. But this approach misidentifies the harming event. It was *your* beating the victim, and that alone, that harmed him. As Hanser puts it, "He is in a harmed state relative to *that* event's occurrence,"[7]

---

[5]  Hanser, "The Metaphysics of Harm," 424 (italics mine).
[6]  This example also highlights that the counterfactual comparative account renders harm indistinguishable from what might typically be thought of as mere prevention of benefit. This is in tension with the fact that there are strong intuitive asymmetries between the two, even when the benefit prevented is comparable to the harm endured.
[7]  Hanser, "The Metaphysics of Harm," 436 (italics mine).

and that is an event you are solely responsible for. He was not (even partially) harmed by some other event that would have occurred had you not beaten him.

Cases of injury during rescue provide further examples of overdetermination that resist a counterfactual comparative analysis of harm. If you are hanging off of a high cliff at an awkward angle, and I break your arm because doing so is the only way to pull you to safety—saving you from a fall that would have broken your arm as well as many of your other bones—I think it is plausible to say I have both harmed you and benefited you. The same would be true of a doctor who causes his patient pain and hair-loss by administering chemo and radiation therapy that prevents the patient's cancer from metastasizing. In both cases, a lesser harm is inflicted in order to bestow a greater benefit. The counterfactual comparative account misses this distinction, however. According to it, the cliffhanger and the cancer patient have not been harmed at all.

I can see why one might be attracted to this conclusion, offset as the harms are by overriding benefits. Undoubtedly, it would reveal a disturbing lack of gratitude if the rescued cliffhanger complained that his rescuer had broken his arm. But, nevertheless, I join Seana Shiffrin in being "not sure what is gained by denying that the rescuer inflicts a lesser harm, whereas the denial seems in tension with recognizing *justified* harms and harming actions."[8] Identifying harms such as broken limbs in cases of overriding benefit is important because it calls attention to the sorts of negative consequences in need of special justification. It also helps us register that certain types of damage are serious and demand certain responses of care and compensation, often regardless of whether they have a positive or negative counterfactual effect on one's well-being. That the counterfactual comparative account of harm fails to identify overdetermined harm as harm is a mark against it.

## The Temporal Comparative Account of Harm

I now turn to the temporal comparative account. According to this account, to suffer harm is to be made worse off than one was previously. Parallel qualifications are necessary to the base version of the temporal comparative account as to the base version of the counterfactual comparative account, resulting in the claim that

a person suffers harm if and only if there are a time *t1* and a later time *t2* such that the person is in some respect worse off at *t2* than he was at *t1*.[9]

---

[8] Seana Valentine Shiffrin, "Wrongful Life, Procreative Responsibility, and the Significance of Harm," *Legal Theory* 5 (1999), 125. Quotes from Shiffrin's article are reproduced throughout this book with permission.

[9] This definition is taken from Hanser, "The Metaphysics of Harm," 425.

This account fares better with cases of overdetermined harm. What is essential to harm according to the temporal comparative account is that the one harmed is worse off than he was previously, not that he is worse off than he would have been otherwise. If one person breaks another's legs, therefore, he harms him by making him worse off in some respect temporally, irrespective of whether anyone else would have done the same or worse to him in the same respect at around the same time.

However, the temporal comparative account joins the counterfactual comparative account in its trouble accounting for the lack of harm in some cases of being made worse off, though not badly off. Suppose we amend the case of Jeter's salary negotiation so that his salary is cut from 20 million to 17 million. Here it is not as obvious whether Jeter has been harmed. We might speak about his interests being harmed. And if his diminished salary caused him serious financial or psychological difficulty, we might speak reasonably about Jeter himself being harmed. But it seems to me that if the consequences of the pay cut for Jeter are not particularly severe, it is most plausible that he has not been harmed. Jeter's salary renegotiation is again problematic, this time because the pay cut makes him, in a financial respect, worse off than he was previously. The temporal comparative account therefore yields the implausible result that the modest salary reduction of a multi-millionaire *necessarily* comes to him as a harm.

The Jeter counterexamples highlight that on the most natural rendering of comparative accounts—whether counterfactual or temporal—"the subject's absolute level of well-being is immaterial. It doesn't matter how high up or down the scale the levels being compared lie; all that matters is the size of the gap separating them."[10] But my case of Jeter and many other relevantly similar cases imply that this is a mistake. We should prioritize helping people who would otherwise be badly off over people who would simply be worse off, especially if they would be pushed below an important threshold in some respect. Hanser seems correct that even when declines are comparatively equivalent, "the duty to avoid causing people to be badly off takes precedence over the duty, if there even is one, to avoid causing people to become merely worse off."[11] Comparative accounts of harm act to obscure this important asymmetry.

Additionally, the temporal comparative account has trouble accounting for a type of harm not yet mentioned—preventative harm. Sometimes we can harm someone by preventing her from receiving a benefit, especially when the benefit is particularly significant. The temporal account fails to accommodate this intuition in cases where the prevention of benefit does not cause someone to be worse off in some respect than she was before.[12] If I actively prevent you from having a

---

[10]  Hanser, "The Metaphysics of Harm," 431.      [11]  Hanser, "The Metaphysics of Harm," 431.
[12]  The counterfactual comparative account has its own problems with cases of benefit-prevention. See n. 6, this chapter.

surgery that would restore your eyesight, I harm you, and seriously so; however, I may not make you any worse off than you were at any time in the past. In fact, if I am the surgeon and I prevent surgery on only one of your eyes while operating successfully on the other, you may even come to be better-off than you were previously. But again, it is implausible to think this precludes the existence of preventative harm in such cases.

## The Non-Comparative Account of Harm

Both comparative accounts have serious failings. To my mind, a non-comparative account fares better. According to the non-comparative account as Hanser understands it,

> a person suffers harm at a time if and only if he is in a non-comparatively bad state (i.e., a state in which one fares badly) at that time.[13]

On the most natural rendering of this account, the seriousness of a given harm is proportionate to the non-comparative badness of the relevant state.

This account does well accounting for all three types of case that cause trouble for the comparative accounts. With respect to preventative harm, the non-comparative account yields the result that one is harmed by being prevented from receiving a benefit when that prevention causes one to remain in a bad state, but not otherwise. That seems plausible. A person is harmed if he is prevented from receiving sight-restoring surgery, but not if he is prevented from receiving a raise to his already multi-million dollar salary. The non-comparative account also has no trouble accounting for the lack of harm in cases—such as the case of Jeter's salary cut—where a person who remains non-comparatively very well-off in some respect is made to be comparatively worse off in that respect. Nor does the non-comparative account have trouble dealing with cases of overdetermination. According to the non-comparative account, being made badly off is sufficient for harm, even when one is not made worse off due to overdetermination.

It is questionable, however, whether the non-comparative account can handle a fourth type of case where, intuitively, one is harmed by being made worse off, though *not* non-comparatively badly off. One example would be of an outstanding amateur pianist who injures one of his hands and as a result cannot play the piano as well as before. Suppose the difference in his playing ability is significant, but that he still plays the piano better than most amateur pianists. The pianist is by no means non-comparatively badly off musically (nor, let's suppose, in other relevant

---

[13]   Hanser, "The Metaphysics of Harm," 425.

ways), but it still seems intuitive to say that the pianist has been harmed. Hanser offers the example of a Nobel Prize winner whose intelligence diminishes to the point of being average.[14] Similarly here, it seems very plausible both that this is a case of harm and that having average intelligence is not a non-comparatively bad state for a person to be in.

I agree with Hanser that this diminishment of intelligence (and not just any resulting non-comparatively bad state (e.g., psychological or professional hard-ship)) comes to the Nobel Prize winner as a harm. Hanser judges that cases of this sort undermine the non-comparative account. My judgment is that cases of this sort expose a problem with Hanser's formulation of the non-comparative account rather than a problem with the account itself.

Hanser admits that "non-comparative" is a somewhat misleading name for this account; perhaps every so-called non-comparative value judgment "implicitly invokes" at least a comparison with some "ideal or norm."[15] But while Hanser concedes that some form of comparison may be essential to so-called non-comparative accounts, he nonetheless understands a non-comparative account to be committed to the claim that "it is bad for a person to be in such a state regard-less of whether a better state was ever a genuine alternative *for him*."[16] That is, Hanser holds that counterfactual and temporal comparisons are *irrelevant* to whether any given state is bad in the sense necessary and sufficient for it to be harm according to what he calls the non-comparative account.

I'm unsure why Hanser endorses such a strong non-comparative condition. As I see it, what is important about the so-called non-comparative account is that—in contrast to the comparative accounts—its identification of harm is not based *solely* on temporal or counterfactual comparisons; being made temporally or counterfactually worse off is neither necessary nor sufficient for harm. But it does not follow from this that such comparisons are altogether irrelevant to the meta-physics of harm. I see no reason to deny that they can contribute to the absolute badness of some bad states.

## The Trans-Comparative Account of Harm

I suggest replacing Hanser's characterization of the non-comparative account of harm with a *trans*-comparative account:

> a person suffers harm at a time if and only if he is in a bad state (i.e., a state in which one fares badly) at that time.

---

[14] Hanser, "The Metaphysics of Harm," 432.        [15] Hanser, "The Metaphysics of Harm," 426.
[16] Hanser, "The Metaphysics of Harm," 426.

According to the trans-comparative account, counterfactual and temporal comparisons can contribute to a more fundamental quality of badness-for-a-person that is not fully explained by counterfactual or temporal comparisons of a person's interests. One's interests in not being made worse off temporally or counterfactually are just two notes to be taken into account when judging whether a person is in a trans-comparatively bad state in some respect.

On a trans-comparative account, we can say that the Nobel Prize winner is harmed because he is in the trans-comparatively bad state of being so much worse off in such an important respect. The badness of this state is not sufficiently explained by its being *so much worse off comparatively*, nor by its being a state of *such an important interest*. But taken together, these comparative and non-comparative elements combine to yield a trans-comparatively bad state.[17]

This raises the question of what it is for a state to be trans-comparatively bad for a person. Why is the Nobel Prize winner's intelligence loss trans-comparatively bad when Jeter's salary cut is not?

Seana Shiffrin proposes a trans-comparative account where the badness that unifies cases of harm is that "harm involves conditions that generate a significant chasm or conflict between one's will and one's experiences…[Harms] forcibly impose experiential conditions that are affirmatively contrary to one's will."[18] This account can be understood as trans-comparative because both the non-comparative badness of a state and the comparativeness worseness of a state can contribute to that state being contrary to one's will. This is the case, for instance, when a

---

[17]  In these cases of harm without non-comparative badness, I'm inclined to think there is a negative correlation between how important the relevant interest is and how much that interest needs to be adversely affected in order to count as harm.

[18]  Shiffrin, "Wrongful life…," 123–4. To quote her at greater length, Shiffrin suggests that what unifies cases of harm is that "harm involves conditions that generate a significant chasm or conflict between one's will and one's experience, one's life more broadly understood, or one's circumstances. Although harms differ from one another in various ways, all have in common that they render agents or a significant or close aspect of their lived experience like that of an endurer as opposed to that of an active agent, genuinely engaged with her circumstances, who selects, or endorses and identifies with, the main components of her life. Typically, harm involves the imposition of a state or condition that directly or indirectly obstructs, prevents, frustrates, or undoes an agent's cognizant interaction with her circumstances and her efforts to fashion a life within them that is distinctively and authentically hers—as more than merely that which must be watched, marked, endured or undergone. To be harmed primarily involves the imposition of conditions from which the person undergoing them is reasonably alienated or which are strongly at odds with the conditions she would rationally will; also, harmed states may be ones that preclude her from removing herself from or averting such conditions. On this view, pain counts as a harm because it exerts an insistent, intrusive, and unpleasant presence on one's consciousness that one must just undergo and endure. Disabilities, injured limbs, and illnesses also qualify as harms. They forcibly impose experiential conditions that are affirmatively contrary to one's will; also, they impede significantly one's capacities for active agency and for achieving harmony between the contents of one's will and either one's lived experience or one's life more broadly understood. Death, too, unless rationally willed, seriously interferes with the exercise of agency. By constraining the duration and possible contents of the person's life, it forces a particular end to the person—making her with respect to that significant aspect of her life merely passive" (123–4). Shiffrin further develops these ideas in Seana Shiffrin, "Harm and Its Moral Significance," *Legal Theory* 18.3 (2012), 382–91.

professional baseball pitcher seriously injures his throwing arm. Because this condition is trans-comparative rather than non-comparative, it gets the desired result in the case of the Nobel Prize winner who, while not reduced to a non-comparatively bad state with respect to intelligence, is nevertheless reduced in that respect to a state that is strongly at odds with his will.

Hanser is suspicious of Shiffrin's trans-comparative version because it seems plausible that some states can be bad for people even when they do not object to (or even welcome) the relevant states.[19] This can be the case in instances of masochism and martyrdom. Think of the wife who welcomes her husband's abuse because she believes that he only loves her if he abuses her, or of Ignatius of Antioch embracing being eaten by the lions. I also would like to hear more about how Shiffrin would account for harm done to animals, to human persons whose brains have been injured such that they are in a permanent unwilling state, or to young children who don't understand enough to will against certain forms of harm.

Elizabeth Harman proposes a different trans-comparative account. She suggests that, for human persons, there is a point of comparison that involves healthy bodily functioning, which includes healthy mental functioning. Sufficient (though perhaps not necessary) for an action's harming someone is that it causes her to be in a state that is worse than life with healthy bodily functioning. A healthy body, according to Harman, involves no damage such as cuts or burns or diseases, no deformity whether genetically or otherwise induced, and living a normal human lifespan.[20] Harman's theory also lends itself to a trans-comparative analysis. One way a bodily state can compare unfavorably with healthy bodily functioning is by being below a certain objective threshold, but because there is a stability to healthy bodily functioning, another way a bodily state can compare unfavorably is by being abnormally worse than its preceding states.

Harman's theory can account for all of the counterexamples I listed against Shiffrin's theory. Her account also yields a plausible result in the Nobel Prize winner case. The state of average intelligence *due to a drastic loss of intelligence*— especially if early in life—is at odds with healthy bodily functioning. But, still, Harman is right to suspect that an unhealthy bodily state is not *necessary* for harm. I'm inclined to think serious pain, for instance, would be a trans-comparatively bad state for a rational being to be in even if consistent serious pain were part of the healthy bodily state of beings of its type.

Harman's theory also does not account for the case of the amateur pianist, for there it seems that the diminished hand function comes to the pianist as a harm

---

[19] Hanser, "The Metaphysics of Harm," 432, n. 13. Shiffrin offers what could form part of a response to Hanser's objection in Shiffrin, "Harm and Its Moral Significance," 383, 390–1.

[20] See Elizabeth Harman, "Can We Harm and Benefit in Creating?," *Philosophical Perspectives* 18 (2004), 97.

primarily because of how it affects his will to play the piano, not because his bodily functioning is no longer healthy. His bodily functioning might remain completely healthy—such that if he were not a piano player he wouldn't notice the difference at all—and yet his diminished ability still comes to him as a harm. Likewise, it is Shiffrin's rather than Harman's theory that fares better with a case of someone being denied the opportunity to have a higher education.[21] That does not necessarily involve a loss of physical or mental health, and it would be wrong to say that only those who have gone to university are normally functioning people. But nevertheless I believe a denial of this sort could be a serious harm, especially if—as Shiffrin presses—it is against one's will.

Given the complex nature of human interests, there may be no one theory that simply and exhaustively identifies all states that are trans-comparatively bad for human persons, but both Shiffrin's and Harman's conditions are good candidates for sufficient conditions for harm. Harman admits that she is "leaving it vague what counts as a healthy bodily state." But that is okay, she claims: "The important point is that the kinds of pain, early death, bodily damage, and deformity described in the radioactive case are clear cases of states and events that are worse than life with a healthy bodily state."[22] Likewise, the cases I am concerned with in this book—primarily cases of *horrendous harm*—will tend to satisfy both Harman's and Shiffrin's conditions for harm.

## The Metaphysics of Benefit

I endorse a trans-comparative account of harm. It is temptingly simplistic, as such, to adopt a trans-comparative account of benefit as well. Both Shiffrin and Harman go this route. While detailing her theory of the metaphysics of harm at some length, Shiffrin assumes without defense a symmetric description of the metaphysics of benefit. She identifies "harms with certain absolute, noncomparative conditions…and benefits with an independently identified set of goods."[23] Harman, as well, moves quickly from her claim that harms stem from the way it would be "non-relatively bad for someone if we acted in a particular way" to the claim that benefits "stem from the way it would be non-relatively good for

---

[21] This example highlights the context-dependency of some harms. If my parents had denied me higher education in late twentieth-century America, I think it's plausible to claim they would have harmed me; however, a knight who failed to have his children learn to read and write in the Middle Ages may only have denied them a benefit.

[22] Harman, "Can We Harm and Benefit in Creating?," 97.

[23] Shiffrin, "Wrongful Life…," 123. More recently, Shiffrin describes her accounts of harm and benefit as asymmetric. As I am using the terms, her accounts are symmetric because they are both trans-comparative. Cf. Shiffrin, "Harm and Its Moral Significance," 366, 376, 389–90.

someone if we acted in a particular way."[24] Moreover, despite their other metaphysical disagreements, on the *symmetry* of the metaphysics of harm and benefit the non-comparative theorists (such as Shiffrin and Harman) and the comparative theorists (such as Joel Feinberg[25]) tend to agree. As Hanser observes, "It is natural, though not logically necessary, for the proponent of the counterfactual comparison view to adopt a parallel account of benefit."[26]

Despite a tendency in the literature on the metaphysics of harm to assume a symmetric metaphysical account of benefit, I argue in what follows that there are reasons to resist this tendency before proposing an asymmetric account of the metaphysics of benefit (the disjunctive comparative account). I then highlight that my asymmetric accounts allow for an intuitive and important ethical distinction between harm-averting and non-harm-averting benefits.

## Asymmetry between Harm and Benefit

Intuitions suggest that there are deep moral asymmetries between harm and benefit, and, if there are, these might reflect deeper metaphysical asymmetries between them than typically assumed.

Beginning with the moral asymmetries: *Ceteris paribus*, intuitions suggest that we have more reason not to harm than to benefit. Choices not to harm others are often obligatory whereas otherwise similar choices to benefit are merely supererogatory. Couples generally have no obligation to create happy children, though they do have obligations not to purposefully create unhappy children. Harman confirms this asymmetry when she notes that "[t]he couple who does not create a happy child does not do anything bad; they merely fail to do something good."[27] The couple who does not create an unhappy child, however, not only fails to do something bad, but fulfills a moral obligation.

This normative asymmetry between harm and benefit is further motivated by our intuitions about compensation and justification. *Ceteris paribus*, harms endured make much better cases for compensation than benefits foregone. The parents who fail to treat their child for a serious medical condition are liable to compensate in a way that the parents who fail to increase their child's already adequate standard of living are not, even if in comparative terms the good of the benefit foregone by the parents outweighs the bad of the damage caused by the medical condition.

---

[24] Harman, "Can We Harm and Benefit in Creating?," 98.
[25] See, for example, Joel Feinberg, "Wrongful Life and the Counterfactual Element in Harming," *Social Philosophy and Policy* 4.1 (1986), 146.
[26] Hanser, "The Metaphysics of Harm," 423.
[27] Harman, "Can We Harm and Benefit in Creating?," 98.

These intuitions suggest that we do not conceive of harm and benefit as opposite extreme determinates of a single determinable. And that raises the question, why think they have the same sort of existence conditions?

Moreover, we do find metaphysical asymmetry in related concepts such as those of one person harming or benefiting another. The intentional states required for harming seem fewer than those required for benefiting. To be due credit for a benefit, one often must not only *foresee* that benefit as a consequence of her action; she must also *desire* it. Asymmetrically, merely *foreseeing* a harm as a consequence of one's action seems in general enough to be credited with harming. Indeed, it is often enough if one *should* have foreseen the harm, even if one did not foresee it.

Take the following case, for instance. A city council is deciding on water policy. One policy will be slightly less difficult to implement and will allow for water fluoridation that will be significantly better for the teeth of those who live in the city. Say the council decides on this policy, but for the sake of ease of implementation rather than for the sake of healthier teeth. It seems the council is not morally praiseworthy for this benefit, even though it knew that it would result from their decision. However, say the council chooses for the sake of ease of implementation an alternative policy that they are aware will cause drastic tooth decay, or that they would have been aware will cause drastic tooth decay had they performed the tests they ought to have performed. Here it does seem that the council is morally to blame for harming the city's inhabitants, even if they had no desire for them to suffer tooth decay.

Perhaps it is not the case that agents get no credit at all for bringing about benefits that are foreseen but unintended, but what is clear is that any credit they get and the extent to which they benefit is generally less than harmers harm and are blameworthy when they bring about unintended but foreseen harms. Foreseen but unintended harms are more plausibly cases of harming than foreseen but unintended benefits are cases of benefiting, an asymmetry one natural explanation of which is that it is derived from metaphysical asymmetry in the more fundamental concepts of harm and benefit.

## The Disjunctive Comparative Account of Benefit

I now develop an account of the metaphysics of benefit by asking which of counterfactual comparative, temporal comparative, and trans-comparative conditions are necessary or sufficient for benefit. That this method independently yields an asymmetric account of harm and benefit results in a cumulatively strong case for metaphysical asymmetry.

I judge that none of the three conditions are *necessary* for benefit. Unlike harm, a trans-comparative condition is not necessary. Whereas only trans-comparatively bad states come to people as harms, it often comes as a benefit to be in states that are not absolutely good in the relevant respect. In cases of harm aversion, for instance, one can be benefited despite remaining badly off and even worse off in the relevant respect. This is the case when a below-the-knee amputation is performed to save the rest of one's leg. While a below-the-knee amputation in a harm-averting situation might come to a patient as a benefit, it does not plausibly leave the patient in a healthy bodily state with respect to his leg. This type of case is also a counterexample to the necessity of the temporal comparative condition for benefit. That cases like this are cases of benefit can only be accounted for by a counterfactual account.

But a counterfactual comparative condition is likewise unnecessary for benefit. It is plain that in cases of overdetermined benefit, we can be benefited by an event *e1* even if we would have been similarly benefited by an event *e2* had *e1* not occurred. I conclude that none of the most commonly employed conditions are necessary for benefit.

Which conditions, if any, are *sufficient* for benefit? Again in contrast to the metaphysics of harm, a trans-comparative condition is not sufficient for benefit. With harm, you harm me by torturing me even if you now torture me less severely than you did previously and less severely than someone else would otherwise have done. This is asymmetric with benefit. Putting someone in a worse state than both their previous state and the state they would have been in otherwise doesn't plausibly benefit even if it leaves her in an absolutely good state in the relevant respect. Our Nobel Prize winner, for instance, is not benefited by a significant loss to his intelligence so long as he is left with good intelligence.

A trans-comparative account of benefit should be rejected because a trans-comparative condition is neither necessary nor sufficient for benefit. Moreover, given a trans-comparative account of harm, a third point against a trans-comparative account of benefit is that symmetric trans-comparative accounts have trouble accounting for why harming for benefit is more easily justified in cases where the harm is overdetermined. For instance, a doctor is more easily justified in performing a painful surgery for the sake of some benefit if equivalent pain to that occasioned by the surgery was already or would be nevertheless the result of the patient's condition. On a symmetric trans-comparative account, this moral distinction is obscured because neither the existence nor the extent of the relevant harm or benefit is affected by the overdetermination. Regardless of whether there is overdetermination, the relevant trans-comparatively bad and trans-comparatively good states are the same. Bringing either a counterfactual or a temporal comparative condition back into the account of benefit would make available a plausible explanation: Overdetermined harm is more easily justified by resulting benefit because the justifying benefit is either counterfactually or temporally greater in cases of overdetermination.[28]

---

[28] This vulnerability in symmetric trans-comparative accounts is usually taken to be reason to prefer symmetric counterfactual comparative accounts of the metaphysics of harm and benefit, but it equally supports asymmetric accounts.

In fact, I judge that *both* temporal and counterfactual comparative conditions are individually sufficient for benefit. If you give me a new tennis racket for my birthday, you benefit me, even if someone else would have given me a better tennis racket had I not received one from you. That I have been made temporally better-off is sufficient for my having been benefited. Likewise, being made counterfactually better-off is sufficient for having been benefited. If you break my arm to save it from being torn off, you benefit me, even if my arm winds up worse off than it was previously. These judgments again contrast with the metaphysics of harm. If Jeter's salary undergoes a 15 percent decrease counterfactually or temporally, it is strained to call this harm. But if his salary is boosted 15 percent in either respect, it is natural to think of him as receiving a benefit.

My recognition of the asymmetries between harm and benefit and my case-based assessment of the existence conditions for benefit lead me to endorse a disjunctive comparative account of benefit:

> a person receives a benefit if and only if either there occurs an event *e* such that had *e* not occurred, he would have been worse off in some respect for some interval of time or there are a time *t1* and a later time *t2* such that the person is in some respect better-off at *t2* than he was at *t1*.

I acknowledge with Shiffrin that sometimes when a great harm is accompanied by a small temporal or counterfactual comparative benefit, it seems strained to say a person has been benefited. But this straining seems to me plausibly accounted for by the fact that it would be callous and patronizing in such circumstances to call attention to the fact that someone undergoing great harm had been benefited in some minor way. Since this explanation is plausible, I don't think such cases demand any modification of my account of benefit.

Also worth noting is that while I take both temporal and counterfactual comparative conditions to be independently sufficient for benefit, the counterfactual condition should be given priority for the purposes of moral assessment. Though you benefit someone if you make her temporally better-off in a case of overdetermined benefit, such benefit will do little to justify harm. Only counterfactual comparative benefit has a plausible claim to justifying significant harm, so it is this type of benefit I will be most concerned with in the construction of my evaluative framework and in my moral assessments of theodicies.

In summation, I propose an asymmetric account of the metaphysics of harm and benefit. For harm, I judge that a trans-comparative condition is necessary and sufficient. Counterfactual and temporal comparative conditions are neither necessary nor sufficient, though sometimes relevant. For benefit, I judge that none of these conditions are individually necessary but that counterfactual and temporal comparative conditions are disjunctively necessary and individually sufficient. That the structure of the metaphysics of harm and benefit is hybrid in this way makes sense of our interests. What we seek to avoid most is what's bad (not just worse) and what we seek to receive most is what's better (not just good).

One result of my hybrid account is that Hanser is wrong when he writes, "What is impossible is that a person should be *simultaneously* in both a harmed and a benefited state with respect to a single aspect of his well-being, relative to the occurrence of a single event."[29] When half of a leg is amputated to save the other half, the patient is both trans-comparatively harmed and counterfactually benefited at the same time with respect to the state of his leg.

## Harm-Averting and Pure Benefits

Another distinction that has a central place in my taxonomy is that between harm-averting and non-harm-averting benefits, and another advantage of the asymmetric accounts of harm and benefit I have outlined is that they allow for an intuitive moral differentiation between these benefit types.

Shiffrin proffers the term "pure benefits" to refer to those benefits which are not also removals from or preventions of harm. She suggests that the central cases involve "the enhancement of one's situation or condition, or the fulfillment of nonessential, though perhaps important, interests."[30] Some preliminary examples include "material enhancement, sensual pleasure, goal-fulfillment, nonessential knowledge, competitive advantage."[31] Those items all involve benefits, but the absence of them would not tend to be characterized as trans-comparatively bad states. (If coming to exist with a worthwhile life is a benefit, it is a non-harm-averting benefit (for non-existence is not a state of harm), but one of a very unique sort. I will, for now, exclude coming to exist as a case of pure benefit and save discussion of its classification and implications for theodicy for Part II.)

Intuitions suggest that there is a significant moral asymmetry between pure and harm-averting benefits. Pure benefits have significantly less justificatory power, *ceteris paribus*, than harm-averting ones. For instance, when a person is unavailable for consent, it is normally morally justified to benefit them by inflicting a lesser harm to avert a greater one. However, it is in general morally suspect to perform a procedure on an unconscious patient that will cause her harm merely because it will also obtain for her greater pure benefit, say increased running speed or superior eyesight.[32]

Another way to see this significant asymmetry in justificatory force is to ask whether it is permissible to bestow a gift on one of two children when you have

---

[29] Hanser, "The Metaphysics of Harm," 425.

[30] Shiffrin, "Wrongful Life...," 124–5. See also Shiffrin's further discussion of the distinction between harm-averting and pure benefits in Shiffrin, "Harm and Its Moral Significance," 364–5.

[31] Shiffrin, "Wrongful Life...," 123, 125.

[32] Shiffrin discusses this point in Shiffrin, "Wrongful Life...," 126–7.

only one gift to give. Fairness presents a problem here. When what's being bestowed is a pure benefit, we sometimes think you should take a miss in order to be fair. But when the benefit will avert a significant harm, it then seems clear that this overrides the badness of any unfairness. No one in their right mind would argue that we should fail to rescue one of two children from serious harm because we do not have the resources to rescue both children.

A plausible account of the metaphysics of harm and benefit should be consonant with this intuitive asymmetry. Perhaps the most popular account, however—the symmetric counterfactual comparative account—collapses the distinction between pure and harm-averting benefits. According to this account, all benefits are by definition harm-averting because all benefits keep their subjects from being counterfactually worse off, and being counterfactually worse off is sufficient for harm. There is therefore no structural difference between benefiting someone by rescuing him from danger and benefiting him by advantaging an interest of his with respect to which he is already well-off. That symmetric counterfactual accounts of harm and benefit obscure the moral asymmetry of pure and harm-averting benefits is a significant mark against them.

Symmetric temporal comparative accounts of harm and benefit can accommodate some asymmetry between pure and harm-averting benefits. A harm-averting benefit would be one that makes one temporally better-off in a respect in which she was becoming temporally worse off. But symmetric temporal comparative accounts fail to recognize the distinction between harm-averting and pure benefits in many other cases in which the distinction is intuitive. For instance, so long as both people were not in the process of becoming worse off financially, symmetric temporal comparative accounts make no structural distinction between a monetary benefit that relieves someone from poverty and one that affords a more extravagant lifestyle to someone who is already wealthy; both simply make someone better-off than they were previously.

Granted, the law of diminishing marginal utility suggests that monetary benefits of equal size will benefit someone in poverty much more than it will benefit someone who is already wealthy. But even adjusting so that the monetary benefit received by the wealthy person is great enough to even out the utilities of the benefits received, intuitions suggests that relieving one from poverty remains much more significant morally than skyrocketing the wealth of someone already well-off.

Symmetric trans-comparative accounts fare better in accounting for this moral asymmetry. They suggest the correct result that the one who is relieved from the trans-comparatively bad state of poverty receives a harm-averting benefit whereas the already wealthy monetary recipient receives merely a pure benefit. However, I argued earlier that a trans-comparative condition is neither necessary nor sufficient for benefit, and that a symmetric trans-comparative account of the metaphysics of harm and benefit faces further difficulties.[33]

---

[33]   See the paragraph on p. 27 directly preceding n. 28, this chapter.

Most importantly, for my purposes, my asymmetric account of harm and benefit accommodates a distinction between harm-averting and pure benefits. According to my hybrid account,

> a person receives a harm-averting benefit if and only if either there occurs an event *e* such that had *e* not occurred, he would have been worse off and badly off in some respect for some interval of time or there are a time *t1* and a later time *t2* such that the person is badly off in some respect at *t1* and is in the same respect better-off at *t2*. Other benefits are pure benefits.

The earlier casuistry supporting my accounts of harm and benefit did not suppose a prior recognition of the moral asymmetries between harm and benefit or between harm-averting and pure benefits. That my accounts accommodate these intuitive asymmetries is therefore further support for them. Moreover, because symmetric counterfactual comparative accounts of harm and benefit are the ones best suited to accommodate the rejection of a distinction between harm-averting and pure benefits, that my casuistry independently undermines the counterfactual comparative account of harm is further reason in favor of acknowledging the intuitive distinction between these benefit types.

I'll be talking in this book about the possibility of justifying harm by its consequent benefits. The type of harm I am most concerned with is *horrendous harm*. As a result, the cases I consider will typically be paradigmatic cases of trans-comparative harm, but will also tend to be clear cases of harm on comparative accounts. The benefits I discuss will come in the form of temporal or counterfactual (and usually both) comparisons, but will often count as benefits on a trans-comparative account of benefit as well. As such, what I have to say may be of interest even to those who disagree with me about the metaphysics of harm and benefit.

## Causation, Permission, and Risk

The third set of distinctions essential to my framework is that between causation, permission, and risk. My project concerns how agents are to be ethically assessed in light of their responsibility for harms. But agents can be responsible for harms to various degrees in virtue of various relations holding between them and harms. I use the terms causing, permitting, and risking to pick out three such relations particularly relevant to theodicy. These terms are used often in the contemporary theodicy literature to describe God's relation to the existence of evils, but they typically are left undefined and inadequately distinguished. In this section, I detail how I will use these terms.

There are several different concepts of causation in regular use including scientific, metaphysical, legal, and what Christopher Hitchcock refers to as folk attributive causation.[34] I will use causing, permitting, and risking in my own technical senses, but these senses are most closely related to folk attributive causation. This, according to Hitchcock, is the type of causation that is of primary concern to the normal person in making attributions of praise and blame. It is this concept that the plain man applies when accusing another of causing him harm and when asserting that the wind caused a tree to fall on his house.

My technical senses of causing, permitting, and risking are intended to help fix the extent of responsibility of personal agents for the outcomes or consequences that follow on their voluntary agency or lack thereof in the world. As such, only persons acting (or omitting to act) voluntarily will count as causers, permitters, or riskers of harm in my technical senses.

I also narrow the scope of my agent-focused technical terms by constructing them out of only two variables central to determining the extent of an agent's responsibility for an outcome. The first variable is the extent to which the outcome was foreseen or foreseeable by the agent in question. The second variable is whether the outcome is a consequence of something the agent does or something he merely allows.

Because I am concerned with the ethical status of an epistemically perfect agent, what is foreseen and what is foreseeable will merge in the cases I consider. Typically, agents can be responsible for even unforeseen outcomes when those outcomes are unforeseen due to culpable ignorance. For my purposes, I can avoid this complication because an epistemically perfect agent is never culpably ignorant.

Furthermore, while folk attributive cases of causation tend to be cases of foreseen or at least reasonably foreseeable harm, the folk attributive concept does include some cases where the outcome is non-culpably unforeseen but nevertheless the desired result of one's action (either as an end in itself or as necessary for some further end). If I aim a gun at you from across a field and shoot you (whether in cold blood or to stop you from shooting someone else in cold blood), I cause you harm even if I did not know I would hit you, in fact, even if I knew it was highly unlikely that I would hit you. It would be odd to say I risked hitting you with the bullet. Hitting you was what I was trying to do; it was what I wished my action would accomplish.

Aiming for harm for its own sake would clearly contradict the supposed ethical perfection of God. But whether God could aim for harm that he cannot foresee for some other—potentially justificatory—end is controversial; it depends in part on whether there are future contingents such as the outcomes of free human choices and whether God has foreknowledge of them. However, with respect to God's actions, the theodicies I consider in this project present God either as

---

[34] Christopher Hitchcock, "Three Concepts of Causation," *Philosophy Compass* 2 (2007): 508–16.

intending foreseen harm or as not intending—in fact hoping against—unforeseeable harm. God aiming for unforeseeable harm does not play a significant role, and thus it is not cumbersome that my technical definitions also leave to one side this second complexity of ordinary usage.

Roughly, in my technical senses, a person causes the foreknown consequences of what he does, permits the foreknown consequences of what he allows, and risks the potential but unknown consequences of what he does or allows. I take an agent to foreknow an outcome when his foresight of it is epistemically strong enough to count as knowledge that it will occur (or, if one is skeptical that there can be knowledge of the future because one thinks the future does not exist and resultantly that the truth condition for knowledge cannot be met by beliefs about the future, when his foresight is strong enough to count as meeting the justification condition for knowledge). Causing and permitting are similar in involving foreknowledge of the relevant consequences.

I understand the distinction between doing and allowing to largely overlap with the distinction between active and inactive agency.[35] The distinction between causing and permitting harm, therefore, is typically between harm occurring primarily because of the existence of one of the agent's actions and harm occurring primarily because the agent did not perform an action he could have performed.

Distinguishing between cases of causation, permission, and risk in my senses will be subject to vagueness between the concepts of action and inaction as well as knowledge and mere belief. For example, there will not be a clearly identifiable line between cases of very high risk and cases of causation. In this, my terms resemble their corresponding folk attributive concepts. Hitchcock records that "ordinary subjects do not seem to view causation as an all or nothing affair. When invited to rate the extent to which they judge one event to be a cause of another, they cheerfully choose intermediate states."[36] More than clear-cut delineation between these concepts, what is important for my evaluative framework is that responsibility for an outcome tends to increase the closer one's relevant agency is to action and the closer one's relevant epistemic state is to knowledge.

Without going so far as committing myself to the view that God never causes what would have happened anyway, it is *horrendous harm* that would not have happened but for God's relevant agency that motivates the problem of *horrendous evils* and that the theodicies I consider focus on. As such, a counterfactual approach to identifying the outcomes or consequences of one's agency is not disturbed in my project by cases of overdetermined outcomes. I will therefore identify caused and permitted harms as those that would not have occurred had the

[35] For an attempt to explain the doing/allowing distinction as roughly that between action and inaction, see Warren Quinn, "Actions, Intentions, and Consequences: The Doctrine of Doing and Allowing," *The Philosophical Review* 98 (1989): 287–312.

[36] Hitchcock, "Three Concepts of Causation," 512. Hitchcock cites results recorded in Mark D. Alicke, "Culpable Causation," *Journal of Personality and Social Psychology* 63 (1992): 368–78.

agent in question acted otherwise, and risked harms as those that would have had a lower probability of occurring had the agent in question acted otherwise.

More formally, then, my technical definitions are as follows:

a person *y causes* a harm *x* if and only if there is an action *A* such that *y* knows *x* will result if he performs *A*, *y* knows *x* will not result if he does not perform *A*, and *y* voluntarily performs *A*.

a person *y permits* a harm *x* if and only if there is an action *A* such that *y* knows *x* will result if he does not perform *A*, *y* knows *x* will not result if he performs *A*, and *y* voluntarily does not perform *A*.

a person *y risks* a harm *x* if and only if there is an action *A* such that *y* knows it is more likely (though not certain) that *x* will result if he performs (or does not perform) *A* than if he does not perform (or performs) *A*, and *y* voluntarily performs (or does not perform) *A*.

I take my technical senses of causing, permitting, and risking harm to be conceptually prior to the moral assessment of the agency in question. This marks another divergence between my technical terms and their corresponding folk attributive concepts. Hitchcock claims that "folk causal attributions are influenced by normative factors, such as the existence of behavioral norms, or the intentions of agents," and offers the following evidence in support:

[I]n an experiment performed by Knobe and Fraser, subjects were presented a vignette in which two individuals, Lauren and Jane, both use the same computer. They can log on from separate terminals, but if they both log on at the same time, the computer will crash. In order to avoid this outcome, the company they work for establishes a policy allowing Lauren to use the computer in the morning, and Jane to use it in the afternoon. Then one morning, both Lauren and Jane log on to the computer, Jane doing so in violation of the company policy. The computer crashes. In this scenario, subjects are more strongly inclined to judge that Jane caused the computer to crash than that Lauren did.

Hitchcock thinks "[t]hese results suggest that Jane's violation of the company's policy inclined subjects to judge that her action was a cause of the crash."[37] But, in fact, the judgment of the subjects in this experiment can be just as naturally explained by epistemic factors as by normative ones. On the most natural fleshing out of the case, Lauren and Jane would know that the company policy was designed to avoid computer crashes caused by them logging on at the same time. We can therefore say that Jane caused the computer to crash because presumably

---

[37]  Hitchcock, "Three Concepts of Causation," 512.

she knew that Lauren would be on (or at least would be likely to be on) the computer in the morning. However, given the company policy, Jane did not have strong reason to believe Laruen would use the computer during this time. Hitchcock is wrong that this example supports his claim that folk causal attributions are influenced by normative factors.

But other cases will support Hitchcock's claim. Here is another experiment that he details:

> Alicke presented subjects with a scenario in which an agent, John, was speeding on his way home. John is then involved in a traffic accident with another car. In one version of the story, John is speeding in order to get home before his parents so that he can hide an anniversary present that he left sitting out; in the other version, he is speeding in order to hide a vial of cocaine that he left sitting out. Subjects were then asked to what extent John's speeding was a cause of the accident. Subjects judged that John caused the accident to a greater extent when he was speeding home to hide the cocaine. Thus John's intentions seemed to affect subjects' judgments of his causal role in the accident.[38]

In folk attributive and legal contexts, risking harm *immorally* is often sufficient for being one of its causes, despite the fact that the agent in question did not and could not know that the harm would occur. While there may be good reasons justifying this normatively-influenced application of causation in some contexts, it is not ideal for the purposes of moral evaluation because it obscures important differences in foreseeability at the time of the act in question. On my classification, the negligent driver counts as risking rather than causing harm. This takes account of the fact that he would be still more to blame if he had not only acted in a way that he knew *might* cause harm, but if he had acted in a way that he knew *would* cause harm.

## The Morality of Human-Induced *Horrendous Harm*

I can now present my taxonomy. The question on the table is this: Under what, if any, conditions would an ethically perfect God create and sustain human persons in a *horror*-ridden world? To help answer this question, I propose an evaluative framework constructed out of two of the most ethically relevant variables: firstly, whether the *horrors* are caused, permitted, or risked in the lives of the individuals who suffer them, and secondly, whether the *horrors* are caused, permitted, or risked in order to bestow a pure benefit or a benefit that averts greater harm.

---

[38]  Hitchcock, "Three Concepts of Causation," 512–13.

While there are six possible combinations of these two variables, the influential contemporary theodicies that I will discuss can be classified as one of four types. These are:

Type A – *Horrendous harm* caused for all-things-considered pure benefit.
Type B – *Horrendous harm* permitted for all-things-considered pure benefit.
Type C – *Horrendous harm* risked for all-things-considered pure benefit.
Type D – *Horrendous harm* permitted for all-things-considered harm-averting benefit.[39]

By "for," I mean that to bestow the stipulated benefit is God's primary reason for causing, permitting, or risking the harm in question. By "all-things-considered," I mean that the resulting benefit is a benefit *in the end* and *overall*. By "in the end," I mean in the context of the relevant subject's entire life. By "overall," I mean with respect to one's well-being, where one's well-being is taken to be the cumulative state of all of one's harm and benefit restricted interests. By "harm and benefit restricted," I mean that the interests are fully accounted for by the subject's interests in being benefited and in not being harmed. I also refer to these as "beneficence-restricted interests." These interests are not the same as one's full set of interests if there are deontological interests—for example interests in being told the truth, having promises kept, and retaining autonomy over one's body—that cannot be fully explained by one's interests in being benefited and in not being harmed.

At various points in the working out of my taxonomy, I will use the phrases "worthwhile life" and "life worth living" interchangeably. I use these phrases to refer, roughly, to a human life that is both a significant objective good and whose subject is able to appropriate enough of that good into her personal meaning-making systems that she will usually judge it to be good for her to have lived it.

I now discuss four cases of human-induced *horrendous harm*, one for each Type, to help us get our intuitional bearings with respect to the moral framework. My review of these cases will recommend an approach to the ethics of *horror* inducement that I will bring to bear on contemporary theodicies in the next two chapters.

## Case A:    *Horrendous Harm* Caused for Pure Benefit

*Sometime in the not too distant future, it is possible to significantly enhance human potential through a surgery that is available only to young children. The individuals who undergo this surgery end up with significantly greater*

---

[39] I will use 'necessary to avert even greater *harm*' and 'necessary to avert even greater *horrors*' interchangeably because I believe any harm greater than *horrendous harm* will have to be *horrendous* itself.

*strength, better eyesight, higher intelligence, and greater empathy than other-wise would have been the case. Almost without exception, people who undergo this procedure judge at the end of their lives—and reasonably so—that they were significantly better-off all things considered for having undergone it.*[40] *However, following the surgery, it takes the body several years to accept the enhancement, and, during those years, the person must undergo a very trau-matic recovery that includes regular rounds of chemotherapy. The physical pain and psychological trauma experienced during these initial years of recovery is universally acknowledged to be among the worst forms of suffering known to human persons. It is rightly classified horrendous. Consider parents who decide for their child to have this enhancement surgery. Otherwise, the child would have been average in the relevant respects but would nevertheless have had a worthwhile and full life.*

Here we have a case of *horrendous harm* being caused for an all-things-considered pure benefit. This is not to say that there is not also risk and permission involved in the parents' decision; however, it is their causation of the *horrendous* suffering in question that is the greatest challenge to the morality of their choice. The high-est level of ownership over the harm in need of justification is due to their causation of it.

Most non-philosophers would agree that the parents in Case A wrong their child by putting her through the enhancement process. Even if the parents were justifiably certain that enhancement of this sort would lead to their child's all-things-considered benefit, the common sense intuition remains that they have seriously wronged their child by *horrendously* harming her in this way.

## Defense by Harm Denial

Suppose, however, that the parents denied this. How might they be inclined to defend themselves? Perhaps they would be assuming that their action in Case A cannot be morally objectionable due to harm done to their child because

(1) If by $y$'s doing $A$, $x$ is foreseeably better-off all things considered than $x$ would have been had $y$ not done $A$, then $y$ does not harm $x$ by doing $A$.

They might argue that because their action leaves their child better-off all things considered, far from their action being immoral due to harm done to their child, their action did not harm their child at all. The parents might cite Derek Parfit

---

[40] I assume that some lives are better or worse than other lives, but not that comparisons of this sort can be made exact or that all lives are commensurable in this way.

who supports this defense when he claims that "if what we are doing will not be worse for some other person, or will even be better for this person, we are not, in a morally relevant sense, harming this person."[41]

I have claimed that this approach to the metaphysics of harm makes two false assumptions: firstly, that harm is primarily a matter of being made worse off rather than of being made badly off, and, secondly, that the negative effect relevant to harm must be true *all things considered*—that is, *overall* and *in the end*—rather than merely "in some respect" and "for some time." One reason to reject this latter assumption is that, in a case like Case A, we have the same reason to alleviate the damage done to the victim regardless of whether that damage has or will have the consequence of benefitting the victim all things considered.[42] A plausible explanation of this is that the child is harmed by the enhancement process regardless of whether she winds up better-off all things considered.

Moreover, what if the all-things-considered consequences of the parents' action in Case A were as yet undetermined? Should we then be agnostic about whether or not the child has been harmed? Or, if we ought to say that she has been harmed, should we do so only tentatively, recognizing that possible future benefits might tip the scales and prove us wrong? Such practices seem to me very counterintuitive. That we can have harmed people when the all-things-considered consequences of that harm remain undetermined or even when the one harmed is made better-off all things considered reliably explains our inclination to name and respond to harm when it occurs.

I conclude with Elizabeth Harman that "there can be harm even when there is not all-things-considered harm, and there can be a reason against an action in virtue of harm even when there is not all-things-considered harm."[43] We should say therefore that the parents in Case A cannot successfully defend themselves by claiming that they have not harmed their child.

## Defense by Rescue Analogy

(1) will not morally excuse the parents in Case A. But perhaps what the parents would have in mind is not (1) but rather

---

[41] Derek Parfit, *Reasons and Persons* (Oxford: Oxford University Press, 1991), 374. Parfit puts this assumption to work three times in Chapter 16 of *Reasons and Persons*. He does so once in his discussion of *The 14-Year-Old Girl* (359), once in his discussion of *Depletion* (363), and once in his discussion of *The Risky Policy* (372). Gregory Kavka endorses a similar position in "The Paradox of Future Individuals," *Philosophy and Public Affairs* 11 (1982), 100: "On the assumption that life as a slave is better than never existing, their [creating a slave child] would not harm the child."

[42] Shiffrin, "Wrongful Life...," 120–1.

[43] Harman, "Can We Harm and Benefit in Creating?," 109.

(2) If by $y$'s doing $A$, $x$ is foreseeably better-off all things considered than $x$ would have been had $y$ not done $A$, then $y$'s doing $A$ is not immoral due to harm done to $x$.

Here the parents concede that they harmed their child, but claim that because they harmed her in the knowledge that she would be better-off all things considered for their harming her, their harming her was morally permissible. The parents might seek to support (2) by claiming an analogy between their situation and that of a rescuer. When a rescuer breaks a person's arm as the only means of pulling him from a life-threatening situation, far from being blame-worthy, he is heralded as a hero. One tempting explanation of our favorable moral assessment of rescuers is that their actions are justified because they do not harm on balance, given the great benefit of rescue. Similarly, the parents in Case A might claim that their benefitting their child on balance justifies any harm that they caused her.

We have already seen how to respond to this line of defense—by highlighting with Shiffrin the justificatory asymmetry between pure and harm-averting bene-fits. Our use of "benefit" tends to be ambiguous between benefits that do and don't avert greater harms. Joel Feinberg's characterization of cases where harm is necessarily conjoined with rescue is an example of this. He suggests that the bestowal of an "overriding benefit" explains why the rescuer's action is morally justified.[44] Shiffrin argues that this characterization

> illegitimately trades upon a common equivocation of "benefit." In the rescue case, the injury is necessarily inflicted to prevent greater harm. Although we sometimes speak as though removing someone from harm *benefits* that person, it does not follow that the *beneficial* aspect of the saving does the moral justifica-tory work for inflicting the lesser harm. Rather, I believe the fact that a greater *harm* is averted performs the justificatory service.[45]

Shiffrin's distinction helps italicize that a rescue case is not a good analogy for Case A. As Case A has it, the parents' child would have lived a worthwhile life even without the enhancement surgery. The surgery is intended not to avert or lessen the bad in her life, but to make the good in her life even better. The parents in Case A harm for pure benefit, not for harm aversion, and cases where harm is caused for pure benefit call (2) into question.

---

[44] Joel Feinberg, "Wrongful Life and the Counterfactual Element in Harming," in *Freedom and Fulfillment: Philosophical Essays* (Princeton: Princeton University Press, 1992), 27.
[45] Shiffrin, "Wrongful Life...," 126.

## Supplementing Shiffrin: The Moral Significance
## of *Horrendous Harm*

The parents would be right to remind us at this point that rejecting (2) is not enough to morally impugn them; harming for pure benefit is not *always* wrong. We do sometimes have the right to harm others in order to purely benefit them all things considered. I take myself to have this right when I take my friend Adam— who is a non-verbal quadriplegic—swimming. The process of getting him to and into the pool requires moving his body in ways that cause him some moderate pain, but it would be hard for anyone who saw the smile on his face once he is in the pool to doubt that he should be taken swimming.

But even if there are cases where we can justifiably harm others for pure benefit, this is a very limited right, and introducing the category of *horrendous harm* to Shiffrin's thought undercuts this line of defense. Where *horrors* are concerned, even harm aversion has trouble justifying their causation. Consider the World War II bombing of Hiroshima and Nagasaki. Even of those who believe that the *horrendous* destruction of these cities was foreseeably harm-averting all things considered, many conclude that the dropping of the atomic bombs was nevertheless immoral. This same negative moral valuation of *horror* causation is all the more strongly intuitive in cases of pure benefit.

Though there may be counterexamples to the claim that *it is always wrong to harm another for pure benefit*, I am inclined to think they will only be cases of minimal or at most moderate harm. I am at a loss for counterexamples to the claim that *it is always wrong to horrendously harm another for pure benefit*. While harming *horrendously* to avert greater harm and harming non-*horrendously* to bestow pure benefit may have reasonable claims to moral exoneration, harming *horrendously* to bestow pure benefit does not.

## Appeals to Parental Rights

Suppose the parents in Case A maintained that it would have been wrong for most people to harm their child in the manner they did, but that they should be morally exonerated due to their special parental rights over their child.

Richard Swinburne observes that "most of us are dependent . . . at various times on other persons and authorities, such as teachers and the state, the latter having certain duties with respect to us, giving rise to certain rights over us."[46] He claims both that the parent-child relationship is one in which such caretaker rights

---

[46] Swinburne, *Providence and the Problem of Evil*, 224.

arise and that these rights include increased rights to harm children for their all-things-considered well-being.[47] Parents, for example, may have a right to send their children to a private school that will provide more opportunities for their children in the long run even if their children will be somewhat unhappy at the school.[48] Swinburne concludes, "I do not have the right to cause some stranger, Joe Bloggs, to suffer for his own good or that of Bill Snoggs, but I do have *some* right of this kind in respect of my own children."[49]

The scope of a carer's right to harm is plausibly taken to be a function of one's capacity, responsibility, and commitment to benefit, together comprising one's *caretaking roles*. Consider three broad ways to understand the relationship between caretaking roles and caretaker rights to cause harm for pure benefit. According to the first, the two are correlated on a simple sliding scale. As caretaking roles increase on the horizontal axis, caretaker rights increase on the vertical, *ad infinitum*. On this understanding, any evil—no matter how bad—could be caused permissibly for the sake of a child's all-things-considered pure benefit by a great enough—for instance a divine—caretaker.

Secondly, there may be a direct correlation between caretaking roles and rights to harm for pure benefit that approaches a threshold. Beyond that threshold are harms that are never permissibly caused for pure benefit, regardless of one's caretaker rights. Similar to the second understanding, the third suggests that rights to harm for pure benefit increase with caretaking roles to a threshold. There is not an absolute ban on harms beyond that threshold, however. They can be permissibly caused only in what I'll refer to as *extreme situations*. (I will say more about such situations shortly.)

The first understanding gives the best chance of justifying the parents' action in Case A. Parents are often morally justified in demanding that their children wear braces—at times a moderately painful and socially debilitating instrument. Likewise, parents sometimes do well to demand that their children stay in school until at least the age of eighteen so that they will have the pure benefit of the greater life-opportunities made available by further education. Such a policy can be to the parents' credit even in countries where this level of education is not a legal requirement and even when it is foreseeably accompanied by not insignificant psychological harms resulting from bullying or pressure to perform.

But it is clear that parental rights to harm for pure benefit do not extend much further than this. We may be inclined to think they do, for instance when parents decide for their young child to undergo a serious surgery in order to fix a

---

[47] Swinburne, *Providence and the Problem of Evil*, 227.

[48] This example is adapted from a related example on page 228 of Swinburne, *Providence and the Problem of Evil*.

[49] Swinburne, *Providence and the Problem of Evil*, 227.

considerable but only cosmetic deformity. But I think cases like this are more plausibly understood to be cases of harm aversion in disguise. Maybe part of what the parents aim for in deciding on a surgery of this sort is pure benefit, but I believe much of the justificatory work is being done by the fact that the surgery will avert the child from very significant psychological harm, harm that would have been the likely result of living in an appearance-centered society with a considerable deformity. We are perhaps distracted from this harm aversion by the fact that the corrective surgery aims *in the first instance* at merely cosmetic modification.

But even if this case of cosmetic surgery were a case of parental harm justified primarily by pure benefit, *horrors* blow right through this level of harm. It is not implausible that Helen Keller was better-off all things considered for the disease she contracted at nineteen months old and its consequences in her life. Suppose Helen's parents somehow knew in advance that this would be so, and caused Helen to contract the sight-and-hearing-negating disease so that it would be so. It seems to me that this knowledge and motive would in no way justify the parents' action. Even on the first understanding of parental caretaking roles and rights, the pure benefits accrued in Helen's life are inadequate to justify such treatment of a daughter by her parents.

The appeal to special parental rights should have a similarly negligible effect on our moral evaluation of Case A. Given that the child in Case A would have a worthwhile life even without the harm caused, and would suffer less, it is hard to see how mere life-enhancement could have justificatory force significant enough to justify *horrendous harm*. Even if parents have greater scope to harm their children for their children's benefit when it comes to minor harm, this does not carry over to cases of *horrendous harm*. If anything is *greater* in these cases as a result of parents' caretaking roles, it is the parents' obligations to protect against and not to cause *horrors* in the lives of their children, making an appeal to parental roles more likely to further impugn the parents than to morally exonerate them.

## Appeals to Retrospective Acceptance

What if as a final defense the parents in Case A appealed to the fact that their child came, in time, to not wish the *horrendous harm* she endured out of her life history, given the great good that resulted from it? Even when foreseeable, retrospective acceptance of this sort does little to justify serious harms caused for pure benefit. Consider again the life of Helen Keller. It is plausible that Helen *did* come to not wish away the suffering she endured as a child. But if we once more imagine that her parents caused her to suffer as she did, having done so with this eventual subjective judgment in view would be as impotent to justify such harm as having done so with an eye to the objective judgment that the harm would result in her life being better-off all things considered.

Robert Adams rightly points out that although a victim's retrospective attitude toward harm is ethically relevant, "it is in general what is preferable [to the one harmed] before the action that is most relevant to the moral perfection of [a harming] agent."[50] Prioritizing the preferences people have prior to actions that will affect them is most relevant morally because it respects human persons' rights to (within limits) exercise autonomy about how their lives will go. And because sanity requires us to adjust to what has been, that someone would be likely to come to retrospectively accept a certain sort of harm is not a good barometer for judging that they would be prospectively in favor of it.

As Case A is described, it is a young child who is caused to suffer, and we can suppose, very plausibly, that the child not only *did* not give prior informed consent to such suffering but *could* not have had the competency to do so. And any appeal to the fact that the child *would* have consented had she been competent to do so is unconvincing. Firstly, I doubt this counterfactual could be true. I doubt this because, following Robert Adams, I do not see what could make it true.[51] The most natural candidate would be something about the child that it pertains to. But at the time of the parents' decision, what is true about the child is not enough to provide competent consent. After the parents' decision, what is true about the child will depend on a great host of variables, including the decision itself. Which potential future self of their child are the parents supposed to imagine when considering whether their child would give hypothetical consent to the enhancement surgery? I don't see any reasonable way of answering this question.

But even if I'm wrong about this, human persons tend to weight an action's temporally near effects over its temporally distant effects and the aversion of harm over the procuring of pure benefit. For these reasons, among cases resulting in all-things-considered benefit, cases of imminent *horrendous harm* caused for merely pure benefit are among those least likely to be prospectively consented to.

And finally, it is very unclear that even actual prospective consent would be sufficient to morally justify harming someone *horrendously* for her pure benefit. Because competency in consenting to an outcome relies on capability to conceive of that outcome, and the badness of *horrendous* outcomes exceeds human conceptual capabilities, there is reason to think human persons could never be in position to competently consent to suffer *horrendous evil*.

---

[50] Robert Merrihew Adams, "Existence, Self-Interest, and the Problem of Evil," in Robert Merrihew Adams, *The Virtue of Faith and Other Essays in Philosophical Theology* (Oxford: Oxford University Press, 1987), 75. This is in tension with Parfit's contention that "[t]here may be no objection to our harming someone when we know both that this person will have no regrets, and that our act will be clearly better for this person" (*Reasons and Persons*, 374).

[51] For a thorough treatment of issues related to this claim, see Robert Merrihew Adams, "Middle Knowledge and the Problem of Evil," in *The Problem of Evil*, ed. Marilyn McCord Adams and Robert Merrihew Adams (New York: Oxford University Press, 1990), 77–93.

Appeals to both retrospective acceptance and prospective consent seem impotent to morally justify the parents' action.

## The Verdict

The parents in Case A knowingly and voluntarily caused their child to suffer harms, those harms were *horrendous*, and they were caused merely for a pure benefit rather than to prevent a greater harm. Intuitions suggest that it is entirely appropriate to find the parents morally at fault for their actions due to the harm they caused their child, and neither appeals to special parental rights nor to retrospective acceptance or hypothetical consent are capable of forestalling this conclusion. Moreover, though I have focused on the *morality* of Case A in this discussion, the parents' action also calls into question their *character* as parents. If you love someone, there are certain ways you cannot bear to hurt them. The *horrendous* harming of child by parents in Case A cannot be reconciled with appropriate parental love. As Austin Farrer puts it, "it would be a strange sort of love which destroyed its object in the process of bettering it."[52]

If you are in doubt about my moral intuition regarding Case A, note that none of the harm I have detailed in Case A is as obviously *horrendous* as some of the examples of actual *horrendous harm* I listed in Chapter 1. I have tried not to taint Case A with forms of harm that are so emotionally difficult to consider that they would make it hard to isolate our intuitions about the harm involved. But it is fair to acknowledge that there are harms in our world that likely go well beyond how many of our imaginations fill out the details of Case A, and this should incline us still more to the conclusion that at least some *horrendous harm* cannot be justified by mere pure benefit.

## Implications for the Ethics of *Horrendous Evil*

Zooming out from this casuistry, important results for ethics come into view. For one, applying the moral asymmetry between harms and benefits to cases of *horrendous harm* in particular highlights an important distinction between the moral justification of actions and the summative value of their consequences. Specifically, whether harms are justified by the foreseeable benefits they produce cannot be easily determined along a better-off/worse off divide. Elizabeth Harman puts it usefully when, reflecting on cases like Case A, she writes that

---

[52] Austin Farrer, *Love Almighty and Ills Unlimited* (London: Collins, 1966), Chapter VI, 119.

there are two different senses in which benefits can *outweigh* harms in a person's life. The benefits in these cases do outweigh the harms in that they are more beneficial than the harms are harmful: the total package of benefits plus harms leaves the person better off than he or she otherwise would be. But the benefits do not outweigh the harms in that they do not render it permissible to cause the harms. Another way of putting this is that the *reasons* to benefit do not outweigh the *reasons* against harm, though the benefits themselves outweigh the harms.[53]

Because consequent harms generally provide greater reason against action than consequent benefits provide for action, an action can be immoral due to its consequent harm even when that harm is foreseeably less harmful than the action's consequent benefits are beneficial.[54] In Harman's words, "Reasons against harm are *morally serious* reasons that are difficult to outweigh; the mere presence of benefits more beneficial than the harms are harmful is not sufficient to render harming permissible."[55]

My casuistry therefore urges suspicion of any ethical theory that proposes the summation of the value of consequences as a barometer for morality. Cases such as Case A—ones of causing *horrendous harm* for pure benefit—are among those that most clearly highlight the problem with moral principles such as

> (U) An action is morally permissible if and only if the sum total of the value of the foreseeable consequences produced by that action is no worse than the sum total of the value of the foreseeable consequences produced by any other actions that the acting agent could have performed.

According to this principle, it could be that any scenario in which the parents in Case A do *not* subject their child to enhancement surgery—by virtue of being worse all things considered than the scenario in which they do—will fail the test of moral permissibility. If we accept (U), we may be forced to conclude that the parents in Case A would have been morally blameworthy if they had *not horrendously* harmed their child!

I take that to be an unacceptable result. A correct theory of morality should take account of more than the summative value of the consequences because persons have morality-relevant interests other than and more specific than their interest in maximizing their all-things-considered well-being. James Woodward gives a deontological example of such an interest when he reflects that

---

[53] Harman, "Can We Harm and Benefit in Creating?," 100.
[54] Shiffrin affirms the point: "[A] harm that does not make a life worse does not always have less or significantly less weight than harms that do worsen lives" ("Wrongful Life...," 134).
[55] Harman, "Can We Harm and Benefit in Creating?," 108.

We have a strong interest in retaining control over central aspects of our lives—an interest which is in part protected by the right to refuse medical treatment. Coercive medical intervention can be wrong and wrong because of the way that it adversely affects this interest or violates this right, even though it affects a patient's other interests in a way which we may regard as, on balance, beneficial.[56]

But in addition to deontological concerns, certain sorts of consequences—notably *horrendous* consequences—also resist mere quantitative moral analysis. I suggest that the right not to be *horrendously* harmed is another example of a morality-relevant interest other than (and in this case stronger than) our general interest in maximizing our all-things-considered well-being. It is by violating this right that the parents in Case A act against the interests of their child, despite their actions predictably enhancing her life taken as a whole.

Elizabeth Anscombe argues in her "Modern Moral Philosophy" that basing morality solely on the value of the foreseeable consequences is a mistake because there are some actions that are absolutely morally prohibited "whatever [the] consequences." Anscombe undermines the plausibility of her critique, however, by citing examples such as "treachery" among the (implied) absolutely morally prohibited.[57]

When *horrendous evils* are substituted as examples and the justificatory asymmetry between pure and harm-averting benefits is applied, I think absolute moral prohibitions become much more plausible. I recommend (V) as a moral principle capturing the morality of *horror* causation:

(V) It is wrong for one individual to voluntarily cause another individual[58] to be *horrendously* harmed for pure benefit.[59]

I believe (V) is very plausible.[60] (If there are counterexamples to (V), they may be cases where victims of *horrendous harm* consent to or even request the relevant

[56] James Woodward, "Reply to Parfit," *Ethics* 97 (1987), 804.

[57] G.E.M. Anscombe, "Modern Moral Philosophy," *Philosophy* 33 (1958), 10.

[58] V is neutral regarding whether it is ever morally permissible for a person to cause or permit *horrendous harm to himself* in order to attain a pure benefit for himself or another.

[59] This principle purposefully does not distinguish between *horrendous harm* caused as a *means* to a pure benefit and *horrendous harm* caused as a foreseen *side-effect*. I am doubtful that this distinction—often central to discussions of the Doctrine of Double Effect—can be stated in a morally significant form. But even if it can be so stated, where *horrendous harm* is concerned, pure benefit will be insufficiently justificatory regardless of whether the harm in question is used as a means to that benefit or is a mere side-effect of it. The plausibility of double effect reasoning as it is commonly employed in just war theory relies on harm being caused for harm aversion.

[60] Even if you disagree with my asymmetric account of harm and benefit and adopt instead a symmetric counterfactual comparative account, (V) could be reformulated as 'It is wrong for one individual to voluntarily cause another individual to be *horrendously* harmed for a non-bad-state-of-affairs-averting good.'

harm. I am not convinced that such cases would provide counterexamples, but if you disagree, "without her consent" can be added to the end of the principle. Because many actual *horrendous harms* are in fact not consented to, this amended version of the principle is also sufficient for my purposes.) Moreover, all I will need for my overall argument is the truth of the claim that no mere pure benefits are sufficient to justify the causation of the *most horrendous harms* of the actual world.

## Challenging the Principle

One might object: Don't we consent to causing *horrendous evils* for pure benefit all of the time? Isn't this the case, for instance, when we approve of raising road speed limits? We have enough predictive sophistication to know, undoubtedly, that raising speed limits will cause more people to be killed in car crashes, and yet—at least sometimes—we deem it permissible to raise speed limits for the non-essential benefit of travel efficiency.

I doubt the fact that there are new intervening agents here—the commissioner of transportation doesn't crash the cars himself—will do enough to get us off the hook because family and work responsibilities make it unreasonable to expect many drivers to stop using road transportation, even if they are strongly averse to speed limit increases. Moreover, this seems like a particularly devastating counterexample to (V) because the motivating pure benefit here is not even a pure benefit for those individuals who will wind up in serious car crashes, but only for the community of travelers as a whole.

I have several responses to this proposed counterexample. Firstly, even if this is a clear case of causing *horrendous evil*, the fact that most accidents are not *horrendous* may be affecting our intuitions. Our intuitions would change markedly if, say, we stipulated that the deaths caused by the policy change would all occur in the most brutal, torturous manner. Once we change the example to a case that calls to mind obviously *horrendous evil*, I doubt most of us remain inclined to register our approval.

Moreover, even if raising speed limits is a case of causing *horrendous* suffering *for a group*—the group of motorists that travel the stipulated road—it is not a case of knowingly and voluntarily causing *horrendous* suffering *for an individual*. The policymaker in the road case does not know who will suffer as a result of his decision. Nor does he in any sense *will* the suffering of any person in particular. His decision to raise speed limits only *risks* suffering for specific individuals. It therefore does not violate (V). What this case surfaces is that causing *horrendous harm* for pure benefit with respect to a group while only risking it with respect to individuals may have a more plausible claim to moral permissibility than causing a specific individual to be *horrendously* harmed for pure benefit.

What if we complicate the case? Suppose that as we were deliberating about whether to raise the speed limit, a road genie appeared and gave us the names, addresses, and personal profiles of each of the people that would be killed in *horrendous* fashion by car crashes as a result of our raising the speed limit. And suppose we had very good reason to trust this road genie. Does this change things? I believe it does. We might be tempted to believe it does not, because, after all, we were already able to predict roughly how many people would be killed by raising the speed limit, and we had counted that cost. Why should it matter that we now have in our possession a record of names, addresses, and other life details?

It matters because of the importance of taking individuals seriously in ethics. *Ceteris paribus*, when harming for benefit, it is worse to procure the benefit by knowingly and voluntarily *horrendously* harming one specific individual than by risking *horrendously* harming numerous individuals, knowing that you will as a consequence *horrendously* harm one of them.[61] Relatedly, procreating ten children, knowing in advance that it is highly likely that one of them will be born with a *horrendous* disease, is less morally problematic than procreating ten children, knowing in advance that the fifth will suffer from the disease. I think this is in part because riskers of *horrendous harm* are able to maintain a rational hope for the well-being of those they potentially harm that causers of *horrendous harm* cannot rationally maintain for those they *horrendously* harm.[62] Consequently, people often have rights not to be caused to suffer certain types of harm that do not extend to being merely risked to suffer the same types of harm. Every time a parent drives with a child in the car, for example, the parent risks harm that it would be immoral for the parent to cause. (I'll have more to say about the ethics of risking in my consideration of Case C below.)

Taking stock, if the harms that raising speed limits would cause would be genuinely *horrendous* and were reliably detailed to us by a road genie, should we then never raise speed limits? For that matter, should we not build any roads at all? We may be inclined to think we can't do without roads, even if we can do

---

[61]   There also could be intermediate cases where, for instance, you know the addresses of the people who will be killed, even if you don't know them by name or other life details. I judge that the greater your knowledge of the person who will be harmed for benefit, *ceteris paribus*, the greater the moral reason against that harm. I'm inclined to think this is related to the fact that the more you know about how an individual will be affected by harm, the less you can rationally hope against potential bad consequences of the harming action. If all I know is a person's address, I can rationally hope that their being harmed will not have bad consequences for a family with young children. However, if I know enough about the person who will be harmed to know he is a father with young children, I can no longer maintain this hope rationally.

[62]   I therefore would be inclined to a different assessment of cases where riskers of *horrors* act without hope for the well-being of those whom their actions will possibly harm—cases of dropping nuclear bombs on cities or of aimlessly and maliciously firing a gun into a large crowd, for instance. Such actions may not be any less bad for the actors' ignorance of the identities of the future casualties of their actions. When harming *for benefit*, whether one knows which individuals will be harmed makes a difference, but harming with mal-intent may sometimes be so bad that knowing the identities of the individuals who will be harmed may add nothing to the badness. What Nazi's did in the crematoria was plausibly no worse for having a detailed list of names.

without raising speed limits. But I'm inclined to think any difference in intuitions here is at least partially explained by the fact that *some* road construction is a disguised case of harm aversion. Roads certainly accrue to their users all sorts of pure benefits, but they also avert significant harms. Moving resources more efficiently results in manifold pure benefits, but it also allows medicine to be more readily shipped to those in need of it, makes hospitals more accessible for emergency visits, and makes a variety of harm-averting benefits available to those in need during humanitarian crises. The effect of road development on the economy and hence on overall harm aversion is complex and unclear. Admittedly, we wouldn't have lots of roads that we actually have if we built roads primarily for harm-averting purposes. But we would have a good number of roads, and given this, I take it to be a plausible result that additional roads should not be constructed—or at least that there should be heavy restrictions placed on using them—if a road genie reliably detailed individuals who would be *horrendously* harmed by further construction and made a compelling argument that such construction would not be harm-averting.

I conclude that even these difficult proposed counterexamples to (V) are vulnerable on several grounds. The harm these cases call to mind is not clearly *horrendous*, is not clearly *caused* in the relevant person-specific sense, and is at least partially justified by its harm-averting power. Such counterexamples should not therefore cause us to doubt the principle forwarded as capturing the immorality of causing specific individuals to suffer *horrors* for pure benefits.

## Extreme Situations

All that said, I admit that one still might reasonably resist (V). What if a potential *horror*-causer (or permitter) were in an *extreme situation*, that is, a situation in which all of his non-*horror*-causing (or permitting) alternatives were *so* inferior that there regrettably seemed no reasonable alternative to *horror*-causation (or permission)? What if, for instance, causing or permitting another to be harmed *horrendously* were (a) necessary for (b) bestowing a pure benefit that (c) would exceedingly outweigh the *horrendous harm*, (d) the possession of which would likely far surpass any alternative all-things-considered state (for the harmed) attained by equal or less harm, and (e) no other alternative courses of action would have been likely to yield lives better than ones minimally worth living for the harmed.

If conditions in the vicinity of (a)–(e) were satisfied, would it be permissible to cause *horrendous evil* for pure benefit? For example, would it be permissible for the parents in Case A to *horrendously* harm their child if the pure benefit procured by the harm made the difference between a life that is a great good for her all things considered and one that, while free from significant harm, is only minimally worth living?

If the harm in question is severe enough, I am doubtful that it would be permissible; but this question does not need to be answered here. The parents in Case A are not in an *extreme situation*; they do not come anywhere close to satisfying (a)–(e). As the case stipulates, their child would have had a worthwhile and fulfilling life even without the enhancement surgery, and this is undoubtedly a reasonable alternative to the parents' *horror* causation. I reaffirm the common-sense intuition, therefore, that the parents in Case A wrong their child by violating her right not to be *horrendously* harmed for pure benefit.

## Case B:   *Horrendous Harm* Permitted for Pure Benefit

*Suppose that the enhancement described in Case A can in very rare cases be passed on by the exchange of bodily fluids, and suppose one child contracted it from another while at school. The parents of the child who contracted the condition now have a decision to make. If the parents do nothing, it will take several years for their child's body to accept the enhancement, during which time he will have to endure the horrendous physical and psychological harms of the recovery period described in Case A, but afterward he will live an enhanced life that will result in pure benefit all things considered. If the parents act to avert the enhancement—which they have the right to do and could do easily (it involves merely feeding their child a pill)—the child nevertheless will have a worthwhile and full life. The parents permit the enhancement for their child's all-things-considered pure benefit.*

This case diverges from Case A in one plausibly morally significant way. The *horrendous harm* is not *caused* by the parents. The primary moral challenge to their decision is due to their *permission* of the *horrendous harm* in question. That is, their responsibility for the harm is due primarily to an inaction of theirs rather than an action of theirs. Do the parents in Case B nevertheless wrong their child? It seems intuitively clear that they do.

The child in Case B has her rights violated—for one, the right to protection of her body from excessive, and especially *horrendous*, harm. All the more so for their caretaking roles, the parents are morally obligated to make a serious effort to avoid the violation of such rights.

An objection to this conclusion might point to there being a morally significant distinction between causing and permitting. One might attempt to defend the parents' *horror*-permissive behavior by appeal to the following principle:

An agent is responsible for her actions in a way she is not responsible for those actions she permits or allows or does not prevent when she could.[63]

---

[63] The wording of this principle is taken from Marilyn Adams, *Horrendous Evils and the Goodness of God*, 35.

This principle has some plausibility, but what is undeniable is that a person *is* morally responsible for *some* of what she permits. Chiefly, she is responsible for permissions foreseeably resulting in *horrendous* suffering that could be avoided at minimal cost, and with respect to which she has the right to intervene.[64] Case B is a clear example of such a permission. So even if the causing/permitting principle is true, it won't morally exonerate the parents. It remains plausible that in choosing to permit the enhancement, they severely wrong their child.

Consideration of Case B motivates a second—to my mind, equally compelling—version of (V):

(V*) It is wrong for one individual to voluntarily cause *or permit* another individual to be *horrendously* harmed for pure benefit when he has the right to avoid the harm and could do so easily and without causing other harm.

### Case C:    *Horrendous Harm* Risked for Pure Benefit

*Parents are choosing to send their child to one of two secondary schools. One is a boarding school with a wonderful educational standard, but also where there is a significant amount of hazing of younger students by their peers. Moreover, there is significant academic pressure at this school; some students fall into depression and suicide is not uncommon. The second school has only an average educational reputation, but is a much safer environment. The parents can predict that if they send their child to the second school, he will have a worthwhile life and be at very low risk of suffering horrendously. If they send their child to the first school, he will be afforded opportunities that likely will give him a significantly better life all things considered, but at the risk of being horrendously harmed by hazing, depression, or worse. Motivated by a desire to enrich their child's life, the parents send their child to the first school.*

Case C diverges from the previous two cases in several respects. Only in Case C is the likelihood that *horrendous harm* will result in a better life all things considered for the child not treated as a morally sufficient reason for the action being evaluated. In Case C, the parents hope against *horrendous harm*, and the possibility and probability of it not occurring in the first place bears on their decision.

In fact, Case C does not commit itself to even the possibility of *horrendous harm* resulting in their child being better-off all things considered than he otherwise would have been. In contrast to Cases A and B, where any remotely plausible defense of the parents had to rely on a high likelihood of all-things-considered

---

[64] Perhaps some *horrors* can be outside the scope of one's legitimate involvement. For example, you might think a single nation should not step in and stop all *horrors* worldwide even if the cost of doing so were not a factor. This is controversial. But nonetheless, neither my cases of parents and child nor the case of God and creature are plausibly understood to be cases of illegitimate involvement.

counterfactual comparative benefit, I will argue that—under certain conditions—the parents in Case C act permissibly even if they have no special knowledge that things will turn out well all things considered if *horrors* do occur.

Moreover, only in Case C is no *horrendous harm* caused or permitted for the sake of pure benefit. The potential *horrors* in Case C are not caused in my technical sense because they are not a known consequence of the parents' action. Nor are they permitted, for I am assuming that the parents will be unaware of any hazing or depression that occurs during their child's tenure at the school. (This is not an unrealistic assumption, given the fact that these things often surface only well after they occur.) Therefore, the parents in Case C avoid the charge that they have violated (V*). The parents have not knowingly and voluntarily caused or permitted an individual to suffer *horrendously*; they have only *risked horror* participation.

One might think to reformulate:

(W) It is wrong for one individual to voluntarily cause, permit, *or risk* another individual to be *horrendously* harmed for pure benefit when he has the right to avoid the harm and could do so easily and without causing other harm.

But (W) is implausible. Even if it is morally objectionable to cause or permit *horrendous harm* for an individual's pure benefit, intuitions suggest that it is nonetheless sometimes morally permissible to *risk* it for this type of good. The romantic who leads his girlfriend (by a sufficiently safe route) to the top of a mountain so that he can ask her to marry him is not to be condemned because he increased the probability that she would be harmed *horrendously* due to a bad fall. Their subsequent marriage presents another *horror* risk. In relationships involving high levels of intimacy and commitment, there is bonding at many and deep levels of personality. This can provide wonderful pure benefits, but only at the expense of significantly increasing the risk of *horrors* if the relationship breaks down. And *horror* risk continues when parents have children and allow them, for instance, to ride bicycles and play dangerous sports such as ice hockey and pole vaulting. Reasonable increases in the probability of *horror* participation are an unavoidable part of living a normal human life.

It is morally permissible to risk *horrendous harm* for an individual's pure benefit sometimes, but when is the risk too great? I suggest that to not wrong another due to risking *horrendous harm* in his life, you must (1) accept liability for incidental harm, (2) know that the expected value of your risk compares favorably for that person with your alternatives, and (3) have no reason to assume that person's dissent, whether explicitly stated or inferred (for instance from your girlfriend's terrible fear of heights). Moreover, in at least some cases of parents making decisions for their children, I'm inclined to think (1) and (2) alone are enough. Parental caretaking rights give parents greater scope for permissible risk even in cases where children actively dissent.

We can build into Case C that condition (1) is met by the parents. What would it take for them to meet conditions (2) and (3)? The answer to this question is reasonably taken to be a function of the probability of *horrendous harm* occurring and the probability of that harm, if it does occur, being balanced-off by benefit in the context of the rest of one's life considered as a whole. Assume that in choosing the educationally superior school, the parents in Case C take either a low, moderate, or high risk that their child will suffer something *horrendous* as a result. Likewise, assume that there is either a low, moderate, or high probability that *horrendous harm*, if suffered, will be balanced-off by benefits in the rest of the child's life. Lastly, assume that the parents have reliable access to these probabilities. The parents may therefore find themselves in any of the following risk-situations:

(1)  Low risk of *horror* with low probability of balancing-off.
(2)  Low risk of *horror* with moderate probability of balancing-off.
(3)  Low risk of *horror* with high probability of balancing-off.
(4)  Moderate risk of *horror* with low probability of balancing-off.
(5)  Moderate risk of *horror* with moderate probability of balancing-off.
(6)  Moderate risk of *horror* with high probability of balancing-off.
(7)  High risk of *horror* with low probability of balancing-off.
(8)  High risk of *horror* with moderate probability of balancing-off.
(9)  High risk of *horror* with high probability of balancing-off.

Note that high risk of *horror* will not be the same as high probability of *horror*. If there is a high probability of *horror*, then plausibly the *horrendous* consequences would be foreknown and would therefore count as being caused rather than risked. There is likely to be disagreement about how high the probability of *horror* can be before risk turns into causation; very roughly, I'm inclined to think of the transition from risk into causation occurring around the 60–70 percent probable range.

It seems to me that people are often justified in risking *horrendous harm* for an individual's significant pure benefit if they find themselves in positions (1), (2), or (3). Position (1) might at first appear dubious, but only until it is recognized that position (1) is often the best-case scenario in any case of human *horror*-risk. It is not common for us to see genuinely *horrendous* suffering balanced-off in the lives of *horror*-participants. Position (6) is difficult. More would have to be said about the motivating pure benefit to come to a proper judgment. Only (4), (5), (7), (8), and (9) seem to me to be positions where it is clearly immoral for the parents to risk *horrendous harm* for significant pure benefit. In (1), (2), and (3), the probable result is that they will benefit their child all things considered. In position (6), the parents can at least be confident that the remainder of their child's life will be worthwhile all things considered. So long as the parents in Case C risk in a morally favorable position, they should be cleared of the charge that they have wronged their child or acted in an unloving manner toward him.

### Case D:    *Horrendous Harm* Permitted for Harm-Averting Benefit

*A family is being held captive and their captors have set up a torture device. If the parents do nothing, the device will horrendously torture one of their children. If the parents flip a switch, the initial torture will be avoided; however, a second device will then torture either the same child or another of their children even more horrendously. The parents are sure that the devices will work as has been described. The parents do nothing.*

In permitting harm not for pure benefit but in order to avert greater harm, the parents in Case D do not violate (V\*), and they act in the best interests of their children.

If the parents had to *horrendously* torture one of their children *themselves* in order to avoid the still worse torture of one of their children, their decision would be more difficult to evaluate morally. As I mentioned earlier, it is a reasonable, if controversial, thought that it would be immoral to *cause horrendous harm* even if it were necessary to avert greater harm.

In Case D, however, the causing/permitting principle seems to do enough work to clear the parents of all charges, even if they know that the child who will benefit will be a different child than the one who will suffer. Although they permit *horrendous harm*, not permitting it—their only alternative—would have been even worse for one of their children. The parents can be likened to rescuers desiring to save two people but only capable of saving one. Their circumstances are revoltingly unfortunate, but it would be unreasonable to fault the parents for allowing the lesser of two evils.

## Conclusions

The person-destroying potential of *horrors* grounds convincing counterexamples to the broadly utilitarian assumption that a metric can be used to weigh the moral significance of consequences. Cases A and B, in particular, suggest that consequences are not in principle capable of being summed such that the calculation tells you what you ought to do.

I conclude that the parents are morally at fault in Cases A and B because it is wrong to cause or permit another to suffer *horrendously* in order to bestow pure benefit. The parents could have acted permissibly in Cases C and D because *horrendous harm* may be risked for pure benefit when the expected outcome compares favorably with other alternatives, and *horrendous harm* may be permitted for the sake of averting still greater harm.

# 3

# Applying the Analogies

## Causing for Pure Benefits

In the previous chapter, I sketched four cases where *horrendous evil* is caused, permitted, or risked by human persons for all-things-considered benefit. *Prima facie* moral intuitions in these cases were strong and philosophical reflection affirmed them. I now apply these four cases to the project of theodicy. Each represents a structural approach to theodicy that is present in the contemporary literature on the problem of evil. I claim that the analogical relations are strong, and that the conclusions reached in the human cases should be brought to bear on their divine analogues.

I will classify each theodicy I consider as Type A, Type B, Type C, or Type D. A theodicy is Type A if God, like the parents in Case A, is depicted as causing particular persons to suffer *horrendous harm* for pure benefit. As with Case A, this does not mean that the harm is *only* caused; God also may be depicted as permitting and risking *horrendous harm*. That he causes at least some *horrors* is sufficient for a Type A classification, and I will evaluate Type A Theodicy with respect to divine *causation* of *horrendous harm* because that is where I take it to be structurally most vulnerable. A theodicy is Type B if God is depicted as permitting particular persons to suffer *horrors* though not as causing any to do so. Again, this is a sufficient condition for Type B classification. God may also risk *horrors* according to Type B Theodicy, though it is his permission of them that I will focus my structural evaluation upon in the first instance.

Type C Theodicy is theodicy that depicts God as risking *horrendous harm* and stipulates that God is *morally obligated* to permit any *horrors* that result from that risk. Type C Theodicy therefore diverges from Case C in depicting God as at least permitting *horrors* in addition to risking them. The parents in Case C, like the policy-makers deciding on highway construction, risk *horrors* in the lives of individuals without causing or permitting them. They don't cause or permit them because they don't know in advance of its occurrence that any particular *horror* will occur. But with God things are different. Because he is omniscient, he has massively greater ability to foresee *horrors*. Even if the occurrence of particular future *horrors* is not causally determined and God lacks Molinist knowledge,[1] it is

---

[1] See Chapter 1, n. 21 on Molinism.

*Non-Identity Theodicy: A Grace-Based Response to the Problem of Evil*. Vince R. Vitale, Oxford University Press (2020).
© Vince R. Vitale.
DOI: 10.1093/oso/9780198864226.003.0003

nonetheless the case that God would see coming many of the *horrors* that occur in the minutes, seconds, and moments preceding their occurrence, when many of them will have become exceedingly probable. And as an omnipotent being, he would have the power to avert these *horrors* with divine ease. Moreover, as Swinburne affirms, "since God is also omnipotent, he is able to ensure that no one remains in such [situations of harm] for longer than he (God) chooses."[2] Most of the theodicies I treat are committed enough to non-Molinist libertarian human free will for them to depict God as risking *horrors*, but God is too knowledgeable and powerful to *merely* risk *horrors*. Maybe God permits *horrors* with good reason—a thesis the remaining chapters will explore—but nonetheless, he permits them.

Though Type C Theodicy diverges from Case C in this respect, it shares with Case C the assumption that if the agents in question are morally at fault, they are so only for the *risk* that they take. In Case C, this is because the parents only risk the harm in question. In Type C Theodicy, this is because God is taken to be morally obligated to permit *horrors* that result from his risk. In Chapter 4, I grant this assumption of Type C Theodicy for the sake of argument and make my evaluation with respect to divine risk. In Chapter 5, I return to question whether the claim of divine moral obligation to permit *horrors* can withstand scrutiny.

Type D Theodicy follows Case D in depicting God as permitting and not causing *horrendous harm* in order to avert still greater harm.

## Type A Theodicy

I will start with three theodicies that are analogous to Case A in depicting God as causing particular persons to undergo *horrendous harm* in order to bestow pure benefits. I will briefly summarize each Type A Theodicy and then evaluate whether it is *structurally promising* with respect to *horrors*. That is, if the set of facts and reasons posited by the theodicy were true, would God be ethically in the clear?

## Type A: John Hick's Soul-Making Theodicy

John Hick presents his Type A Theodicy in his classic book *Evil and the God of Love*. There he rejects any historical notions of Augustinian original righteousness and a subsequent cosmic fall as arguably unintelligible[3]—suffering from

---

[2] Swinburne, *Providence and the Problem of Evil*, 232.
[3] John Hick, *Evil and the God of Love*, 2nd ed. (London and Basingstoke: The Macmillan Press, 1977), 278–80. See also 172–6.

"insuperable scientific, moral, and logical objections"[4]—and any attempt to shift ultimate responsibility for evil away from God as undermining divine sovereignty. Affirming an Irenaean approach to theodicy as developed in Friedrich Schleiermacher, Hick accepts God as the ultimate cause of evil. In his words,

> [God's] decision to create the existing universe was the primary and necessary precondition for the occurrence of evil, all other conditions being contingent upon this, and He took His decision in awareness of all that would flow from it.[5]

And again, "it is … an inevitable theological inference, to which we must not blind ourselves, that the actual universe, with all its good and evil, exists on the basis of God's will."[6]

Hick argues that the fatal mistake of many theodicies is that they conceive of humanity more like animal pets, for whom we are inclined to construct environments as pleasurable as possible, than like human children, "who are to grow to adulthood in an environment whose primary and overriding purpose is not immediate pleasure but the realization of the most valuable potentialities of human personality."[7] According to Hick, reconceiving the purpose of humanity in this way makes possible conceiving the human benefits for which evils are divinely caused.

Most broadly, Hick suggests that the benefit of soul formation plays the central role in justifying God with respect to evil. God's primary purpose in creating is to initiate a soul-making process, and all evils can be justified in terms of their pedagogical usefulness in that process. Hick depicts the world as a classroom for a course on moral development, and claims that the sort of environment appropriate to such development would have to be one of "challenge and response."[8] In fact, he goes much further, maintaining that a world well-suited for such development would be "broadly the kind of world of which we find ourselves to be a part."[9] To support this conclusion, Hick argues systematically that "[the world's] imperfections are integral to its fitness as a place of soul-making."[10]

He proceeds with this systematic reflection without recognizing the justificatory asymmetry between pure benefits and benefits that avert greater harm. Thus, the moral objection to causing *horrors* when those *horrors* are not necessary to avert greater harm remains outside Hick's dialectical radar.

---

[4]  Hick, *Evil and the God of Love*, 249. He refers to the Augustinian approach as "fatally lacking in plausibility" (John Hick, "An Irenaean Theodicy," in *Encountering Evil: Live Options in Theodicy*, eds. Stephen T. Davis and John B. Cobb (Edinburgh and Atlanta: John Know Press, 1981), 40).
[5]  Hick, *Evil and the God of Love*, 290.        [6]  Hick, *Evil and the God of Love*, 363.
[7]  Hick, *Evil and the God of Love*, 258.
[8]  John Hick, "An Irenaean Theodicy" (1981), 46.
[9]  Hick, "An Irenaean Theodicy" (1981), 48.        [10]  Hick, *Evil and the God of Love*, 237.

Hick's first step is to claim the logical impossibility of free persons being created ready-made in the state that is to constitute the end of the soul-making process.[11] Hick concedes that human persons could have been constituted so as to guarantee that they would always act freely and rightly in relation to one another, but suggests that "one who has attained to goodness by meeting and eventually mastering temptations, and this by rightly making responsible choices in concrete situations, is good in a richer and more valuable sense than would be one created *ab initio* in a state either of innocence or of virtue."[12]

Moreover, Hick claims that it is logically impossible for God to produce by sheer fiat the authentic fiduciary attitudes *toward him* that he values from human persons.[13] To illustrate the point, Hick describes a case of hypnotism. He admits that even if a person is hypnotized, the actions of one carrying out post-hypnotic suggestions are free actions. However, he thinks we must say that the patient is not free as far as these particular actions are concerned "*in relation to the hypnotist*."[14] If God in his omnipotence plays hypnotist, "there would be something inauthentic about the resulting trust, love, or service."[15]

Hick concludes, therefore, that a necessary condition of the soul-making process—of coming to trust and love God and to "[embody] the most valuable kind of moral goodness"[16]—is being created at an epistemological distance from God.[17] The world must be to some extent "as if there were no God." God must be a hidden deity, veiled by his creation, because "man can be truly *for* God only if he is morally independent of Him, and he can be thus independent only by being first *against* Him!"[18]

Sin is the inevitable result of humanity's epistemic distance from God,[19] but our world is filled not only with sin, but with pain and suffering as well. Hick considers these categories consecutively and suggests that each makes possible various second-order benefits conducive to soul-making. For instance, by promoting withdrawal, pain has the biological function of a warning signal and therefore helps to preserve life.[20] We first gain invaluable knowledge, for example that it is painful to have our bodies collide at high speed with large, hard objects

---

[11] Hick, *Evil and the God of Love*, 255–6. See also 239–40 and Hick, "An Irenaean Theodicy" (1981), 43: "Indeed, if the end-state which God is seeking to bring about is one in which finite persons have come in their own freedom to know and love him, this requires creating them initially in a state which is not that of their already knowing and loving him. For it is logically impossible to create beings already in a state of having come into that state by their own free choices."

[12] Hick, *Evil and the God of Love*, 255.       [13] Hick, *Evil and the God of Love*, 273.

[14] Hick, *Evil and the God of Love*, 272.       [15] Hick, *Evil and the God of Love*, 273.

[16] John Hick, "An Irenaean Theodicy," in *Encountering Evil*, ed. Stephen T. Davis (Louisville and London: John Knox Press, 2001), 43.

[17] Hick claims that being created directly in God's presence would have the result that we could not exist as "independent autonomous persons." He writes, "In order to be a person, exercising some measure of genuine freedom, the creature must be brought into existence, not in the immediate divine presence, but at a 'distance' from God" ("An Irenaean Theodicy" (2001), 42).

[18] Hick, *Evil and the God of Love*, 287.       [19] Hick, *Evil and the God of Love*, 288.

[20] Hick, *Evil and the God of Love*, 298.

or to move too close to burning fires. Such knowledge leads in turn to the formation of protective habits conducive to guiding our movements successfully within our material environment, and hence to preservation.[21]

Hick recognizes that this value of pain presupposes a material environment with causal regularities. One might object that an omnipotent God could have created an environment in which causal regularities are always miraculously suspended when they are about to cause pain or suffering. But then, Hick responds, "there could be no sciences, for there would be no enduring world structure to investigate. And accordingly the human story would not include the development of the physical sciences and technologies with all that they have meant for the exercise of man's intelligence and the drawing out of his adaptive resourcefulness."[22] Nor would such a divinely manipulated environment demand the inventiveness, human skill, and cooperation between persons essential to the development of culture and the creation of civilization. In short, "a soft, unchallenging world would be inhabited by a soft, unchallenged race of men."[23]

According to Hick, suffering differs from pain in that it refers beyond the present moment. To suffer is "to be aware of a larger context of existence than one's immediate physical sensations, and to be overcome by the anguished wish that this wider situation were other than it is."[24] Hick now claims that even more than culture and civilization would be lost in a world in which there is not only no pain, but no suffering of any kind.[25] For one thing, moral qualities would no longer have any point or value in such a world. There would be nothing wrong with stealing because no one could ever lose anything by it. There would be no such crime as murder because no one could ever be killed. If to act wrongly means basically to harm someone, there would no longer be any such thing as wrong action.

Symmetrically, there would be no such thing as morally right action. In a ready-made paradise, Hick argues, there would be no way to benefit because there would be no possibility of lack or danger. Nor would there be any virtues in such a world, for virtues exist for and arise out of the function of benefiting, a function that would be entirely absent. In short, Hick claims that suffering underlies virtually the whole range of the more valuable human characteristics,[26] the acquisition and development of which is essential to the end goal of mature souls.

## Dysteleological Evil

So the divinely desired great good of made souls requires a world with moral evil, pain, and suffering, but still, "need the pedagogic programme include the more

---

[21] Hick, *Evil and the God of Love*, 301.    [22] Hick, *Evil and the God of Love*, 306.
[23] Hick, *Evil and the God of Love*, 307.    [24] Hick, *Evil and the God of Love*, 319.
[25] Hick, *Evil and the God of Love*, 324.    [26] Hick, *Evil and the God of Love*, 324–7.

extreme forms of torture, whether inflicted by man or disease? As well as bearable pain, need there be unendurable agony protracted to the point of the dehumanization of the sufferer?"[27] Hick's answer to this question is given in his discussion of dysteleological evil, which he defines as any evil seemingly devoid of soul-making value. A subset of such evils are *horrendous evils*. Hick admits that dysteleological evils seem to be "far beyond anything that can have been intended in any divine plan"[28] and considers their existence the "final and most difficult problem of theodicy."[29]

Hick recognizes that accounting for such evils is particularly challenging due both to their exceptional intensity and to their apparent lack of utility in the soul-making process. With regards to the first point, Hick argues that

> evils are exceptional only in relation to other evils which are routine. And therefore unless God eliminated all evils whatsoever there would always be relatively outstanding ones of which it would be said that He should have secretly prevented them…There would be nowhere to stop, short of a divinely arranged paradise in which human freedom would be narrowly circumscribed, moral responsibility largely eliminated, and in which the drama of man's story would be reduced to the level of a television serial.[30]

In this way, Hick hopes to dissolve the problem of the intensity of *horrors* completely. What's left is to determine their soul-making value. He admits that the prospects are not initially encouraging. When we conceive of some evils, "their effect seems to be sheerly dysteleological and destructive. They can break their victim's spirit and cause him to curse whatever gods there are."[31]

Hick's solution is "a frank appeal to the positive value of mystery."[32] Mystery contributes to the world as a place in which human sympathy and self-sacrifice are called forth and in which the right must be done for its own sake. In a world without dysteleological suffering, "human misery would not evoke deep personal sympathy or call forth organized relief and sacrificial help and service,"[33] for such responses are motivated or enhanced by the fact that the suffering is not observably instrumentally useful. Further, the systematic apportioning of suffering to desert would entail that happiness would be the predictable result of virtue and misery the predictable outcome of wickedness.[34] Such a world would lack the great good of doing the right simply because it is right and without any expectation of reward. So, upon reflection, Hick concludes that "in a world that is to be the scene of compassionate love and self-giving for others, suffering must fall

---

[27] Hick, *Evil and the God of Love*, 309.     [28] Hick, *Evil and the God of Love*, 289.
[29] Hick, *Evil and the God of Love*, 289.
[30] Hick, *Evil and the God of Love*, 327–8. See also 303.
[31] Hick, *Evil and the God of Love*, 330.     [32] Hick, *Evil and the God of Love*, 335.
[33] Hick, *Evil and the God of Love*, 334.     [34] Hick, *Evil and the God of Love*, 335.

upon mankind with something of the haphazardness and inequity that we now experience."[35] *Prima facie* dysteleological suffering is in fact teleological.

## Eschatology

Finally, Hick brings in the eschatological aspect of his theodicy, claiming that the soul-making environment can be justified only by its intended result—the universal salvation of souls. He claims that "the needs of Christian theodicy compel us to repudiate the idea of eternal punishment," which is "incompatible either with God's sovereignty or with His perfect goodness,"[36] and moreover Hick claims it would contradict God's love for lost human persons if he annihilated them or allowed them to dwindle out of existence while the benefits he hoped for them were still so largely unattained. Hick concedes that there would be a logical contradiction in its being predetermined in the strict sense that creatures endowed with free will shall come to love and obey God, but he believes we can say that God will never cease to desire and to actively work for the salvation of each created person.[37] Thus, Hick concludes, "despite the logical possibility of failure the probability of His success amounts…to a practical certainty."[38]

For Hick, not only is the universal salvation of souls a necessary condition of reconciling the existence of God with as yet non-made souls, but it is also suggested to be sufficient to justify God's choice to actualize what might appear an abnormally evil world. Hick claims his theodicy "must find the meaning of evil in the part that it is made to play in the eventual outworking of [the soul-making] purpose; and must find the justification of the whole process in the magnitude of the good to which it leads."[39] Seen retrospectively from the point of fulfillment of God's soul-making purpose, all evil will receive a "new meaning" because it will be recognized as a necessary constituent of the end to which it has led;[40] in Roderick Chisholm's language, it will be *defeated*.[41] Moreover, "The 'good eschaton' will not be a reward or a compensation proportioned to each individual's trials, but an infinite good that would render worthwhile *any* finite suffering endured in the course attaining to it."[42]

## Evaluation

On Hick's theodicy, God chooses a world that will be *horror* producing so that the pure benefit of human soul-formation will take place. If Hick is being precise

---

[35] Hick, *Evil and the God of Love*, 334.　　[36] Hick, *Evil and the God of Love*, 342.
[37] Hick, *Evil and the God of Love*, 343.　　[38] Hick, *Evil and the God of Love*, 344.
[39] Hick, *Evil and the God of Love*, 261.　　[40] Hick, *Evil and the God of Love*, 363.
[41] See Chapter 1, n. 11 on *defeat*.　　[42] Hick, *Evil and the God of Love*, 341.

when he writes that God "took His decision in awareness of *all* that would flow from it,"[43] then his theodicy depicts God as *causing* the specific evils—including the *horrendous evils*—that followed. This reading is suggested by the fact that Hick contrasts God's creative choice with the choice of a human person to make alcohol easily accessible to a recovering alcoholic. Hick says that while the human person in this scenario is only guilty of "*risking*" the bad outcome, "in the case of God no such qualification is possible."[44] On this reading, Hick's theodicy is structurally analogous to Case A and, as such, the *horror* causation it attributes to God is *prima facie* morally objectionable.

There is some lack of specification in Hick, however, about the extent to which God can know in advance the specific evils that will occur. There are places where Hick can reasonably be read as implying that—even for God—if a person is free, it may be "unpredictable as to the actual form that his behavior will take."[45] Even so, one might nevertheless wonder whether God would be responsible for causing *horrors* in the lives of the first generation of free human persons, before the unpredictability of their freedom had sufficiently moved them from the path of what God could reliably foresee. Or one might wonder whether God would remain responsible for *horrors* (or something akin to *horrors*) in generations of humanoids immediately preceding the advent of free human choice.

But even if Hick further specified that, while God knew all of the *sorts* of evil that would flow from his choice, all of the specific evils that would flow were initially hidden from him by quantum indeterminacy,[46] for instance, God nevertheless would be responsible for *permitting* specific *horrors*. Hick's theodicy would then be structurally analogous to Case B rather than Case A, but would remain *prima facie* morally objectionable by analogy.

Frederick Sontag challenges Hick with a question that homes in on the problem *horrendous evils* raise for Hick's theodicy: "We would not be able to develop without danger, it is true, but my problem is why the dangers were designed so that they actually break and destroy so many?"[47] Otherwise put, how can soul-breaking be necessary for soul-making?[48] We have already seen Hick's response to this in *Evil and the God of Love*. It is twofold. He claims that (1) the badness of any evil is only measurable relative to other actual evils and that (2) even dysteleological evils have instrumental value because they provide an air of mystery favorable for the soul-making process. Hick makes the same first move in a more

---

[43] Hick, *Evil and the God of Love*, 290 (italics mine).    [44] Hick, *Evil and the God of Love*, 290.

[45] Hick, *Evil and the God of Love*, 369. Cf. 271–5.

[46] Hick does say at one point that "the world…is not a deterministic system but a living realm involving important elements of freedom and contingency" ("An Irenaean Theodicy" (1981), 64), but he says this in a discussion of human freedom and is unclear about whether the elements of contingency he has in mind are exhausted by those due to free human choice.

[47] Frederick Sontag, "Critique of John Hick: 'An Irenaean Theodicy,'" in *Encountering Evil*, ed. Stephen T. Davis and John B. Cobb (Edinburgh and Atlanta: John Knox Press, 1981), 56.

[48] Hick also raises this objection in *Evil and the God of Love*, 329–30.

recent essay as well, claiming that in a less evil world, something else would qualify as the worst natural evil and hence be intolerable to us, and so on *ad infinitum*.[49]

One concern at the heart of Sontag's objection is that so many evils break "so many [*people*]." As in Marilyn Adams's definition of *horrendous evils*, what is most important is not the badness of *horrendous evils* relative to other evils, but rather the objective criterion of being *prima facie* life-ruining. Hick is surely right that in a less evil (but not evil free) world there would still be some worst evil. But it is not true that there would always be *horrendous evil*. There are possible worlds, for instance, in which a headache would be both the worst of actual evils and fail to satisfy the objective criterion for counting as *horrendous*. Hick is wrong that evils are exceptional only in relation to other actual evils and, as a result, his *ad infinitum* argument does not resolve the problems *horrendous evils* pose for theodicy. Moreover, Hick's thesis seems to imply that no amount of evil could ever be inconsistent with the existence of a perfectly good God. As Stephen Davis puts it, the problem with Hick's argument about there being less evil worlds *ad infinitum* is that "it appears to cut the other way too."[50] For *any* degree of human suffering, there would always be some greater degree compatible with the existence of a perfectly good God. Surely this is false.

Having side-stepped the problem of the intensity of *horrors*, Hick thinks he only has to deal with their dysteleological nature. He responds with his second move, that the mysteriousness of apparently dysteleological evil is itself an intrinsic feature of a soul-making world. But the failure of Hick's first move calls into question this second move as well. Even if the mystery of dysteleological evil contributes to soul-making generally, when *horrors* are appreciated for the *prima facie* life-ruining evils that they are, it becomes clear that Hick has not said enough to make plausible the claim that the mystery of *horrendous* dysteleological evils in particular is more soul-making than soul-breaking, especially for those who suffer *horrendously*.[51]

Moreover, even the success of Hick's second move would not salvage his theodicy. Even if *horrendous* dysteleological harms contributed to the all-things-considered benefit of soul-making, Hick's theodicy nonetheless depicts God as causing *horror* for pure benefit. Hick might want to respond that his

---

[49] Hick, "An Irenaean Theodicy" (1981), 49–50.

[50] Stephen T. Davis, "Critique of John Hick: 'An Irenaean Theodicy,'" in *Encountering Evil*, ed. Stephen T. Davis and John B. Cobb (Edinburgh and Atlanta: John Knox Press, 1981), 58.

[51] Though not a central part of his theodicy, Hick seems at least inclined to the position that any evil must be justified by the soul-making role it plays in the life of the one who suffers it. He writes, "A person's sin and suffering can be redeemed, retrospectively, by becoming part of the history by which *that person* arrives at the fulfillment of God's purpose" ("An Irenaean Theodicy" (1981), 66) (italics mine). And more recently Hick claims that his theodicy does not "in any way mean that 'my moral development is offered as the justification of the sufferings of others'" ("An Irenaean Theodicy" (2001), 71).

theodicy depicts God in something similar to an *extreme situation* or even as averting greater harm—the harm of not being united with God in the way only made-souls can be. But for this response to be successful, Hick would have to argue that all of God's non-*horrendous* alternatives were so inferior or so harmful as to make *horror* causation ethically preferable. Given the resourcefulness of omnipotence, I take this to be a very tall order. To participate freely in making one's soul is indeed a great good, but it is not the only good God could aim for. Seeing God face-to-face and as a result always acting rightly also has much to recommend itself. Moreover, even if allowing souls to be freely made were God's only attractive option, experience shows that experiences of the good are often as useful as experiences of the bad—and experiences of both the good and the (serious but non-*horrendous*) bad typically more useful than experiences of the *horrendous*—for making souls.

Hick's insistence on measuring all actual evils only in relation to each other results in his failing to appreciate the distinctive justificatory demands that *horrors* make on those responsible for them, in particular the moral obligation not to cause *horrendous evil* to procure mere pure benefits. Without more said, the structural similarity between Hick's theodicy and Case A is strong reason to think Hick's approach is flawed. It fails to recognize the asymmetry between harms and benefits, the objective badness of *horrors*, and the consequent moral objection to causing *horrors* when those *horrors* are not necessary to avert greater harm. I judge that when *horrors* are seen for the *prima facie* life-ruining evils that they are, a system of *horror* causation cannot "find the justification of the whole process in the magnitude of the good to which it leads."[52]

## Type A: Richard Swinburne's Theodicy

I judge Swinburne's theodicy also to be a Type A approach according to which God causes at least some particular *horrors* in order to bestow pure benefits. While Hick's ambiguity regarding the extent of God's knowledge of the future leaves open the possibility that his theodicy is Type B rather than Type A, Swinburne's explicit commitments to libertarianism and the rejection of Molinism might seem even more conducive to depicting God as permitting specific *horrors* but not causing them. This classification might seem to be recommended by Swinburne himself when he claims that because "God's knowledge of the future is limited by the libertarian free will which he gives to humans, even God cannot know in advance for certain the actual amount of harm one individual will suffer at the hands of another in a given situation."[53]

---

[52] Hick, *Evil and the God of Love*, 261.
[53] Swinburne, *Providence and the Problem of Evil*, 232.

But Swinburne makes a distinction between God's agency relative to moral evils (roughly, evils brought about by the "deliberate actions or negligent failure"[54] of humans) and natural evils (roughly, evils "uncaused by humans (and not negligently allowed to occur by them)"[55]), and suggests that God *causes* natural evils. This is suggested, for instance, when he writes, "I need to argue in due course for the greater good which allowing (and when we are dealing with free human actions, it is only allowing, not *causing*) such horrible things to occur makes possible."[56] Here Swinburne implies that moral evils are to be differentiated from natural evils because God causes the latter but not the former. I take it that this is also the differentiation Swinburne has in mind when he writes of God "allowing or *making* others suffer"[57] and of "God's right to create, *cause*, and allow suffering,"[58] and when he affirms the following passage from Aquinas: "Moral evil (*malum culpae*) God in no way wills... but the evil of natural defect (or the evil of punishment) he does will by willing some good to which such evil is attached."[59] That harm is caused by God with respect to natural evil, even if not with respect to moral evil, explains why—despite his non-Molinist libertarianism—Swinburne writes in several places of God *causing* harm to human persons.[60] It likewise explains his regularly talking of God "bringing about" suffering,[61] which Swinburne introduces as a synonym for "causing" in his discussion of action.[62]

Even so, Swinburne might be read as implying that God causes harm only with respect to the community of human persons taken as a whole, not with respect to any particular individual. Swinburne's frequent reference to the consequences of "natural processes" might suggest this. If God merely sets up natural processes at

---

[54] Swinburne, *Providence and the Problem of Evil*, 4.

[55] Swinburne, *Providence and the Problem of Evil*, 163.

[56] Swinburne, *Providence and the Problem of Evil*, 107. See also Swinburne, *The Existence of God*, 2nd ed. (Oxford: Oxford University Press, 1991), 236.

[57] Swinburne, *Providence and the Problem of Evil*, 165 (italics mine).

[58] Swinburne, *Providence and the Problem of Evil*, 243 (italics mine).

[59] Thomas Aquinas, *Summa theologiae*, Ia. 19.9. Quoted in Swinburne, *Providence and the Problem of Evil*, 160.

[60] Two instances are "But it must remain the case that God must not cause harm to us which is uncompensated by benefit to us" (*Providence and the Problem of Evil*, 230) and "God's right to allow some other free agent to cause harm to us is likely to be greater than his right to cause that harm directly. (He can allow wicked men to do things to us that mere inanimate processes will not cause.)... It will inevitably be the case that God will only cause harm for the sake of good" (*Providence and the Problem of Evil*, 231).

[61] For example, "It remains to be shown, first, that it is morally permissible for God to *bring about* these bad states for the sake of good states which they make possible" (*Providence and the Problem of Evil*, 223) (italics mine).

[62] For instance, "Now I move on to consider the goodness of action, that is causing or bringing about" (Swinburne, *Providence and the Problem of Evil*, 82). However, Swinburne is not always consistent in using "bringing about" in this way. In the following passage he seems to interchange it with "permitting" rather than with "causing." "So by permitting (by *bringing about*) the natural evil of physical pain and other suffering God provides a bad state such that allowing it, or an equally bad state, to occur makes possible and is the only morally permissible way in which he can make possible good states" (*Providence and the Problem of Evil*, 167) (italics mine). See 238 for similar usage.

the beginning and then lets them do their thing in a world influenced by libertarian actions and possibly randomness as well, then perhaps he should be understood as merely permitting even all natural evils with respect to individual persons.

Against this is the fact that Swinburne is not at all inclined to this more deistic position. In addition to affirming God's "general providence"—that "arising from the general structure of the world, the natural order of things"—Swinburne affirms God's "special providence"—"his intervening in the natural order of things" in his "dealings with particular individuals."[63] It is by God's special providence that "to each is given a different package of various things, good and bad, to be used in different ways. Thus God treats us as individuals, each with her own vocation."[64] These packages and vocations can be highly individualized because "God may be bending nature to answer prayers and thus interact with individuals and groups all the time."[65] Indeed, evidence "that God very seldom intervenes in nature...would show something very much in error in the Christian tradition."[66] This all is consistent with one of Swinburne's preferred analogies—that of parental care for children—where he describes parents as intervening by *causing* one son to suffer either for his own good or that of his brother.[67]

All told, I judge that Swinburne's assumptions about special providence make it most natural to read him as depicting God as causing at least some particular *horrors* in the form of natural evils. But, as with Hick, if his theodicy can be read or reformulated such that God merely permits all *horrors*, it then could be assessed as a Type B Theodicy.

Swinburne's theodicy is consonant with Hick's in many ways over and above their shared ambiguity about whether God causes or only permits *horrors*. Like Hick, Swinburne downplays the justificatory value of an Augustinian fall.[68] He accepts God's bottom-line responsibility for evil. God is responsible for setting up a world in which other libertarian free agents are prone to moral evil, and God is a sufficient cause of at least some natural evil.

Swinburne then seeks to justify God by appealing to various pure benefits that evils make possible, including the abilities to choose to acquire well-justified knowledge of good and evil, to choose freely and meaningfully between good and evil, to develop one's character, to display virtues, to love, to contemplate beauty, and to be of use (to others and to God). Achieving all of these goods to a significant degree, Swinburne argues, requires a good deal of suffering. He makes the

---

[63] Swinburne, *Providence and the Problem of Evil*, 116.
[64] Swinburne, *Providence and the Problem of Evil*, 236.
[65] Swinburne, *Providence and the Problem of Evil*, 117.
[66] Swinburne, *Providence and the Problem of Evil*, 118.
[67] Swinburne, *Providence and the Problem of Evil*, 227.
[68] Despite this downplaying, Swinburne does accept a historical view of the fall. Similarly, he is inclined to accept the existence of angels but not to credit them with significant responsibility for earthly evil. See *Providence and the Problem of Evil*, 37–41, 106, 108–10.

bolder claim, in fact, that when all of these goods are taken into account, the quality and quantity of evil in the actual world should not be surprising.

Swinburne's descriptions of evil-types and their logically dependent goods are often consistent with and plausible elaborations of Hick's. The two major disagreements between the theodicists refer to the beginning and end of human life. Against Hick's presentation in *Evil and the God of Love*, Swinburne says he cannot see why God could not have made perfectly virtuous human persons apart from any suffering-laden soul-making process. Hick claims that because "personal life is essentially free and self-directing…it cannot be perfected by divine fiat but only through the uncompelled responses and willing co-operation of human individuals in their actions and reactions in the world in which God has placed them."[69] Swinburne disagrees with this Irenaean position, saying that "he cannot see why God could not have made man perfect from the first."[70] Nonetheless, he maintains that "it is good that humans have the opportunity to choose freely over a significant period whether or not to become perfect."[71] According to Swinburne, our being created as morally weak beings in a harsh environment makes possible various goods different from those possible had we been created perfect *ab initio*.[72] Heaven is "a marvelous world with a vast range of possible deep goods, but one lacking a few goods which our world contains, including the good of being able to choose to reject the good."[73] Note that this divergence makes the claim that *horrors* are necessary to avert the greater harm of failing to be united with God even less available to Swinburne than it is to Hick.

With regards to the end of life, Swinburne opposes Hick by rejecting universalism. Hick claims that in the end we shall all through our own free choices become formed enough for union with God. Swinburne agrees with Hick that if God always refuses to take no for an answer, we shall all yield in the end. However, he thinks that "if God is to give someone real freedom to reject him, he must after a finite time take no for an answer. To give us the choice to reject God, but never to allow that choice to be permanently executed, is not to give us a real choice at all."[74]

The result of these divergences is that, for Swinburne, eschatology cannot play the primary justificatory role that Hick assigns to it. Swinburne cannot claim that

[69]  Hick, *Evil and the God of Love*, 255.
[70]  Swinburne, *Providence and the Problem of Evil*, 257.
[71]  Swinburne, *Providence and the Problem of Evil*, 257.
[72]  In more recent writings, Hick's view appears less Irenaean on this point and closer to Swinburne's. Cf. "An Irenaean Theodicy" (2001), 43–4, 67–8 and *Evil and the God of Love*, 2nd ed., supplemental final chapter "Recent Work on the Problem of Evil," 379–80. Some difference remains, however, in that while Swinburne speaks of the goods of meaningful free choice and of being created perfect *ab initio* as merely different, Hick maintains that "freely chosen goodness…leads in the end to a different *and higher* quality of happiness" ("An Irenaean Theodicy" (2001), 68) (italics mine). Cf. Swinburne, *Providence and the Problem of Evil*, 250–1.
[73]  Swinburne, *Providence and the Problem of Evil*, 250.
[74]  Swinburne, *Providence and the Problem of Evil*, 257.

all people will be able to look back on evil and recognize it as logically necessary for their attaining the infinite good of eternal union with God, for two individually sufficient reasons: God could have created us in this eternal state without evil and some of us will never be recipients of this infinite good.

Thus, rather than putting much stock in the eschatological redemption of evil, Swinburne seeks to justify evils principally by the greater *earthly* benefits that they make possible. Foremost among these, he claims—and most significant among his additions to Hick's list of goods—is the great good of being of use.

## The Greatness of Being of Use

According to Swinburne, suffering for another's good is a great benefit *for the sufferer*. Being of use in this way is a great benefit even when it is done involuntarily and unknowingly. Swinburne suspects that his contemporaries will resist the point. Commenting on Jesus's proverb that "[i]t is more blessed to give than to receive,"[75] he writes, "We do not, most of us, think that most of the time. We think that our well-being consists only in the things that we possess or the experiences we enjoy."[76]

In support of his modified beatitude—"Blessed is the man or woman whose life is of use"[77]—Swinburne notes that "almost all peoples, apart from those of the Western world in our generation, have recognized that dying for one's country is a great good for him who dies, even if he was conscripted."[78] And in another supporting example, he remarks that when a tragic death leads to an important reform, we generally believe that the deceased did not die in vain.[79] Swinburne claims the great good of being of use makes sense of these intuitions.

God benefits us greatly if he gives us the opportunity to be of use. But, Swinburne reminds us, he can only do so "by building a world in which natural processes ensure that by our actions we can bring benefits to others which they cannot easily secure in any other way."[80] Only if I feel pain that I cannot easily eradicate, for instance, are you given the opportunity to show sympathy and to help to relieve it.

Swinburne thinks we vastly underestimate the value of being of use for at least three reasons. Firstly, we overestimate and tend to focus on the goodness of mere pleasure and the badness of mere pain. Secondly, we fail to recognize that the

---

[75]   Acts of the Apostles 20:35.
[76]   Swinburne, *Providence and the Problem of Evil*, 101.
[77]   Swinburne, *Providence and the Problem of Evil*, 104.
[78]   Swinburne, *Providence and the Problem of Evil*, 102.
[79]   Swinburne, *Providence and the Problem of Evil*, 103.
[80]   Swinburne, *Providence and the Problem of Evil*, 167.

effects which make a case of being of use valuable may lie far away in space and time.[81] Large scale human suffering, for example, provides innumerable opportunities for virtuous responses to it in distant places and later centuries.[82] Thirdly, and most significantly according to Swinburne, we fail to consider that all human suffering that is of use to others will also be of use to God, who has designed the world so that suffering does benefit those others. "One who is of use to the perfectly good source of all being is indeed fortunate."[83]

When the great good of being of use is properly accounted for, Swinburne thinks we should recognize that our normal estimates of the value of individual lives are likely to be "wildly in error; and that most lives that seem to be bad on balance are not really so."[84] However, he adds, if there are any lives on balance bad, God would be under obligation to provide life after death for the individuals concerned—even ones who ultimately will be annihilated—during which they would be compensated. Thus, the package of life will be an overall good one for each created person.[85]

In summation, then, by causing or permitting each evil to occur, "God makes possible a good which he could not make possible without allowing it (or an equally bad state) to occur."[86] Moreover, a perfectly good God would make sure that the suffering he has caused or permitted is ultimately compensated.[87] Combining the points, every bad must result in (or make probable) a greater good, and each individual must have a life that is worth living all things considered.[88]

## Accounting for the Worst Evils

Swinburne's appraisal of the value of being of use is essential to his attempt to justify *horror* causation within his Type A schema. Even the intentional bringing about of the worst defects of this world is justified because it makes possible greater goods, for example good actions which can only be done in response

---

[81] Swinburne, *Providence and the Problem of Evil*, 244–5. Swinburne attributes this failure to "two characteristic human vices: short-term and short-distance thinking. [We tend] to think of the worth of a sentient life as dependent on things that happen during that life and fairly close in space to that life" (245).

[82] Swinburne, *Providence and the Problem of Evil*, 246.

[83] Swinburne, *The Existence of God*, 2nd ed., 261.

[84] Swinburne, *Providence and the Problem of Evil*, 235.

[85] Swinburne, *The Existence of God*, 2nd ed., 263.

[86] Swinburne, *Providence and the Problem of Evil*, 217.

[87] Swinburne, *Providence and the Problem of Evil*, 236.

[88] In Chisholmian terminology, "very loosely, every bad must be defeated by some good; but in the life of one individual the bad needs only to be outweighed by some good" (Swinburne, *Providence and the Problem of Evil*, 238–39, n. 1).

to very bad states. Accordingly, Swinburne offers the following account of the Holocaust:

> The suffering and deaths of the Jewish victims of the Nazi concentration camps were the result of a web of bad choices stretching back over centuries and continents...And the sufferings and deaths in the concentration camps have in turn caused or made possible a whole web of actions and reactions stretching forward over the centuries of sympathy for victims, helping their relatives (to set up the state of Israel), avoiding any such event ever again, etc. The possibility of the Jewish suffering and deaths at the time made possible serious heroic choices for people normally (in consequences often of their own bad choices and the choices of others) too timid to make them (e.g. to harbour the prospective victims) and for people too hard-hearted (again as a result of previous bad choices) to make them, e.g. for a concentration camp guard not to obey orders. And they make possible reactions of courage (e.g. by the victims), of compassion, sympathy, penitence, forgiveness, reform, avoidance of repetition, etc., by others.[89]

Note that most of the goods listed above are most naturally construed to be pure benefits. However, in a couple of places, Swinburne makes the intriguing suggestion that the allowance and causation of *horrors* may be justified in part by being necessary for the avoidance of still greater harm. He firstly points out that the formation of one's character through free choices is a great good and can only occur by choosing the believed good rather than the believed bad. But many, he continues, as a result of past bad choices or bad environments, do not recognize much bad or wrong as bad or wrong. They are "close to the brink of total insensitivity to moral goodness."[90] Rather than watch idly as they fall,

> A good God will be desperately anxious to rescue the hard-hearted before they become incorrigibly hard-hearted, and to rescue them means to help them to make choices which will put them on the road to sanctity. But...the choices for the hard-hearted who have immunized themselves to moderate amounts of suffering in others can only be ones where the wrongness of the bad choice is very evident and very great.[91]

That means giving them the opportunity to resist temptations to perpetrate and perpetuate *horrors*—giving them the opportunity to feed the dying beggar on the street or to leave him to die, to disobey an order to kill a Jewish person imprisoned

---

[89] Swinburne, *Providence and the Problem of Evil*, 151.
[90] Swinburne, *Providence and the Problem of Evil*, 169.
[91] Swinburne, *Providence and the Problem of Evil*, 245.

for his race or to execute him.[92] Yet such opportunities "are only available if these terrible evils will happen if the chooser refuses the right choice."[93] And even when terrible evils are wrought upon individuals, it is still a great good *for them* that they are being used to make serious free choices available, perhaps especially—according to Swinburne—to the hard-hearted.

## Evaluation

I affirm a number of elements of Swinburne's theodicy. I am not convinced with Swinburne that the world will be better overall and in the end for its *horrors*, but I take Swinburne's point that *horrors* make possible some good states that would not be possible otherwise. I think Swinburne is right that we are apt to underestimate the good of being of use, though I think he profoundly overstates his case when—after referencing an officer faced with orders to kill a Jewish prisoner—he claims "it is a great privilege for anyone to be the means of making available serious choices, even or possibly especially for the hard-hearted."[94] I would also like to hear more about why our underestimation of our being of *good* use is any greater than our underestimation of our being of *bad* use. Doesn't being of use multiply in both directions? I think Swinburne does well to appreciate more than Hick the objective badness of *horrors* and the heightened justificatory demands that *horrors* place on those responsible for them. I further concur that "God might well be expected to ask a lot from us in order to give a lot to us."[95]

Nonetheless, my judgment is that—by analogy with Case A—God could not be expected, nor morally permitted, to ask *horrors* from us in order to give us pure benefits. Swinburne claims that "the issue of whether the goods are great enough to justify the bad states which make them possible is the crux of the problem of evil."[96] This is one beam of the crux of the problem of evil, but the other, I suggest, is what types of goods those goods are.

Like Hick, Swinburne emphasizes pure benefits that he regards as made possible by evils, for example in his discussion of the Holocaust quoted above.

---

[92] Swinburne, *Providence and the Problem of Evil*, 169–70. Swinburne lists these as well as torturing animals as examples of "cruel acts," which he implies are (at least partially) attributable to the libertarian free choices of evildoers. I understand Swinburne as claiming that while God *causes* natural evil, he only *permits* or *allows* the worst evils (*Providence and the Problem of Evil*, 107), which he takes to be a subset of the set of cruel acts. In his words, "the worst states of the world are cases of suffering...which humans deliberately and maliciously inflict on other humans together with the evils of their inflicting them" (*Providence and the Problem of Evil*, 241). Still, some natural evils are *horrendous* in the technical sense I inherit from Marilyn Adams, and so Swinburne does not avoid the charge that God *causes horrendous evil.*

[93] Swinburne, *Providence and the Problem of Evil*, 170.

[94] Swinburne, *Providence and the Problem of Evil*, 170.

[95] Swinburne, *The Existence of God*, 2nd ed., 265.

[96] Swinburne, *Providence and the Problem of Evil*, 239.

I argued in Chapter 2 that this will not do where *horrendous evil* is concerned. A further vulnerability of Swinburne's approach arises out of who must receive the benefits attained by evils in order for those evils to be justified. I find Hick to be ambiguous about whether it is the sufferer herself whose soul must be benefited by an instance of suffering, but in some places Hick does insist that his theodicy does not "in any way mean" that one person's "moral development is offered as the justification of the sufferings of others."[97] If you think it is more morally objectionable and contrary to ideal love to force someone to suffer *horrors* for another's pure benefit than for his own—a plausible thought in my opinion—this is reason to think Swinburne's structure is still more vulnerable than Hick's. While Swinburne maintains that being of use is a good for the one who is of use, he nevertheless admits that much of the suffering of this world finds much of its justification in goods that do not accrue to the sufferers. Nor can Swinburne claim with Hick that God's policy with respect to suffering will at least lead to all being well-off in the end. For Swinburne, the end for some will be either eternity in hell or annihilation.[98] Swinburne's approach is also more vulnerable than Hick's because whereas Hick implies that God created "in awareness of all that would flow from it,"[99] including the goods that would result from the evils caused, Swinburne's non-Molinist libertarian assumptions mean that God makes choices to cause *horrors* based on it being only *probable* that they will lead to many of the greater goods that justify them. Alter Case A so that the parents are acting on only the likelihood rather than the knowledge that their child will be better-off all things considered, and the intuition that they have wronged their child and not treated her in a loving manner is even more obvious.

Swinburne does supplement Hick's approach with the suggestion that some *horrors* are justified at least in part by their being necessary to rescue the hard-hearted from the still greater evil of complete moral indifference. This is a biblical line and worthy of further development; however, the rest of Swinburne's assumptions are in tension with this harm-aversion theory. Remember that for Swinburne, contraire Hick, God had among his initial alternatives the possibility of creating human beings perfect *ab initio*. To cause *horrors* in order to avoid perfection from the start hardly has a plausible claim to being classified as a rescue operation. Additionally, Swinburne suggests that God could have made a world where pain and suffering had only 10 percent of the intensity of the actual world. He claims that this—plausibly non-*horror*-producing—world would remain meaningful, just not as meaningful as the actual world.[100] Nowhere is it suggested that an omnipotent being's attempt to create rational creatures in a meaningful

[97]  Hick, "An Irenaean Theodicy" (2001), 71.
[98]  See Swinburne, *Providence and the Problem of Evil*, 196–201.
[99]  Hick, *Evil and the God of Love*, 290.
[100]  Swinburne, *Providence and the Problem of Evil*, 242–3.

world with less suffering would be frustrated by the inevitability of greater harms or of bad states of affairs of any sort. The way Swinburne oscillates without warning between justifying *horrors* by pure benefits and by the aversion of greater harm (and the emphasis he places on the former) shows that he has not recognized nor incorporated into his account the justificatory asymmetry intrinsic to this division of goods.

To be fair, Swinburne would join me in rejecting his theodicy at this point, for there is one more essential element of it yet to be mentioned. Swinburne claims that the greater goods made possible by the worst evils are only sufficiently justificatory when the causer or permitter of those evils is God. So, for example, after a discussion of the greater goods brought about by the eighteenth-century slave-trade, Swinburne qualifies, "but to repeat quickly—yet again before anyone misunderstands—only God our creator had the right to allow bad people to promote the slave-trade."[101] Swinburne's thought is that God is justified in causing and permitting much worse evils than any human person would be because of his unique role as ultimate caretaker and surrogate decision maker in human lives. Swinburne claims that due to these roles, God has rights to harm human persons analogous to but vastly greater than the rights of human parents to harm their children for their children's own good.

My preliminary conclusion is that Swinburne's theodicy is structurally insufficient to deal with *horrendous evils* unless his discussion of divine rights requires a contrary appraisal. I will argue later in this chapter that Swinburne's understanding of caretakers' rights to harm is misconceived in several respects, and therefore that his theodicy remains *structurally unpromising* by analogy with Case A.

## Type A: Alvin Plantinga's "O Felix Culpa" Theodicy

In "Supralapsarianism, or 'O Felix Clupa,'"[102] Alvin Plantinga tries his hand at theodicy for the first time. Applying a similar methodology to Hick and Swinburne's, Plantinga concedes that God is ultimately responsible for evil and claims the justification for God's creating our *horror*-strewn world comes from the non-harm-averting goods that evils make possible. However, in comparison with those of Hick and Swinburne, Plantinga's justification is distinctively global and Christian. Global, because his justification focuses on the overall value of the world

---

[101] Swinburne, *Providence and the Problem of Evil*, 245–6.

[102] Alvin Plantinga, "Supralapsarianism, or 'O Felix Culpa,'" in *Christian Faith and the Problem of Evil*, ed. Peter van Inwagen (Grand Rapids: Wm. B. Eerdmans Publishing Co, 2004). The words "O Felix Culpa" also feature among the closing words of Hick's classic book: "'O felix culpa quae talem ac tantum meruit habere redemptorem' (O fortunate crime which merited such and so great a redeemer). In their far-reaching implications these words are the heart of Christian theodicy" (Hick, *Evil and the God of Love*, 364).

God weakly actualizes[103] rather than on the distinctively person-benefiting goods of that world. Christian, because he focuses on the distinctively Christian goods of the incarnation and atonement of God. Plantinga suggests that in addition to the normal list of good-making characteristics, "there is also a contingent good-making characteristic of our world—one that isn't present in all worlds—that towers enormously above all the rest of the contingent states of affairs included in our world: the unthinkably great good of divine incarnation and atonement."[104]

Plantinga claims that there could not be a contingent good-making feature of a world to rival this one. In his words, "I believe that the great goodness of this state of affairs, like that of the divine existence itself, makes its value incommensurable with the value of states of affairs involving creaturely good and bad."[105] Plantinga thus concludes that "any world with divine incarnation and atonement is a better world than any without it."[106] All possible worlds with divine incarnation and atonement reach a level of value L that no worlds without them reach. Any world whose value equals or exceeds L, Plantinga deems a "highly eligible world."[107] (Here Plantinga's thought is reminiscent of a suggestion of Roderick Chisholm.[108])

Accordingly, if God's intention in creating is to actualize a highly eligible world, he will actualize a world in which he will incarnate and atone. But, Plantinga adds, all the worlds including divine incarnation and atonement contain also something to be atoned for. Therefore, "You can't have a world whose value exceeds L without sin and evil; sin and evil is a necessary condition of the value of every really good possible world. O Felix Culpa indeed!"[109]

This is why Plantinga thinks we should not be surprised by the coexistence of God and evil, at minimum the evil of sin. Next, he presents and responds to three

---

[103] Plantinga assumes there are nontrivial, true counterfactuals of freedom that God has to work with. (See Chapter 1, n. 21.) So, following Thomas Flint, he claims that "the worlds God could have weakly actualized are the feasible worlds" (Plantinga, "Supralapsarianism...," 6). These worlds are, on this Molinist view, a subset of the set of all logically possible worlds.

[104] Plantinga, "Supralapsarianism...," 7.

[105] Plantinga, "Supralapsarianism...," 10. By "incommensurable," Plantinga means that "the value of incarnation and atonement cannot be matched by any aggregate of creaturely goods" (10).

[106] Plantinga, "Supralapsarianism...," 10. Plantinga calls this the "strong value assumption" and says he is inclined to accept it, though he points out that his argument does not depend on anything nearly as strong.

[107] Plantinga, "Supralapsarianism...," 10.

[108] Chisholm says "a state of affairs p is *absolutely good* provided, first, that p is good and provided, further, that *any* possible state of affairs entailing p is better than any possible state of affairs not entailing p, no matter how good or bad the other constituents of those states of affairs may happen to be," ("The Defeat of Good and Evil," *Proceedings and Addresses of the American Philosophical Association* 42 (1969): 33) and "[w]hat if the evils of the world were defeated by some wider state of affairs that is *absolutely good* in the sense we have defined—what if the evils of the world were defeated by a certain state of affairs q such that q is good and such that any possible state of affairs entailing q is better than any possible state of affairs not entailing q?" (37).

[109] Plantinga, "Supralapsarianism...," 12.

objections as a way of thickening his theodicy to account for all extant evils. The objections are formulated in the following interrogative fashion:

(1)  Why does God permit suffering as well as sin and evil?
(2)  Why does God permit so much suffering and evil?
(3)  If God permitted human suffering and evil in order to achieve a world in which there is incarnation and atonement, wouldn't he be manipulative, calculating, treating his creatures like means instead of ends?[110]

To the first objection, Plantinga gives a twofold response. Why does God permit suffering?

> Because, first, some of the free creatures God has created have turned their backs on God and behaved in such a way as to cause suffering; and second, because suffering itself is of instrumental value, and thus will be found in really good worlds.[111]

With regard to the first point, Plantinga assumes that "in general, the more free creatures resemble God, the more valuable they are and the more valuable are the worlds in which they exist."[112] It follows, then, that creatures who have power to do a great deal of good and evil are more valuable, *ceteris paribus*, than creatures whose power is limited or meager, and that a God intending to create a very good world would have reason to create creatures with a great deal of power.[113] Plantinga then makes the additional assumption that the counterfactuals of creaturely freedom come out such that the conjoining of significant creaturely power with creaturely sin always causes suffering.[114]

To account for so-called natural evil, Plantinga takes a similar line at one metaphysical remove and postulates that "much of the natural evil the world displays is due to the actions of Satan and his cohorts."[115] Here we observe a distinction between Plantinga's theodicy and the other Type A Theodicies already considered. Only for Plantinga are there free agents intervening between God and all *horrendous evils*—moral and natural. Nonetheless, Plantinga depicts God as

---

[110]  Plantinga, "Supralapsarianism…," 14.    [111]  Plantinga, "Supralapsarianism…," 19.

[112]  Plantinga, "Supralapsarianism…," 15.

[113]  Plantinga echoes Swinburne here who, in a discussion of humans being made in the image of God, reflects that "the glory of humans is not just their very serious free will, but the responsibility for so much which that free will involves" (*Providence and the Problem of Evil*, 106).

[114]  This addition of "significant creaturely power" responds to Stephen Boër's objection that even if Plantinga's initial free will *defense* could justify God actualizing a world with moral evil because it is the feasible world with the greatest balance of morally good choices over morally bad ones, this does not yet justify God's allowing the bad *choices* to have bad *consequences*. See Steven E. Boër, "The Irrelevance of the Free Will Defence," *Analysis* 38 (1978): 110–12.

[115]  Plantinga, "Supralapsarianism…," 16.

*causing horrors* in my technical sense. The counterfactuals of creaturely freedom make *horrendous evils* a certain consequence of one of God's actions—the actualization of this world—and he knew them to be so.

As for the instrumental value of suffering, Plantinga hypothesizes that worlds with free powerful creatures who sin but do not cause suffering are not as good as worlds in which such creatures produce suffering because suffering is of instrumental value in producing non-harm-averting goods. Plantinga references Hick and Peter van Inwagen as allies here: "[S]ome suffering has the effect of improving our character and preparing God's people for life in his kingdom; this world is in part a vale of soul-making...Some suffering may also be the price of a regular world, as Peter van Inwagen suggests."[116]

Moving on to the next objection, even conceding that a good God would have reason to create a world with some suffering, "why does there have to be as much of these dubious quantities as our world in fact manifests?"[117] Again, Plantinga suggests two responses. Firstly, perhaps the counterfactuals of creaturely freedom come out in such a way that a world as good as ours will contain as much suffering as ours. If so, God could only actualize a world as good as ours by bringing about at least as much suffering as the actual world contains.

Secondly, "there is the question how much sin and suffering a highly eligible world contains."[118] Because incarnation and atonement is an essential feature of all highly eligible worlds, this depends on how much sin and suffering is required to justify incarnation and atonement. Plantinga suggests that in a world where only one creature told a single white lie, a reaction of divine incarnation and atonement would be something like overkill.[119] Hence, although divine incarnation and atonement do not entail any suffering at all, perhaps the counterfactuals of powerful creaturely freedom are such that sin in the amount necessary to warrant incarnation and atonement would always cause at least as much suffering as the actual world exhibits.

Considering both our lack of knowledge of the relevant counterfactuals of freedom and the fact that suffering is of instrumental value, especially as a necessary precondition for divine incarnation and atonement, Plantinga concludes that "we have no way at all of estimating how much suffering the best worlds will contain, or where the amount of suffering and evil contained in [the actual world] stands in comparison with those worlds. This objection, therefore, is inconclusive."[120]

Plantinga admits that the third objection is powerful. According to Plantinga's theodicy, "God's ultimate aim...is to create a world of a certain level of value."[121] God requires suffering on the part of his creatures not to advance *the creatures'* good or welfare but so that he can achieve *his own* magnificent end of actualizing

---

[116]   Plantinga, "Supralapsarianism...," 17.      [117]   Plantinga, "Supralapsarianism...," 19.
[118]   Plantinga, "Supralapsarianism...," 20.
[119]   Pace Anselm of Canterbury. Cf. Anselm, *Cur Deus Homo*, Chapter 21.
[120]   Plantinga, "Supralapsarianism...," 21.      [121]   Plantinga, "Supralapsarianism...," 12.

a highly eligible world, "one in which he incidentally plays the stellar role."[122] Wouldn't God be like a father who throws his child into a river so that he can then play hero? Wouldn't it be inconsistent with God loving his creatures to act in such a coldhearted way, to achieve his own ends at their extreme expense?

Plantinga resists this conclusion. He firstly notes that it is not always wrong to treat one as a means rather than an end, for example when a car mechanic is used to fix a car.[123] The important point according to Plantinga is not that creatures are used as means rather than ends but that they are so used without their consent.

But again, Plantinga claims that it is not always wrong to use others as means without their consent. It depends on why their permission is withheld. Plantinga claims—without supporting argument—that if God knew his creatures would consent if they could or if he knew their unwillingness was due only to ignorance, God would be morally in the clear. Further, he claims, even if God knew their unwillingness was due to disordered affections, "in this case too, as far as I can see, his being perfectly loving would not preclude his allowing me to suffer. In this case God would be like a mother who, say, insists that her eight-year-old child take piano lessons or go to church or school."[124]

Finally, Plantinga speculates that even if God's reason for making me suffer is not so that I can be benefited, "nevertheless, perhaps it is also true that he would not permit me to suffer for that end, an end outside my own good, unless he could also bring good for me out of the evil."[125] He motions toward Jonathan Edwards and Abraham Kuyper in speculating that fallen creatures who suffer before being redeemed can be admitted to greater intimacy with God than creatures who have not fallen and suffered. Three reasons for thinking this are that only creatures who have fallen and suffered can be in solidarity with God in his suffering, can receive divine forgiveness by atonement, and—as Julian of Norwich has suggested—can receive God's gratitude for having suffered for his plans.[126]

## Evaluation

To be successful—a quality Plantinga is inclined to grant his theodicy and to deny most others[127]—a theodicy must show some significant plausibility. While my primary concern in this section is to assess the *structural promise* of Plantinga's

---

[122] Plantinga, "Supralapsarianism...," 21.   [123] Plantinga, "Supralapsarianism...," 22.
[124] Plantinga, "Supralapsarianism...," 24.   [125] Plantinga, "Supralapsarianism...," 24.
[126] Plantinga, "Supralapsarianism...," 18–19. In coming up with these three reasons I am reading into Plantinga somewhat, but I hope charitably so.
[127] Plantinga, "Supralapsarianism...," 12: "So if a theodicy is an attempt to explain why God permits evil, what we have here is a theodicy—and, if I'm right, a successful theodicy." Compare this with his earlier claim that "most attempts to explain why God permits evil—theodicies, as we may call them—strike me as tepid, shallow, and ultimately frivolous" ("Self-Profile," 35). Cf. also Alvin Plantinga, "Epistemic Probability and Evil," in *The Evidential Argument from Evil*, ed. Daniel Howard-Snyder (Bloomington: Indiana University Press, 1996), 70.

theodicy, it is worth noting that, independently of my evaluation of its *structural promise*, I have serious doubts about the plausibility of Plantinga's approach. I'll briefly note three of these doubts.

For one thing, I'm skeptical that his appeals to what Molinist counterfactuals of creaturely freedom "perhaps" are lend any substantial support to a claim of plausibility. Even if there are such counterfactuals—a controversial position in its own right—it strikes me as very implausible that, given all of the beings and world-types that omnipotence would allow one to create, "it wasn't within the power of God to create free creatures who are both capable of causing suffering and turning to evil, but never in fact do cause suffering."[128] Without further support, such claims of what "perhaps" is the case seem better suited for the purposes of offering a *defense*—as Plantinga has done elsewhere—than a theodicy.

A second plausibility concern of mine has to do with the explanatory power Plantinga grants "Satan and his cohorts." Plantinga claims, "The thought that much evil is due to Satan and his cohorts is *of course entirely consistent* with God's being omnipotent, omniscient, and perfectly good."[129] I think this is an overstatement, and will discuss why I think so in Chapter 5.

Thirdly, even if significant sin and suffering is necessary for incarnation *and* atonement, it is less plausibly necessary for incarnation. Plantinga fails to distinguish between incarnation and atonement despite the fact that some of the most celebrated Christian theologians (including Robert Grosseteste, Duns Scotus, and Karl Barth) have argued that neither sin nor suffering is necessary for incarnation. If incarnation and atonement has value so great as to be incommensurable with all creaturely goods, as Plantinga suggests, I'm inclined to think incarnation on its own will also have such incommensurable value. This surfaces a new challenge for Plantinga to tell us what is so valuable about atonement *over and above incarnation* that it justifies all of the sin and suffering of the actual world.

On to *structural promise*. My earlier evaluation of Case A morally impugned the parents for causing *horrors* for pure benefit—that is, for causing a certain type of suffering (*horrendous* suffering) with a certain sort of instrumentality (as a means to pure benefit). Plantinga's theodicy has worrying structural similarities. According to it, God is justified in causing the *horrendous* suffering of the actual world because suffering of this sort is instrumentally required as a means to achieving the goods of incarnation and atonement.

Plantinga does not describe these goods as pure benefits, but his description of them may leave his theodicy even more vulnerable for it. Whereas Hick is concerned with *horrors* being beneficial in the end for those who suffer them, and Swinburne at least with humanity as a whole being benefited, Plantinga's approach

---

[128]  Plantinga, "Supralapsarianism...," 17.
[129]  Plantinga, "Supralapsarianism...," 16 (italics mine).

does not depict God as causing *horrendous evils* for creatures' benefit at all, but rather for the non-person-specific good of a world of a certain value. Maybe Plantinga is thinking of God himself as the beneficiary of having such a stellar role in attaining such a valuable good. If so, then like parents who cause serious suffering in their children's lives so that they can then play hero, Plantinga's theodicy threatens to diagnose God with an egocentric savior complex.[130] In any case, I have argued that causing *horrendous harm* to others is not permissible even when done for the pure benefit of the *horror* sufferers themselves, let alone when done for a non-person-specific good or for one's own benefit.

Perhaps Plantinga's approach could be reformulated to put primary justificatory emphasis on the supposed sin-and-suffering-entailing benefits of solidarity with God in suffering, forgiveness by divine atonement, and divine gratitude for suffering. Even so, these could at best be construed as pure benefits. The possibility of justifying *horrors* as avoiding a still worse harm is—as with Swinburne—unavailable to Plantinga who implies that there are non-*horrendous*, feasible worlds containing many excellent creatures with "rich and beautiful and sinless" lives and who "live in love and harmony with God and each other, and do so, let's add, through all eternity."[131]

By analogy with Case A, then, Plantinga's theodicy seems guilty of depicting God as causing *horrendous evils* as a means to ends which are at best pure benefits. Plantinga attempts to avoid this charge by unfairly dissecting it. His objection (2) discusses the magnitude of suffering; his objection (3) discusses the instrumentality of suffering. But he never deals with the conjunctive objection that his theodicy depicts God as using suffering of a *horrendous* magnitude *with* a certain sort of instrumentality.

After referencing Marilyn Adams as a proponent of objection (3), Plantinga formulates the objection thus: "God's love for his creatures is incompatible with his requiring them to suffer in order to advance divine aims or ends that do not advance the creatures' good or welfare."[132] But this is not Adams's challenge. Her challenge is concerned more specifically with how requiring creatures to suffer *horrendously* bears on God's love for them.

I have argued for narrowing this challenge further still: God's love for his creatures is incompatible with his requiring them to suffer *horrendous evils* in order to bestow pure benefit. In these more accurate forms, the relevant challenge that *horrendous evils* pose is a combination of Plantinga's objections (2) and (3). Neither the amount of suffering nor the instrumentality of the suffering is enough on its own to formulate the problem.

---

[130]  The technical term for this psychological condition is Münchausen syndrome by proxy.
[131]  Plantinga, "Supralapsarianism...," 10.    [132]  Plantinga, "Supralapsarianism...," 23.

Returning to Plantinga's *apropos* example, when the father throws his son into the river so that he can play hero, it's not the amount of suffering caused or its instrumentality that is sufficient to condemn the father. The father would have been justified in causing still more harm had he performed on his child a life-saving open heart surgery that he was medically qualified to perform, and the father would have been justified had he *used* his child to help clean the house before company arrived. But considering the amount of suffering and its instrumentality in tandem, the charge is that a good God could not be justified in causing his creatures to suffer this much (i.e., *horrendously*) for an instrumental purpose that aims for creaturely pure benefit at best.

Once Plantinga moves on to objection (3), he seems unaware that the severity of suffering concerned will have bearing on the charge of instrumentality. In his formulation of objection (3), Plantinga likens God to a father who abuses his child,[133] but in responding to the objection he shifts the analogy to "a mother who insists that her eight-year-old child take piano lessons or go to church or school."[134] His doing so highlights that he has failed to fully appreciate the justificatory asymmetry between *horrendous* and less severe evils.

When the badness of *horrors* and the instrumentality of causing them for non-person-specific goods are considered in concert, it becomes clear that containing the minimum amount of evil necessary in order to achieve global value L is not sufficient to justify God's actualizing a world of value L. Early in his article, referring to incarnation and atonement, Plantinga asks the question, "Could there be a display of love to rival this?" And then, as if to correct himself, he continues, "More to the present purpose, could there be a good-making feature of a world to rival this one?"[135] My evaluative framework suggests that the order of the questions should be reversed. Irrespective of the world-enhancing effects of atonement, to cause *horrendous harm* for a non-person-specific good (or at best a pure benefit) would be neither moral nor consistent with the particularity of divine love.

## Divine Right to Harm

Perhaps the best chance of overriding the *prima facie* case against Type A Theodicy is by appeal to divine caretaker rights. In the previous chapter, I suggested that parents have some rights over their children in virtue of accepting and fulfilling certain caretaking roles in their children's lives, for example rights to keep their children in school longer than legally required or to move the family to pursue a job promotion, even when doing so will occasion some harm.

---

[133] Plantinga, "Supralapsarianism…," 21.     [134] Plantinga, "Supralapsarianism…," 24.
[135] Plantinga, "Supralapsarianism…," 7.

Nonetheless, I called attention to the fact that when harm is aimed at pure benefit rather than harm aversion, these parental rights are decidedly limited, and that causing truly *horrendous harm* for pure benefit blows right through plausible cases of parental right to harm. I concluded that on no plausible account of the relationship between caretaking roles and rights to harm would parental rights be sufficient to justify *horror* causation for pure benefit.

Could God have rights so much greater that they are capable of doing the justificatory work? Swinburne thinks so. He recognizes that his theodicy stands and falls with his claims that God has extraordinary caretaker rights over his creatures and that these rights demand modification of our moral judgments. He suggests:

> Since God is so much more the source of our being than our human parents (who can only give us what they give us because God keeps them in existence and keeps operative the laws of nature which enable them to benefit us), he must, by analogy, have far greater duties and rights than they do.[136]

In my treatment of Case A, I outlined three understandings of the relationship between caretaking roles and caretaker rights to cause harm for pure benefit. On the first understanding, the two are directly correlated along a sliding scale *ad infinitum*—the more significant the caretaking *roles*, the more significant the caretaker *rights*. If this is the correct relationship, then Swinburne's elevation of divine rights could plausibly justify God's causing *horrendous evil* for pure benefit.

I join Swinburne in rejecting this first understanding. Swinburne affirms that "the greater the duty to care, the greater (if the duty is fulfilled) the consequent rights."[137] But he several times qualifies the point by noting that the rights of caretakers to cause or permit harm are always limited rights, and that even a divine caretaker would have limits on the intensity and length of bad states he could permissibly have his creatures endure.[138] There seems to be a widely-shared and strong intuition that each person has certain "absolute rights" by which others' caretaker rights are necessarily limited.[139] I have suggested that the right not to be *horrendously* harmed for pure benefit is one such right.

---

[136] Swinburne, *Providence and the Problem of Evil*, 224.
[137] Swinburne, *Providence and the Problem of Evil*, 224.
[138] Swinburne, *Providence and the Problem of Evil*, 228, 232–3, 238. Swinburne concludes that even God only has the necessary rights to impose evil for the sake of greater goods "if...the bad periods are not too long or too bad" (238). See also Swinburne, *The Existence of God*, 2nd ed., 263.
[139] In Swinburne's words, "The right of a carer who provides a life overall good for the dependant to cause some harm to the dependant is, I stress, a very limited one. Clearly someone who rescues a child from poverty and starvation and gives him on the whole a good life does not have the right in return to abuse him sexually from time to time. The obvious reason why there is no such right is that any human has certain absolute rights, such as the right to choose how to use their own sexual organs, by which the carer's rights are limited" (*Providence and the Problem of Evil*, 228).

Resultantly, the moral objection to the parents' action in Case A does not seem to be in any way diminished by their caretaker roles. This will remain true, I'm inclined to believe, even if future technological advances allow "parents" to be "much more the source of [their children's] being" than is presently the case, for instance by allowing them to biologically construct android children in great detail and to sustain their existence through a substantial daily maintenance routine. Alongside increased rights to harm, those in caretaker roles also acquire increased obligations to protect those in their care, especially from the most severe forms of harm. On balance, the parents' caretaking roles—in both normal and technologically enhanced scenarios—seem to render them more rather than less culpable.

If parental and even technologically enhanced parental rights to cause children harm for pure benefit are significantly greater than those of a stranger, and yet in no way diminish wrongdoing in cases of *horror* causation, this is reason to think, *mutatis mutandis*, that even the divine rights grounded in God's much greater caretaking roles are irrelevant to the justification of causing *horrendous harm* for pure benefits. Moreover, if God's greater responsibility for our coming to be and sustained existence results in his having unique rights to harm us for pure benefit, it equally plausibly results in his having unique obligations to protect us from the most severe forms of harm. The result is that there are certain outcomes we don't have a right to cause regardless of our caretaking duties or roles; *horrors* caused for pure benefit are very plausible candidates.

What's behind these intuitions is not that God's rights are not great enough to justify *horror* causation but rather that caretaking rights are not of the correct *type* to do such justificatory work. Swinburne errs in understanding the right of carers to harm those in their care *primarily* as a right to inflict greater harm rather than as a greater right to harm. More plausible, I think, is the reverse emphasis; caretaker rights are more about having the right *to be the one to decide when to harm the one cared for* than about having the right *to harm the one cared for more severely*.

That this emphasis is the more salient one is confirmed by the fact that in the case of parents' death, the guardians that their child is entrusted to (even if only temporarily and even before they have fulfilled substantial caretaking roles in the child's life) seem to have similar rights as the biological parents did in terms of the extent to which the child can be harmed permissibly for the child's benefit. The caretaker rights of the parents gave them primary authority to make surrogate decisions on behalf of their child, but I doubt they justified the parents in harming their child significantly more than others ought to harm their child were the parents not to exist.

I do not deny that caretaker rights can do some work of this latter sort. Perhaps caretaker rights to harm more severely help explain, for instance, why it is illegal for foster parents to physically discipline the children in their care while some forms of minor physical discipline are legal for those with the status of full guardians. Though even here, greater legal rights for parents may have more to do with the state having greater reason to trust them than with their roles. In any case, I take it that caretaking roles do more to help us identify who should be entrusted with deciding when to harm than to identify how severe permissible harm can be. I suspect this latter identification has much more to do with what the potentially harmed object is and how it ought not to be violated than with who is caring for it.

I have suggested that if caretaker rights are understood primarily as rights to harm more severely, there is nonetheless a threshold of harm severity above which caretaker rights to harm no longer increase, regardless of caretaking roles. I am now suggesting that there is a plausible alternative explanation of the primary function of caretaker rights which, if correct, would act to significantly lower that threshold, making it still less likely that even *divine* caretaker rights to harm could ever extend to harming *horrendously*.

This alternative offers a simple explanation of why examples such as Case A imply that some *horrors* are well beyond the threshold of caretaking relevance, not because God's caretaker rights are not great enough but because increasing the amount one can harm permissibly is not their primary function. We should expect God's caretaker rights to give him the right to make even many more decisions on our behalf than our human parents, but not to give him the right to harm us in exceedingly more severe ways.

As a final point, it is worth questioning whether—even if God has, contrary to my opinion, a caretaker right to *horrendously* harm us for our pure benefit—it would be *loving* for him to exercise that right.[140] Theodicy is concerned with God's ethical perfection, which demands not only that he fulfill all of his moral obligations but also that he display a flawless character, and preeminently a character of love. Exercising one's rights is not always the loving thing to do, especially when exercising them is likely to damage important relationships.

Say, for instance, that my brother accidentally broke a picture frame in my house. I take it that I have the right to ask him to either replace it or give me money for it, but I would never exercise this right. To do so would damage our relationship. It would likely cause my brother to question whether I had really forgiven him for his clumsiness. As a result, it would also call into question how much he means to me, given that to me compensation was more important than assuring him that he was forgiven. To exercise this right over my brother would

---

140   In making this point, I am reminded of Marilyn Adams's words: "I can believe I *deserve* this and worse; after all, so many authorities have declared me incorrigibly bad. But if You're the kind of person who visits this sort of thing on people just because we deserve it, then life is a desperate nightmare. It would have been better never to have been born" (Marilyn Adams, "Love of Learning, Reality of God," in *God and the Philosophers: The Reconciliation of Faith and Reason* (Oxford: Oxford University Press, 1994), 155).

be to treat him like a stranger rather than like a brother, with the result that he would no longer feel comfortable and amid family in my home. Similarly, it would be unfitting for God as a perfect lover to exercise a right to *horrendously* harm his creatures for pure benefit even if he had such a right. To do so would make him responsible for engendering precisely the sort of estrangement, shame, and mistrust that *horrendous evils* tend to engender. Moreover, the way *horrendous harm* tends to destroy relationships supports the previously elicited intuition that having caretaking roles makes the causation of *horrors* for pure benefit more rather than less morally suspect.

At least three points, then, tell against Swinburne's claim that God has rights to *horrendously* harm his creatures arising from his being "moment to moment the source of our being."[141] Firstly, intuitions about cases of ascending caretaking roles suggest that where *horrors* are concerned, caretaker rights to harm will not significantly aid attempts to morally justify God's ways. If the status of caretaker has any bearing on obligations with respect to *horrors*, it seems more reasonable to suppose that carers are to be condemned even more severely for the perpetration of *horrors* due to their greater obligation as carers for the well-being of those in their care. Secondly, there is reason to think that the temptation to suggest otherwise in the divine case relies on a misunderstanding of the type of right a caretaker right is. And finally, even if God has caretaker rights to *horrendously* harm his creatures, it seems inconsistent with his being perfectly loving for him to exercise those rights. I conclude that divine caretaking considerations do not give me strong reason to modify my evaluations of the Type A Theodicies considered.

## Summing Up

The three theodicies considered thus far are analogous to Case A in attempting to justify a caretaker's causation of at least some *horrors* by describing the ways in which those *horrors* are necessary for pure benefits.

One disanalogy is that the power to benefit is so much greater in the God case than in the parental case. To Hick especially, it is important that the benefit for human persons for which God causes *horrors* is infinitely good. But the problem with this line of defense is that if you have a God so powerful and resourceful that he can bring an infinitely good benefit out of *horrors*, then intuitions suggest that you have a God powerful and resourceful enough to achieve very great goods without *horrors* as well. By claiming that God has the power to create us perfect *ab initio* and to actualize worlds full of love and harmony for all eternity, both Swinburne and Plantinga commend this intuition, and even Hick suggests that

---

[141] Swinburne, *Providence and the Problem of Evil*, 243.

God could make our souls without anything that would meet the objective criterion of the *horrendous*. None of the theodicies considered make anything close to a plausible case for God being in an *extreme situation*. Without more said, Type A Theodicy fails structurally by analogy with Case A.

Let me say again that these attempts to work out a Type A structural approach to theodicy have much to offer. They suggest plausible candidate reasons for much and many types of evil. In a world without *horrors*, perhaps they would be sufficient. But in our world, a world where *horrors* abound, they are structurally deficient. Even were they fully accurate in the ways they depict God's causation of and reasons for *horrendous evils*, they would fail to successfully defend God's ethical perfection.

# 4
# Applying the Analogies

## Permission and Risk; Benefit Production and Harm Avoidance

### Type B Theodicy

Case B differs from Case A because in it the parents merely permit—rather than cause—the *horrendous* suffering of their child. They can easily avert this great harm, but they decide to permit it because they know that the pure benefits it will make possible will result in their child's life being better-off all things considered than it otherwise would have been. A theodicy structurally analogous to Case B would depict God as never directly causing individual *horrendous evils*. All such evils would have to be merely permitted by God, caused by some other intervening agents such as humans or angels.

Of course, it would seem that God must remain at least a partial cause of evil if (as has been traditional in much Western religious thought since Augustine) God created everything out of nothing and sustains everything at all times. One response to this is to question whether God's continuous sustenance, even if technically continuous action, relevantly resembles inaction. When I am driving, I sometimes don't stop to let pedestrians cross when I could. I like to think my "staying the course" in these instances is something I allow rather than something I do, and that I permit the car to continue forward rather than causing it to. Contrastingly, I would cause the car to stop if I hit the brakes.

Peter van Inwagen in particular makes room for this sort of move due to what Alfred Freddoso refers to as "an excessively deistic conception of God's causal relation to the world" that is "stigmatized as (in effect) a form of *deism* by almost every important medieval Christian philosopher."[1] In the ordinary course of nature, van Inwagen conceives of God sustaining the existence of things and their causal powers, but beyond this he lets them do their own thing. The more traditional Christian views of occasionalism and concurrentism suggest, respectively, that God is always either the only efficient cause or one of a number of efficient

---

[1] Alfred J. Freddoso, "Comment on van Inwagen's 'Place of Chance in a World Sustained by God,'" Unpublished work (Notre Dame, 1987), 23 Aug 2011, <http://www.nd.edu/~afreddos/papers/chance.htm>

*Non-Identity Theodicy: A Grace-Based Response to the Problem of Evil*. Vince R. Vitale, Oxford University Press (2020). © Vince R. Vitale.
DOI: 10.1093/oso/9780198864226.003.0004

causes by which natural effects are immediately derived. Additionally, Van Inwagen supposes that "God can, if he chooses, 'decree' that it shall either be the case that *p* or [exclusive] be the case that *q*, without either decreeing that it shall be the case that *p* or decreeing that it shall be the case that *q*…It may well be, then, that such matters as whether a given person dies in some natural disaster is something God has left to chance."[2] If van Inwagen is correct on these points, perhaps it would limit divine foreknowledge and distance divine action enough to make meaningful conceptual space between divine causation and divine permission of *horrendous* outcomes.

Still, how we should categorize my "staying the course" while driving is unclear. You might be inclined to think that my saying I permit the car to continue forward is an instance of rationalization on my part. The difficulty in categorizing this example highlights that even if there is meaningful conceptual space between divine causation and divine permission, there are always divine actions causally relevant and near to any outcome. Recognizing God's continuous sustaining influence on the world is reason to be suspect of any framework that suggests *very* different ethical assessments of God based on whether he is taken to cause or permit the relevant outcomes. My evaluative framework yields no such suggestion. I critique theodicies that do suggest this in Chapter 5.

The main distinction between most Type A and Type B Theodicies is that Type B Theodicies tell causal stories that attempt to shift significant responsibility for *horrendous evils* away from God and onto non-divine free agents. I find a theodicy analogous to Case B in van Inwagen's work. By following his detours to this structure, I will simultaneously draw out many of the elements of theodicies analogous to Cases C and D.

## The Pieces of van Inwagen's Theodicy

Van Inwagen claims that if his theodicy is true, God's reasons for permitting all of the evil of the actual world are sufficient to maintain his ethical perfection,[3] and as to whether it is true, he confidently asserts, "I certainly don't see any reason to reject any of it."[4]

---

[2] Peter van Inwagen, *The Problem of Evil* (Oxford: Oxford University Press, 2006), 167. For a more thorough discussion of these matters, see van Inwagen's "The Place of Chance in a World Sustained by God," in Peter Van Inwagen, *God, Knowledge & Mystery: Essays in Philosophical Theology* (Ithaca: Cornell University Press, 1995).

[3] Van Inwagen writes, "What I claim for the theodicy presented in this essay is this: it alleges a reason, or an interconnected set of reasons, that God has for allowing evil—of the amounts and kinds we observe—to come to be and to continue; if these were the only reasons God had for permitting evil, they would by themselves justify this permission" (Van Inwagen, "The Magnitude, Duration, and Distribution of Evil: A Theodicy," 97).

[4] Van Inwagen, *The Problem of Evil.* 92.

Van Inwagen offers different reasons for human and non-human animal suffering. Because *horrendous evils* (in the technical sense I have inherited from Marilyn Adams) are person centered, I will concentrate on the former. Here I list the essential components of van Inwagen's theodicy for human suffering as first presented in "The Magnitude, Duration, and Distribution of Evil: A Theodicy:"[5]

(1) Necessarily, only beings with sin in their possibility of choice are capable of freely loving God. Human beings are among these beings, and freely loving God is of great value.

(2) Necessarily, the natural consequences of human beings' sin are catastrophic and horrendous.[6] These consequences account for all of the human suffering in the world.

(3) Necessarily, because God is *ex hypothesi* not a deceiver, he must permit much of the natural consequences of human sin.

(4) The horrors[7] of this world are a necessary postlapsarian condition of the great good of God's plan of atonement, and the expected overall value of God's plan of atonement for human persons—given potential horrors—is highly positive.

Firstly, a rundown of van Inwagen's support for these four claims. Van Inwagen takes (1) to follow from the fact that

love implies freedom: for A to love B is for A freely to choose to be united to B in a certain way. Now even an omnipotent God cannot *ensure* that some other being *freely* choose x over y. For God to create beings capable of loving him, therefore, it was necessary for Him to take a risk: to risk the possibility that the beings He created would freely choose to withhold their love from Him.[8]

As for (2), van Inwagen proposes that we are living with the natural consequences of separation from God, including a radical vulnerability to natural processes. By claiming that these consequences are "natural," van Inwagen means to imply that God could not have made it such that the natural consequences of human sin were not *horrendous*. As he writes,

---

[5] Van Inwagen, "The Magnitude, Duration, and Distribution of Evil: A Theodicy," in *God, Knowledge, and Mystery, Essays in Philosophical Theology*, ed. Peter van Inwagen (Ithaca and London: Cornell University Press, 1995), 96–122.

[6] Van Inwagen refers to the beginning of Genesis as "a mythico-literary representation of actual events of human pre-history" (*The Problem of Evil*, 84–5).

[7] By his own admission, van Inwagen uses the term horrors more loosely than Adams's technical sense (Van Inwagen, *The Problem of Evil*, 168), but he does claim for his theodicy that it accounts for even the worst evils of the actual world. It is therefore fair to apply his general approach to *horrors* in Adams's technical sense and to test its efficacy when thus applied.

[8] Van Inwagen, "The Magnitude, Duration, and Distribution of Evil," 98.

It is simply a part of the mechanics of nature that intrinsically harmless but potentially destructive things like avalanches or viruses or earthquakes should exist…Such things are a part of God's design in the sense that the ticking sound made by a clock is a part of the watchmaker's design.[9]

And putting the point from the divine perspective:

Even I can't make a world which is suitable for human beings but which contains no phenomena that would harm human beings *if* they were in the wrong place at the wrong time.[10]

A radical human vulnerability to the magnitude, duration, and distribution of evil is the metaphysically unavoidable cost of creating a "structurally and nomologically coherent world complex enough to contain [human beings]."[11]

Van Inwagen's story is one whereby God intervened at some point in the evolutionary process to miraculously raise a small breeding community of pre-*Homo sapiens* primates to the status of human beings. Not only did he give them "the gifts of language, abstract thought, and disinterested love—and, of course, the gift of free will,"[12] but, prior to the fall, they were also protected from natural evil by special powers. These powers depended on their union with God and allowed them to always avoid being in the wrong place at the wrong time.[13] Earthquakes and tornadoes existed, but they did not cause suffering because human persons always knew how and when to avoid them.[14]

Perhaps recognizing that human suffering is due to more than just being in the wrong place at the wrong time, van Inwagen expands on his description of the first human beings' preternatural powers in his more recent writings:

God not only raised these primates to rationality—not only made of them what we call human beings—but also took them into a kind of mystical union with himself, the sort of union that Christians hope for in Heaven and call the Beatific Vision. Being in union with God, these new human beings, these primates who had become human beings at a certain point in their lives, lived together in the harmony of perfect love and also possessed what theologians used to call preternatural powers—something like what people who believe in them today call 'paranormal abilities.' Because they lived in the harmony of perfect love, none of them did any harm to the others. Because of their preternatural powers, they

---

[9]  Van Inwagen, "The Magnitude, Duration, and Distribution of Evil," 118. See also 106.
[10]  Van Inwagen, "The Magnitude, Duration, and Distribution of Evil," 118–19.
[11]  Van Inwagen, "The Magnitude, Duration, and Distribution of Evil," 119.
[12]  Van Inwagen, *The Problem of Evil*, 85.
[13]  Van Inwagen, "The Magnitude, Duration, and Distribution of Evil," 106.
[14]  Van Inwagen, "The Magnitude, Duration, and Distribution of Evil," 105–6.

were able somehow to protect themselves from wild beasts (which they were able to tame with a look), from disease (which they were able to cure with a touch), and from random, destructive natural events (like earthquakes) which they knew about in advance and were able to escape.[15]

This first generation of human persons used their free will for bad; in doing so, they separated themselves from God and lost their preternatural powers. That their protective powers were lost in the fall "is as natural a consequence of our ancestors' separation from God as is the loss of the capacity to acquire language a natural consequence of the feral child's separation from the human community."[16] Moreover, the first human persons "ruined not only themselves but their posterity, for the separation from God that they achieved was somehow hereditary."[17]

Van Inwagen thus elides the problem of natural evil into the problem of moral evil by redefining the suffering of human persons due to natural evil as a special category of moral evil. The result is that, in contrast to Type A Theodicies, God does not sufficiently cause any *horrors*. According to van Inwagen, any *horror* that occurs is one God permits as part of the "catastrophic consequences" of the fall.[18]

God risks; humans rebel. The next question is whether God would permit the *horrendous* natural consequences of humans turning away from him. Van Inwagen offers two reasons why God might be justified in doing so. The first is that he can't but permit them; the second is that he permits them for benefit. Consider the first reason:

(3) Necessarily, because God is *ex hypothesi* not a deceiver, he must permit much of the natural consequences of human sin.

Van Inwagen poses a challenge to his story: "Why didn't God immediately restore His fallen creatures to their original union with Him?"[19] He responds with a secular analogue of two brothers who quarrel violently and eventually come to hate one another. Their mother then prays to God and asks that the mutual love between her sons would be restored immediately. For God to grant this request would involve, according to van Inwagen, at least deleting all memory of what happened just before they began quarreling. Van Inwagen claims God would not do such a thing because "as Descartes has pointed out, God is not a deceiver, and such an act would constitute a grave deception about the facts of history."[20] God

[15] Van Inwagen, *The Problem of Evil*, 85–6.
[16] Van Inwagen, "The Magnitude, Duration, and Distribution of Evil," 106.
[17] Peter van Inwagen, "Non Est Hick," in van Inwagen, *God, Knowledge, and Mystery: Essays in Philosophical Theology*, ed. Peter van Inwagen (Ithaca and London: Cornell University Press, 1995), 196.
[18] Van Inwagen, "The Magnitude, Duration, and Distribution of Evil," 99.
[19] Van Inwagen, "The Magnitude, Duration, and Distribution of Evil," 108.
[20] Van Inwagen, "The Magnitude, Duration, and Distribution of Evil," 108.

would not put the sons in an epistemic position that gives them strong reason for believing they have not quarreled if in fact they have.

Similarly, van Inwagen concludes, God would not *always* step in and miraculously cancel the effects of sin. To do so would be to "engender an illusion with the following propositional content: It is possible for human beings to live apart from God and not be subject to destruction by chance."[21] God could stop the world altogether, but opting for human annihilation rather than the natural conse-quences of sin may be to trade *horror* for *horror*. And moreover, it is at least as plausibly contrary to the character of an ideal lover to give up on human persons altogether by annihilating them as it is to deceive them. So long as God remains committed to the human project, severe suffering is the unavoidable result of the impossibility of God acting deceptively.

The second reason why God might permit *horrendous* consequences of the actions of intervening human agents is that such consequences are a necessary condition of some outweighing benefit. For van Inwagen,

(4) The horrors of this world are a necessary postlapsarian condition of the great good of God's plan of atonement, and the expected overall value of God's plan of atonement for human persons—given potential horrors—is highly positive.

Van Inwagen's recommendation of (4)'s second independent clause is consistent throughout his work but most explicit in a more recent passage:

[B]efore there were human beings, God knew that, however much evil might result from the elected separation from himself, and consequent self-ruin, of his human creatures—if it should occur—the gift of free will would be, so to speak, worth it. For the existence of an eternity of love depends on this gift, and that eternity outweighs the horrors of the very long but, in the most literal sense, temporary period of divine-human estrangement.[22]

Once we have entered this eternity of love, we will be able to recognize its depend-ence on *horrors* for at least two reasons. Firstly, the *horrors* of this world are the "only motivation fallen human beings have for turning to [God]."[23] Secondly, the memory of the "hideousness" that is "living disunited from God" will allow for a heavenly security that might not be otherwise possible.[24] Those in heaven will

---

[21] Van Inwagen, "The Magnitude, Duration, and Distribution of Evil," 117–18. See also 108. A similar theme is found in the work of Simone Weil: "Affliction contains the truth about our condition" (Weil, "The Love of God and Affliction," 194).

[22] Peter van Inwagen, "The Problem of Evil," in *The Oxford Handbook of Philosophy of Religion*, ed. William Wainwright (Oxford: Oxford University Press, 2005), 209. See also a very similar passage in van Inwagen, *The Problem of Evil*, 90, and a related passage on 72.

[23] Van Inwagen, "The Magnitude, Duration, and Distribution of Evil," 113.

[24] Van Inwagen, "The Magnitude, Duration, and Distribution of Evil," 112.

know what it is like to be separated from God. "Continuing in their restored state," therefore, "will be no more puzzling than the refusal of the restored Prodigal Son to leave his father's house a second time."[25]

## Constructing van Inwagen's Theodicy

Van Inwagen endorses each of these four claims as a significant line in his story; however, exactly what work each is doing is less than perspicuous. It is especially unclear in "The Magnitude, Duration, and Distribution of Evil" how van Inwagen's claim that God cannot be a deceiver and his claim that God's plan of atonement will result in all-things-considered benefit relate to one another. The two are frequently mentioned side-by-side in concluding statements as if they each count as a sufficient reason for, and together overdetermine, God's ways. Consider the following two selections:

> I cannot see how God could simply, by sheer fiat, immediately have restored fallen humanity other than by a similar grave deception. And, we may add, if He did, what would happen next? What would prevent the fall from immediately recurring?[26]

> If, therefore, God were miraculously to "cancel" the natural consequences of separation from Himself, He would not only be a deceiver but would remove the only motivation fallen human beings have for turning to Him.[27]

Van Inwagen appears to be concluding that God could not step in to cancel *horrors* and, moreover, that even if he could, he would not in order to allow for the benefits they make possible.

Note, however, that (4) is ambiguous between (4a) and (4b):

(4a) The horrors of this world are a necessary postlapsarian condition of the great good of God's plan of atonement, the expected overall value of God's plan of atonement for human persons—given potential horrors—is highly positive, and the expected good of God's plan of atonement *averts still worse harm.*

(4b) The horrors of this world are a necessary postlapsarian condition of the great good of God's plan of atonement, the expected overall value of God's plan of atonement for human persons—given potential horrors—is highly positive, and the expected good of God's plan of atonement *bestows pure benefit.*

---

[25]  Van Inwagen, "The Magnitude, Duration, and Distribution of Evil," 112.
[26]  Van Inwagen, "The Magnitude, Duration, and Distribution of Evil," 108–9.
[27]  Van Inwagen, "The Magnitude, Duration, and Distribution of Evil," 113.

Adjusting for this ambiguity, I believe there are two charitable readings of van Inwagen's theodicy in "The Magnitude, Duration, and Distribution of Evil"—that is, two responses to the problem of evil that are both plausible elaborations of his four main claims and *structurally promising* in how they account for *horrors*. Van Inwagen needs the truth, together with (1) and (2), of either (3) and (4b) or (4a) on its own. In the former case, God's relationship to *horrors* is analogous to that of the parents in Case C. He risks *horrors* for the sake of pure benefit, knowing that if *horrors* do occur, he will be helpless to stop them. We might be inclined to think that God is not the sort of being who could ever find himself helpless to accomplish his will, that he knows too much and is too powerful to ever be merely risking. But on (3) and (4b), van Inwagen suggests that God's hands are tied by his nature as a non-deceiver. In the latter case of (4a)'s truth, God's relationship to *horrors* is analogous to the parents in Case D. His hands are not tied; he could easily stop *horrors*. But he permits them as the best means to averting still greater harm. If both (3) and (4a) are true, then God's justification is overdetermined.

## Evaluation

I find van Inwagen to be ambiguous between (4a) and (4b) in "The Magnitude, Duration, and Distribution of Evil." There is some evidence there for reading van Inwagen's (4) as (4a). At one point, for instance, van Inwagen likens God to a doctor who doesn't prescribe a pain killer "on the grounds that he knows that his patient will curtail some beloved but self-destructive activity—long-distance running, say—only if the patient continues to experience the pain that his condition signals."[28] By analogy, then, God permits *horrors* because only by so doing can he avert the still worse state of our rebellion against him and our becoming increasingly and eternally separated from him.

However, in his subsequent monograph, *The Problem of Evil*, van Inwagen shows his cards. There he retells his theodicy at greater length. Again, it initially seems as if van Inwagen is favoring a reading of his (4) that has God permitting *horrors* in order to avert greater harm. He refers to God's plan of atonement as a *rescue* operation, for example in the following passage: "For human beings to cooperate with God in this rescue operation, they must know that they need to be rescued. They must know what it means to be separated from him. And what it means to be separated from God is to live in a world of horrors."[29]

But it soon becomes clear that the greater good van Inwagen has in mind in (4) is a pure benefit. He writes,

---

[28] Van Inwagen, "The Magnitude, Duration, and Distribution of Evil," 111–12.
[29] Van Inwagen, *The Problem of Evil*, 88.

The best that could come of a miraculous prevention of each of the horrors that resulted from our separation from God would be a state of perfect natural happiness—like the state of the souls of infants who die unbaptized, according to traditional Roman Catholic theology. But allowing horrors to occur opens the possibility of a supernatural good for humanity that is infinitely better than perfect natural happiness.[30]

Perfect natural happiness is still pretty good! If God could avoid the *horrors* of this world while still giving perfect natural happiness to his creatures, then his permission of those *horrors* cannot be claimed to avert any greater *horror*. There is nothing *horrendous* about perfect natural happiness. We are forced to ascribe (4b) to van Inwagen.

Unfortunately, van Inwagen also leaves behind (3) almost entirely in his most recent treatment. There is only one reference to deception: "[H]owever much evil God shields us from, he must leave in place a vast amount of evil if he is not to deceive us about what separation from him means."[31] And it is not clear from this passage if God cannot deceive us because he is *ex hypothesi* not a deceiver or only because if we are deceived, we won't reap the pure benefits of turning back to God. If the latter, this lone mention of deception reduces to an aspect of (4).

With (3) more or less dismissed from van Inwagen's treatment and the ambiguity in (4) clarified as (4b), the hopeful structures forming in "The Magnitude, Duration, and Distribution of Evil" are undermined in *The Problem of Evil*. Van Inwagen's approach reduces to permitting *horrors* for pure benefit, analogous to Case B. Moreover, van Inwagen's theodicy may be still more vulnerable than Case B, for whereas the suffering in Case B is justified by all-things-considered benefit accrued *to the sufferer*, van Inwagen implies that at least some *horror* sufferers will "exist forever in a state of elected ruin—those who, in a word, are in Hell."[32] As such, I judge van Inwagen's theodicy morally unjustifiable and in tension with ideal divine love for human persons.

Van Inwagen is explicit that his theodicy rests on the claim that "it is at least very plausible to suppose that it is morally permissible for God to allow human beings to suffer if the inevitable result of suppressing the suffering would be to deprive them of a very great good, one that far outweighs the suffering."[33] This may be true in many cases where the suffering is not *horrendous* and in many cases where the very great good is one that averts harms worse than the initial suffering, but van Inwagen's theodicy satisfies neither of these conditions. His approach fails structurally because it is not sensitive to normative asymmetries between harms and benefits and between *horrendous* and non-*horrendous* evil.

---

[30]   Van Inwagen, *The Problem of Evil*, 104.
[31]   Van Inwagen, *The Problem of Evil*, 88.
[32]   Van Inwagen, *The Problem of Evil*, 89.        [33]   Van Inwagen, *The Problem of Evil*, 88.

## Reconsidering Divine Rights and the Causing/ Permitting Distinction

Like Swinburne, van Inwagen appeals to divine right in his attempt to justify the ways of God. I have already mentioned that at one point in "The Magnitude, Duration, and Distribution of Evil," van Inwagen makes an analogy between God and a doctor who doesn't prescribe a pain killer "on the grounds that he knows that his patient will curtail some beloved but self-destructive activity…only if the patient continues to experience the pain that his condition signals."[34] Van Inwagen admits that this may be a morally objectionable course of action for the doctor to take; "it would be presumptuous of him to act in such a paternalistic way" toward his fellow adult and citizen. We might even accuse the doctor of "playing God." "But," says van Inwagen, "we can hardly accuse *God* of playing God…God is justifiably paternalistic because He is our Father and because He is perfect in knowledge and wisdom, and because, or so I would argue, He has certain rights over us."[35]

For van Inwagen, God's rights over us derive from the fact that "everything we have…we have received from him."[36] We are utterly dependent on God for our coming to exist, for our being sustained in existence, and for everything we think, feel, or do. We therefore owe him the right to use us for his good purposes, much in the same way that a son who lives and eats at home for free may owe his father a weekly mowing of the lawn.

There are several reasons why the doctor-patient analogy is not a good one for van Inwagen's theodicy. Firstly, the example as described has no claim to being genuinely *horrendous*, and it is van Inwagen's explicit purpose to explain the permission of even the worst evils. Secondly, one reason we feel suspicious about the doctor's actions is that the patient has it in his own power to avoid the greater harm, and we feel he should be given the chance to do so. But with many of the *horrors* of this world, God's creatures have no such choice. When tsunamis threaten to strike, if God doesn't initiate a plan of aversion, nothing else will. Thirdly, the human analogue is clearly a case of permitting harm to avert greater harm. But as we have just seen, this is untrue to van Inwagen's professed position that God permits *horrors* in order to bestow a supernatural pure benefit rather than to settle for perfect natural happiness.

When the analogy is modified on all three points, the major structural distinction left between van Inwagen's approach and those of Hick, Swinburne, and Plantinga is that only for van Inwagen are all *horrors* the result of the fall. Only

---

[34] Van Inwagen, "The Magnitude, Duration, and Distribution of Evil," 111–12. Van Inwagen makes a related analogy in *The Problem of Evil*, 88.

[35] Van Inwagen, "The Magnitude, Duration, and Distribution of Evil," 112.

[36] Van Inwagen, "The Magnitude, Duration, and Distribution of Evil," 112.

for van Inwagen is there always an unpredictable intervening agent standing between God and *horrors*, and potentially diminishing his responsibility for them.

But as I have already argued in my discussion of Cases A and B, this distinction won't do nearly enough (if any) work toward justifying divine permission of *horrors* for pure benefit. Though it may be true that we are often permitted or even obliged to allow more evil than we have a right to cause, this effect tends toward negligibility where the evils are *horrors* and the permitters have caretaking roles in the lives of those suffering.

Moreover, the causing/permitting principle will do even less justificatory work in the divine scenario, for at least four reasons. Firstly, God can always avert harm with divine ease, whereas human persons sometimes have to accept significant costs to themselves in order not to permit harm. Secondly, whereas human persons are sometimes obliged not to meddle in others' affairs, no harm is outside the scope of God's legitimate involvement. Thirdly, God, if he exists, has ultimate authority in all matters, and persons in authority are often as much or more to blame than their subjects when their inaction is a condition of their subjects' action. It is ultimate authority of this sort that makes the commanding general responsible for a slaughter when he permits it by watching inactively from a nearby vantage point. Fourthly, as previously noted, there is nothing that God permits that doesn't have divine acts factoring prominently, both in their ancestry and in their occurrence.

Resultantly, the gap between causation and permission is significantly narrower in cases of divine agency than in paradigm cases of human agency. Perhaps God does not determine free human actions, but nevertheless, for a God who sustains everything at every moment, causing and permitting will not warrant as significant moral asymmetries as they may sometimes do in cases of human agency. All told, I see no reason to think God's rights should extend to permitting *horrors* for pure benefit any more than to causing them for this type of good.

In Case B, I judged the parents guilty of using a readily avoidable *horror* for pure benefit, despite the fact that they permit and do not actively cause the *horror*. By analogy, van Inwagen's Type B Theodicy was judged *prima facie* structurally suspect. Combining my criticisms of appeals to divine right to harm from last chapter with my reflection on the nature of divine permission here, I retain the judgment that Type B Theodicy fails to depict God as ethically upright in his relation to *horrors*.

## Type C Theodicy

I now return to one of the two *structurally promising* readings of "The Magnitude, Duration, and Distribution of Evil." This is the reading that conjoins (1), (2), (3), and either version of (4). On this theodicy, God turns out to be in a position structurally similar to the parents in Case C. Both are deciding whether or not to do something with the knowledge that if they do, it will increase the likelihood that those affected by their action will suffer *horrors*, and if *horrors* do occur, they will be helpless to avert them. This approach leans on the fact that the parents in Case C are rightly said to *risk horrors* rather than to permit or cause them. They do not know they will occur. They hope against their occurrence and only risk them if the probable results for their child—given the probability of *horrors* and the probability of balancing them off—are at the very least positive.

Type C Theodicy is somewhat different. Because God is constrained to allow the *horrendous* natural consequences of sin due only to his character and not to any lack of knowledge or strength, he might still be thought to at least permit these consequences in addition to risking them. But Type C Theodicy stipulates that permitting the consequences of divine *horror* risk is consistent with, in fact demanded by, God's ethical perfection. I will return to question this stipulation in Chapter 5. Presently, I evaluate Type C Theodicy as an example of *risking* for pure benefit because it shares with Case C the assumption that if the agents in question are morally to blame for the bad consequences of their agency, it is only due to the immorality of their initial risk.

Nonetheless, one might assume a disanalogy between Case C and Type C Theodicy at the time of supposed risk. Even if the parents are rightly said to risk rather than to cause or permit the hazing by sending their child to boarding school, surely this is not the case with God. In his omniscience, God would not have to rely on risks and probabilities but would know infallibly—prior to bringing persons into the actual world—whether they would sin, and therefore whether the *horrendous* consequences of a fall would occur.

On libertarian and non-Molinist commitments, this assumption is false. God determines everything that does not depend on created free choices or created random events. For the rest, God has to wait to see what occurs. And this is true regardless of whether you accept a tensed or tenseless theory of time. Either way, God's decision to create human persons is logically prior in the order of explanation to his knowledge of creaturely free-willed events. God knows all that might happen and exactly how probable it is that things turn out in any possible way, but creatures determine to some extent what God conserves.[37] Like the parents in Case C, even God must risk *horrors* and hope.

Robert Adams and Brian Leftow reach the same conclusion. To cite them in succession:

Without middle knowledge God must take real risks if he makes free creatures (thousands, millions, or trillions of risks, if every free creature makes thousands

---

[37] Some of these thoughts were aided by Brian Leftow's lectures on the nature of God given at the University of Oxford in Hilary Term of 2005.

of morally significant free choices). No matter how shrewdly God acted in running so many risks, His winning on *every* risk would not be antecedently probable.[38]

If Molinism is false, God does not, in deciding what to create, know what free agents would do in various possible circumstances. There was nothing of this sort to know.[39]

On the assumptions of a theodicy structurally analogous to Case C, God could not know with certainty that the world would turn *horrendous*. God's only options are either to seek to enhance the lives of human persons by risking *horrors*, or to give such pure benefit a miss. Now, faced with a tough decision, his knowledge of the likelihood of the world turning *horrendous* and of his ability to balance-off potential *horrors* weighs into his decision.

## Divine Benefit of the Doubt

In Chapter 2, I outlined nine positions in which the parents in Case C could find themselves, and I claimed they could be justified in risking *horrendous harm* for pure benefits in some positions in which the expected all-things-considered result is positive for those who might be harmed. There is at least one reason why divine *horror* risk may be more morally suspect than human *horror* risk, however. In typical cases of human *horror* risk, *horror* risk is unavoidable. Human persons choose not between risking and not risking *horrors* but between risking them to greater and lesser degrees. Though controversial, it is arguable that increasing the likelihood of *horrors* from zero to some positive probability provides stronger reason against acting, *ceteris paribus*, than increasing the likelihood of *horrors* from one positive probability to another.

That said, I am still inclined to think that the disanalogies between divine and human *horror* risk favor God overall. Among the disanalogies favoring God are these:

- In human cases of *horror* risk, parents have very limited power to make good on *horrors*. On the contrary, God can undoubtedly at least balance-off any *horrors* that occur within the context of each *horror* sufferer's life (including afterlife). He can know this with certainty in every case, not just with some

---

[38] Robert Merrihew Adams, "Middle Knowledge and the Problem of Evil," 125.
[39] Brian Leftow, "No best world: creaturely freedom," *Religious Studies* 41 (2005), 276. We have already seen that van Inwagen reaches the same conclusion. Cf. van Inwagen, *The Problem of Evil*, 71–2.

degree of confidence. This is one reason to think the moral constraints on human risk-taking are more stringent than on God's.

• You might think that God (in his creative omnipotence) is able to organically *defeat* (in Roderick Chisholm's sense[40]) *horrors* and that a human parent never (or almost never) could. Receiving divine gratitude for one's *horrendous* suffering and being in solidarity with God in *horrendous* suffering may suggest two possibilities for *horror defeat* that are only open to God.[41]

• The length of *horror* participation in proportion to eternity is miniscule when compared to several years in proportion to an average earthly lifespan. This is reason to think the same potential *horrors* are a more reasonable risk from God's perspective than from that of a human risker.

• If being justified in inferring retrospective consent or acceptance plays some justificatory role in risking *horrors* for pure benefit, this too favors God. God can be substantially more confident that someone ultimately may not wish *horror* risk out of their lives because God knows just how wonderful the experience of divine compensation and eternal heavenly existence can be.

• In the divine but not the human case, even those who wind up being *horrendously* harmed as a result of *horror* risk can be better-off all things considered for that risk. The opportunities provided by even the greatest of schools are not plausibly so great as to outweigh *horrors*. It may be more plausible, however, that the value increase from "perfect natural happiness" to "eternal loving union with God" is more positive than the value of earthly *horrendous harm* is negative.

Given all of the disanalogies favoring divine risk taking, I suggest that divine *horror* risk is at least as *structurally promising* as human *horror* risk.

As discussed in Chapter 2, moral permission is a function of the probability that a given individual will suffer *horrors* and the probability of making good on them in the life of that individual if *horrors* do occur. Due to God's unrestricted ability to compensate for *horrors*, there are only three pre-creation positions he could have been in:

(3)   Low risk of *horrors* with high probability of at least balancing-off.
(6)   Moderate risk of *horrors* with high probability of at least balancing-off.
(9)   High risk of *horrors* with high probability of at least balancing-off.

I judge that God would have morally sufficient reason for creating human persons in position (3). Positions (6) and (9) are more difficult. I am inclined to think

---

[40]  See Chapter 1, n. 11.
[41]  For a discussion of these and other potential divine options for *defeat*, see Adams, *Horrendous Evils and the Goodness of God*, 155–80.

that even if human *horror* risk in position (6) is suspect, infinite divine resources for balancing-off are enough to justify divine creation in this position.

I am not sure what to say about position (9). If the risk of *horrors* becomes high enough, the act of creating approaches *causing horrors* for pure benefit, which I have condemned. God does have an advantage over human riskers, however, because any probability of *horrors* less than 1 will be lower than the probability of God being able to balance-off potential *horrors*. My opinion is that God might be justified in risking *horrors* by creating in position (9) if this were his only attractive option. Roughly, God might be justified in creating in position (9) only if he were in something like an *extreme situation*.[42]

Of the theodicies considered so far, none make a plausible case for God being in anything like an *extreme situation* with respect to *horrors*. I have already criticized Hick's attempt to approach this conclusion by reducing what is so bad about *horrors* to their relation to other actual evils, and arguing from this that there must be *horrendous evils* in any world in which there is any evil at all. Swinburne and Plantinga are both explicit that God had highly valuable non-*horrendous* options at his disposal when choosing whether and what to create. This *extreme situation* move is also unavailable to van Inwagen because according to him God had a world inhabited by humans who enjoy "perfect natural happiness" among the divine options.

## Which Position Is God in Prior to Creation?

What's left is to determine which of these three positions God is in prior to creation. This can be determined by multiplying the probability that humanity would fall by the probability of a post-fall individual of the actual world suffering *horrendous evil*. There is some disagreement about the latter of these probabilities. Marilyn Adams thinks *horrors* are inevitable for human persons because she judges all human death to be *horrendous*.[43] I sympathize with this claim, but I think that for many people who pass on in relative peace and without significant pain, death need not be *horrendous*, even if it is very bad. That said, it is clear that death (or at least the dying process) is often *horrendous*, and also that *horrors* not resulting in death are not uncommon. I'm inclined to think that on average human persons have been at moderate risk of suffering *horrors*.

---

[42] In Chapter 2, I made an attempt at specifying some sufficient conditions of such situations. Those conditions were met if causing or permitting *horror* were (a) necessary for (b) bestowing a pure benefit that (c) would exceedingly outweigh the *horrendous harm*, (d) the possession of which would likely far surpass any alternative all-things-considered state (for the harmed) attained by equal or less harm, and (e) no other alternative courses of action would have been likely to yield lives better than ones minimally worth living for the harmed.

[43] Marilyn McCord Adams, *Christ and Horrors: The Coherence of Christology* (Cambridge: Cambridge University Press, 2006), 207–11.

As for the former probability, assuming the first human persons were superior beings along the lines that van Inwagen suggests, with how strong a propensity to sin would God create them? Here intuitions tend to clash, and I think we should be wary of putting too much stock in them. Van Inwagen might opt for a low probability that humanity would fall, claiming that although God could not "*ensure*" that human beings remained united with him in love, "we may be sure that he did everything omnipotence could do to raise the probability of their doing [so]."[44]

Swinburne thinks differently. He claims that God might be justified in creating us with a greater propensity to sin as a condition of the possibility of more meaningful free will.[45] He writes,

> The chance that the agent will do what he believes to be the best will be greater the less is the temptation to do otherwise, but the less the temptation, the less is the goodness of the act done in resisting it. I have no easy algorithm for working out which kind of free will is best to have.[46]

While Swinburne may not offer any calculation of just how high a propensity to sin God would create us with, he does offer one reason God might have for creating us with a significantly greater propensity than need be: "The more serious the free will and the stronger the contrary temptation, the better it is when the good action is done."[47]

Marilyn Adams's view is that if God created human persons (at least, if he did so in a world like this), he would have to create them with a high propensity for actualizing *horrors*. She claims that

> not even God could place human beings in a world like this without their being radically vulnerable to horrors. It seems to me that the metaphysically necessary constitution of created natures is something God has to work with and around in deciding whether and which sorts of things to produce in what circumstances.[48]

On this view, *horrors* are a necessary constraint on human existence (at least in this type of world). It is a modal truth that joining material creation to animal

---

[44] Van Inwagen, *The Problem of Evil*, 145.
[45] Hick's educational model is similar in this respect.
[46] Swinburne, *Providence and the Problem of Evil*, 88. Cf. Swinburne, *Responsibility and Atonement* (Oxford: Oxford University Press, 1998), 40.
[47] Swinburne, *Providence and the Problem of Evil*, 87. Swinburne reaffirms the same point on p. 137: "The stronger the temptation to do bad, and the more significant are the good or bad actions, the greater the possibilities for good that God gives us and the less the chance that those possibilities will be realized."
[48] Adams, *Horrendous Evils and the Goodness of God*, 171.

personality requires a radical vulnerability to *horrors*.[49] Some *horrors* are practically inevitable, even if not this or that *horror* in particular. If God chooses to love beings like us, he has no choice but to set us up for a fall.

I believe we should remain very humble vis-à-vis our intuitions on this matter. We have seen that—on libertarian, non-Molinist assumptions—God has already taken trillions of risks, for he could only be in complete control of human action by abrogating human freedom, and the results of each of these trillions of risks affects how probable *horrors* are today. Moreover, if quantum theory is correct that there is considerable randomness on the quantum level (and assuming God has a good reason for causing or permitting the truth of quantum theory), God may be in even less control.[50] The cash value of all this is that—on the assumptions of Type C Theodicy—the fact that we live in a world where we are apt to produce and suffer *horrors* is not good reason to conclude that the initial human persons had a particular proneness to them, any more than concluding that an excellent billiards player with one million balls to sink winds up with the cue near to where his initial plan would have it when he reaches the last ball. Things could turn out a lot different than even an omnipotent and omniscient being predicts. To quote Leftow once more,

> Given created free will but without Molinist resources, the best God can do is actualize an initial world-segment whose possible continuations give Him the best overall chance of realizing the best overall outcome. For all we know, the continuations of the segment God chose include every world above a given point on the scale of value—which would not be a case of attempting to do less good than He might. That an initial segment has all these good continuations is compatible with some of its possible continuations leading to a very bad outcome: all that follows about God's choice is that He chose this initial segment despite this possibility, because it was more likely that a much better outcome ensue…[F]or all we know about the actual world, it *is* a continuation of the initial world-segment that gave God His best chance at a best possible result (if there are such).[51]

I conclude that on the assumption that God created the first generation of human persons with preternatural powers, no present-day empirical evidence is helpful in determining whether they were at low, moderate, or high risk of losing their *horror*-averting powers. Our judgment in this regard should be a priori, and there is room for reasonable disagreement. That being so, I judge God's initial *horror*

---

[49]  Adams, *Horrendous Evils and the Goodness of God*, 132: "I have traced the root of human vulnerability to horrors in the incongruity of welding spirit and matter, in the misfitting of personality and animality together in the same nature."

[50]  This depends on the extent to which randomness on the micro-level results in randomness on the macro-level.

[51]  Leftow, "No best world: creaturely freedom," 281–2.

risk for individuals of the actual world to be no worse than position (6). Position (6) would be the result of multiplying a presently moderate risk of individual *horror* endurance with a high probability that humanity would fall. If the probability of the fall was low or moderate, then God's risk could even have been taken in position (3).

Theodicy analogous to Case C seems *structurally promising*. With respect to God's initial decision to create human persons, I have suggested that only position (9) is morally problematic, and that our empirical data makes it likely that—on Type C assumptions about the fall of humanity—God created in a position no worse than position (6). With respect to what followed on from divine creation, Type C Theodicy defends it as the necessary result of God being a non-deceiver. If Type C Theodicy is not only *structurally promising* but plausible, I judge that it would be successful. (In Chapter 5 I'll return to question the plausibility of Type C Theodicy, including its use of the claim that God is a non-deceiver.)

## Type D Theodicy

In the previous approach, God (being essentially a non-deceiver) is morally bound to permit the *horrendous* consequences of his initial creative risk. A second reason he might be justified in permitting *horrendous* consequences—this one analogous to Case D—is that permitting them is necessary in order to avert still greater harm.

## Eleonore Stump: Divine Rescue in "The Problem of Evil"

Eleonore Stump begins to develop such an approach in "The Problem of Evil,"[52] with "hope of a successful solution to the problem of evil along the lines developed [there]."[53] Stump suggests that God permits the *horrendous* consequences of human sin because those consequences provide an environment that is the "most conducive" and "maybe the only effective means"[54] to rescuing fallen human persons from "perpetual living death."[55]

Her starting point is reflection on three Christian beliefs that seem to her particularly relevant to the problem of evil: "Adam fell,[56] natural evil entered the

---

[52] Eleonore Stump, "The Problem of Evil," *Faith and Philosophy* 2 (1985): 392–423.
[53] Stump, "The Problem of Evil," 418.   [54] Stump, "The Problem of Evil," 409.
[55] Stump, "The Problem of Evil," 415.
[56] Recognizing that the fall of Adam has been interpreted in many ways, Stump specifies what she is committing herself to in affirming the fall of Adam: "[A]t some time in the past as a result of their own choices human beings altered their nature for the worse, the alteration involved what we perceive and describe as a change in the nature of human free will, and the changed nature of the will was inheritable" ("The Problem of Evil," 402–3).

world as a result of Adam's fall, and after death, depending on their state at the time of their death, either a. human beings go to heaven or b. they go to hell."[57]

To these three beliefs she adds that "all human beings since Adam's fall have been defective in their free wills, so that they have a powerful inclination to will what they ought not to will, to will their own power or pleasure in preference to greater goods. It is not possible for human beings in that condition to go to heaven, which consists in union with God."[58] While this doesn't entail the Irenaean claim that God could not have created human persons perfect *ab initio*, it does imply that it is impossible for him to miraculously transport fallen human persons to a heavenly existence. In her words,

> It seems clear to me that [God] cannot fix the defect by using his omnipotence to remove it miraculously. The defect is a defect in *free* will, and it consists in a person's generally failing to will what he ought to will. To remove this defect miraculously would be to force a person's free will to be other than it is.[59]

However, not only is God helpless to fix the defect miraculously, but self-repair is not possible for human beings with postlapsarian free will because the will itself is the problem and it would have to be the will that initiates the repair.

Stump suggests a solution well-known to Christian tradition:

> The fixing of a defective free will by a person's freely willing that God fix his will is, I think, the foundation of a Christian solution to the problem of evil.

And this naturally leads to the question,

> What sort of world is most conducive to bringing about both the initial human willing of help and also the subsequent process of sanctification?[60]

The answer, Stump proposes, is an environment conducive to a humble recognition of and dissatisfaction with our own evil and "a desire for a better state."[61] She suggests that broadly the quantity and quality of evil in this world may be the best—and maybe even the only[62]—hope for influencing human beings to seek God freely and to develop repentant hearts that lead to reconciliation with God. Both moral and natural evil contribute to this means. Moral evil teaches us of the depravity of human nature. The worst moral evils in the course of human history highlight this nature, and each individual's experience of his own evil willing

---

[57] Stump, "The Problem of Evil," 398.          [58] Stump, "The Problem of Evil," 406.
[59] Stump, "The Problem of Evil," 406.
[60] Stump, "The Problem of Evil," 408–9.          [61] Stump, "The Problem of Evil," 409.
[62] Cf. Stump, "The Problem of Evil," 416.

serves to remind him that he too is in this respect human. Natural evil "takes away a person's satisfaction with himself. It tends to humble him, show him his frailty, make him reflect on the transience of temporal goods, and turn his affections towards other-worldly things."[63]

Stump judges infant suffering to be the most difficult type of evil to account for on her view, but she hypothesizes that "for some persons the molding of the personality produced by suffering in infancy may be the best means of insuring a character capable of coming to God."[64] She claims that because even the earliest stages of human life are "tremendously important in molding the personality and character,"[65] even the suffering of those who die in infancy may be necessary to effect the divinely desired change from their painful existence in this world to "a permanently blissful existence."[66]

Stump grants that her contention that evils serve to make human persons recognize their own sin, become dissatisfied with this world, and ultimately turn to seek God's help is a controversial claim. Marilyn Adams would press doubts on this point, especially where entrenched *horrors* and their agency-wrecking powers are concerned. Nonetheless, Stump insists that "there is *some* historical evidence for [her claim] in the fact that Christianity has tended to flourish among the oppressed and decline among the comfortable."[67]

To the related objection that God's plan for permitting evil is an utter failure because "the vast majority of people in the world are not Christians or theists of any kind; and even among those who are Christian many die in serious unrepented evil,"[68] Stump responds that "it is not incompatible with Christian doctrine to speculate that in the process of their dying God acquaints them with what they need to know and offers them a last chance to choose."[69] Just as in any deathbed repentance, "the sufferings of the dying person will have had a significant effect on that person's character and consequently on the choices he makes on his deathbed."[70] Hence, Stump thinks it is not at all clear that the majority of people end in hell, and therefore not at all clear that God's plan for evil is a failure.

In a final caveat, Stump insists that for God to be morally in the clear, every instance of suffering must contribute to the salvation of the one who suffers it. She writes,

---

[63] Stump, "The Problem of Evil," 409.
[64] Stump, "The Problem of Evil," 411.   [65] Stump, "The Problem of Evil," 411.
[66] Stump, "The Problem of Evil," 411.   [67] Stump, "The Problem of Evil," 410.
[68] Stump, "The Problem of Evil," 412. This is quite a controversial claim. Perhaps the vast majority of people teaching or pursuing graduate degrees at elite Western universities are not Christians or theists of any kind, but I suspect this is decidedly not the case for the world's population taken as a whole.
[69] Stump, "The Problem of Evil," 412.
[70] Stump, "The Problem of Evil," 412.

It seems to me none the less that a perfectly good entity who was also omniscient and omnipotent must govern the evil resulting from the misuse of that significant freedom in such a way that the sufferings of any particular person are outweighed by the good which the suffering produces *for that person*...[T]he suffering of any person will be justified if it brings that person nearer to the ultimate good in a way he could not have been without the suffering.[71]

## The Development of Stump's Response in *Wandering in Darkness*

In her subsequent *Wandering in Darkness: Narrative and the Problem of Suffering*,[72] Stump further develops her response to the problem of evil, now more explicitly presenting Thomas Aquinas's theodicy and deploying it as a *defense*—that is, a description of a possible world in which suffering of the amount and sorts that we find in the actual world coexists with an omnipotent, omniscient, perfectly good God.[73] Stump takes herself to be proposing a *defense* rather than a theodicy because in this context she argues for the possibility rather than the truth of a number of Thomistic claims that her theory relies on. However, "readers who do share Aquinas's theological views," Stump affirms, "can take what follows [in *Wandering in Darkness*] as a theodicy, as Aquinas himself supposed it to be."[74]

In *Wandering in Darkness*, Stump continues her focus on the good of being united to God in loving relationship, claiming that such union is both the best thing for a human person and the only way to avert the worst thing for a human person. She is careful to distinguish her approach from a soul-making approach. For Stump, the justification for suffering is not to be found in virtues or other internal properties of individual persons,[75] "but rather in relationship, and especially in...relationship to God."[76] Stump again emphasizes that loving union with God is not something God can produce unilaterally.[77] It requires from human persons a free act of will "in which a person hates his own moral wrong and longs for the goodness that is God's."[78] In the possible world of Stump's *defense*, suffering, when it occurs, is the "best available means"[79] by which God can shepherd us

---

[71] Stump, "The Problem of Evil," 411.

[72] Eleonore Stump, *Wandering in Darkness: Narrative and the Problem of Suffering* (Oxford: Oxford University Press, 2010).

[73] Stump, *Wandering in Darkness*, 81.

[74] Stump, *Wandering in Darkness*, 155. Stump also extends Aquinas's theodicy to take into account "suffering stemming from the loss of the desires of the heart" (420).

[75] Cf. Stump, *Wandering in Darkness*, 256, 408.    [76] Stump, *Wandering in Darkness*, 256.

[77] Stump, *Wandering in Darkness*, 138.    [78] Stump, *Wandering in Darkness*, 163.

[79] Stump, *Wandering in Darkness*, 455. Stump also uses the phrase "best possible means" (e.g., 633, n.3).

toward freely giving up our resistance to him,[80] thereby enabling God to be close to us in loving union.[81]

The argument in *Wandering in Darkness* differentiates from that in "The Problem of Evil" by offering two distinct justifications for divine allowance of suffering depending on whether or not the sufferer is already united to God. Stump's interpretation of Aquinas's theodicy, in summary, is that God's allowing a human person to suffer is morally justified either because it averts the worst thing for that person or because it leads to the best thing for that person.[82] For those not yet freely united to God, suffering provides the chance to avert the still greater and worst evil of hell (or annihilation, or cycles of purgation)[83]—understood as self-willed isolation from God. This claim continues the harm-prevention line of reasoning from "The Problem of Evil." However, in *Wandering in Darkness* Stump adds a new line of reasoning by recommending a different justification for the suffering of those already freely united to God and for whom heaven awaits. For these people, suffering provides not the aversion of the hellish state of being alienated from God (for they are already united to God) but rather the chance[84] of deepened union with God: "[T]he experience of suffering enables them to open in a deeper way to the love of God."[85]

Stump corrects a frequent omission in the literature by conceding that pure benefits alone generally will not justify serious suffering the way harm prevention will.[86] However, this raises a problem for Aquinas's theodicy and Stump's *defense* because, according to them, those already in relationship with God suffer not to prevent harm but for the pure benefit of deepened union with God. The problem is further intensified because, as Stump explains, Aquinas thinks those who are already closest to God will not only continue to suffer but will suffer more severely:[87] "[S]trenuous medical regiments are saved for the strongest patients, in the hopes of bringing them to the most robust health and functioning."[88]

While Stump recognizes that pure benefits alone won't justify the allowance of the worst instances of suffering, she believes pure benefits plus *consent* will.[89] She makes a distinction between suffering that is involuntary *simpliciter* and suffering that is involuntary *secundum quid*,[90] and suggests that "[i]t is possible for someone to endure a particular suffering involuntarily and yet to have given a kind of assent to the general endurance of suffering of that type."[91] She gives the example

---

[80] Stump, *Wandering in Darkness*, 166.       [81] Stump, *Wandering in Darkness*, 456.

[82] Cf. Stump, *Wandering in Darkness*, 387, 390, 396–7, 452.

[83] Stump, *Wandering in Darkness*, 377.

[84] Stump speaks in terms of chances rather than certain outcomes (e.g., *Wandering in Darkness*, 404), allowing that our wills are free in such a way that our choices are not causally determined by God.

[85] Stump, *Wandering in Darkness*, 399.

[86] See Stump, *Wandering in Darkness*, 392–4.       [87] Stump, *Wandering in Darkness*, 401.

[88] Stump, *Wandering in Darkness*, 400.       [89] See Stump, *Wandering in Darkness*, 392–3.

[90] Stump, *Wandering in Darkness*, 381.       [91] Stump, *Wandering in Darkness*, 382.

of a cross-country coach forcing his team to run another sprint up a hill against their vocal complaints.[92] Again taking a cue from Aquinas, Stump takes commitment to Christianity to include consent of this sort to endure suffering.[93]

In addition to this new way of accounting for the suffering of people already united to God, there is a second major way in which *Wandering in Darkness* alters the approach of "The Problem of Evil." In "The Problem of Evil," Stump sought to provide a "successful solution to the problem of evil" for broadly the quantity and quality of evil in the actual world, including grave moral and natural evil and including infant suffering, which she took to be the most difficult type of evil to account for. In *Wandering in Darkness*, however, Stump makes her project less difficult by aiming to develop a *defense* that covers only the suffering of "mentally fully functional adult human beings."[94] This rules out a number of the hardest cases: the suffering of infants, animal suffering,[95] the suffering of adults with various forms of mental dysfunction, and perhaps—a point I will return to later—suffering so severe that it seriously damages the mental functioning of an otherwise mentally fully functional adult human being. Stump defends this bracketing by saying, "It is not possible to do everything in one book."[96]

A third major addition in *Wandering in Darkness* is Stump's focus on narrative, which she believes has a substantial role to play in theodicy and *defense*. Stump begins her discussion of narrative by distinguishing between what she terms Dominican knowledge (knowledge which is or can be reduced to knowledge *that*) and Franciscan knowledge (knowledge which is difficult or impossible to formulate in terms of knowledge *that*).[97] She argues that a broad array of Franciscan knowledge exists[98] and that the knowledge that contributes to her *defense* is partly Dominican knowledge and partly Franciscan knowledge.

This suggests a skepticism that could be mistaken for skeptical theism.[99] Stump thinks skeptical theism is false because she thinks we *can* know, even propositionally, the general reasons that justify God in allowing suffering. But what Stump *is* skeptical about is our ability to identify instances of those general reasons in particular cases. Often a particular sufferer's psychology is not sufficiently known to us, and even when it is, it may be difficult or impossible to express this knowledge propositionally.

A problem arises, then, about how Franciscan knowledge—if it cannot be expressed propositionally—can be included in a *defense*. An analogy helps both to underscore and to resolve this problem. Suppose I have been a frequent visitor to China and have come to value Chinese culture to such an extent that I am now planning on moving there. When I discuss my plans with good friends of mine

---

[92] Stump, *Wandering in Darkness*, 393.   [93] Stump, *Wandering in Darkness*, 383.
[94] See Stump, *Wandering in Darkness*, 4–5, 378, 476.
[95] Cf. Stump, *Wandering in Darkness*, 379.   [96] Stump, *Wandering in Darkness*, 379.
[97] See Stump, *Wandering in Darkness*, 51, 53.   [98] Cf. Stump, *Wandering in Darkness*, 81.
[99] Cf. Stump, *Wandering in Darkness*, 373, 408.

who have never been to China, I may have difficulty expressing to them my full reasons for moving. As Stump puts it, "What an American learns after numerous extended trips to China cannot be reduced to particular claims about the country, the culture, and the people; the experienced traveler will not be able to explain in numbered propositions what his previous trips have taught him."[100]

This is where narrative is intended to provide assistance. If my friends remain confused about why I am so eager to spend time in China despite my best efforts to explain it to them, I might give them a really good novel set in China. Reading the novel could act as something akin to experiencing what it is like to spend time in China, and my friends might then better know why I want to live there. Stump makes a similar move by presenting her readers with four biblical stories that she believes impart Franciscan knowledge about human psychology that helps us to see how the general reasons justifying God's allowance of suffering apply to particular cases of suffering. The four stories Stump presents are the biblical narratives of Job, Samson (drawing insights from John Milton's life and his biblical interpretation), Abraham (including his binding of Isaac and Søren Kierkegaard's interpretation of it), and Mary of Bethany (including Jesus's raising of Lazarus).

I find Stump's claim that narrative has a role to play in theodicy and *defense* intriguing, and I am impressed by the extent of non-propositional knowledge that Stump makes plausible. That said, I do not think her retelling of biblical narratives accomplishes her goal of imparting substantial Franciscan knowledge. Stump claims that the telling of stories often has an advantage over real life cases in the amount of detail they can give,[101] and she thinks presenting stories "in all their messy richness"[102] is the best way to re-present to the reader the experiences through which the relevant Franciscan knowledge can be acquired.[103]

However, there is not a lot of detail in several of the biblical stories Stump chooses, and Stump frequently interrupts her storytelling with discussions of disputes over interpretation contained in sections with headings such as "two worries, a response, and a workaround."[104] The result was to make my overall experience of Stump's presentation of the biblical stories more Dominican than Franciscan, with the narrative section of *Wandering in Darkness* at times reading more like a travel book about China than like a novel set in China.

If the biblical stories do have something like the Franciscan effect Stump attributes to them, I suspect this has more to do with their sparseness than with their abundance of detail. A more minimalist approach to detail can have the effect of inviting the reader to imagine herself into the story and thereby experience something of the emotions and decisions contained therein. Greater detail sometimes hinders this process because with increasing detail the reader can be

---

[100] Stump, *Wandering in Darkness*, 373.
[101] See Stump, *Wandering in Darkness*, 372–3, 409.     [102] Stump, *Wandering in Darkness*, 373.
[103] Stump, *Wandering in Darkness*, 81.     [104] Stump, *Wandering in Darkness*, 336.

more likely to experience the characters as *other* than as *possibly herself*. My suggestion for getting the most out of Stump's narrative section is to read it through, with the analysis providing context, but then to return to the biblical narratives on their own, looking to their invitation to imagine oneself into the stories, and not to their level of detail, for Franciscan knowledge.

I also have one suggestion for extending Stump's thoughts on the contribution of non-propositional knowledge to *defense* and theodicy. What my friends might come to know through reading a novel set in China is not only about my psychology, but also about the nature and value of the goods that provide me with reasons for moving country. Likewise, might what can be known Franciscanly include truths about the general goods that provide God with reasons for allowing suffering? If so, then even if we did not (or even could not) have sufficient Dominican knowledge of the general reasons justifying God in allowing suffering, we might nevertheless know justifying reasons when our Dominican and Franciscan knowledge is combined. This result would have the significant consequence that successful *defense* and theodicy do not require expressing morally sufficient reasons in propositional form.

I note this to say that, in her focus on narrative, Stump has pointed in a direction worth exploring further for the purposes of theodicy. But that exploration is beyond the scope of my current project. For now, therefore, I will proceed in my assessment of whether the propositional content of Stump's arguments yields a *structurally promising* response to the problem of evil.

## Evaluation

Though I disagree with a number of her claims, I find in Stump's work the components of a *structurally promising* theodicy.

Firstly the disagreements. In both "The Problem of Evil" and *Wandering in Darkness*, Stump suggests that the primary benefit of any (non-voluntary and undeserved) divinely allowed suffering has to accrue to the sufferer *himself*; otherwise the suffering is unjustified.[105] I find this constraint implausible. Where minor suffering is concerned, it certainly seems at times permissible to harm one person for the good of another, even without consent and even when the good in question is a pure benefit. I would gladly punch my brother in the arm if it meant my mom would receive five million dollars. Or to take a more realistic example, many parents act permissibly in allowing their babies to "cry it out" during sleep training for the sake of a better quality of life for the rest of the family. Admittedly, *horrors* change things. I have argued that it is either universally or nearly universally impermissible to cause or permit *horrendous evil* for the pure benefit even of

---

[105] See Stump, *Wandering in Darkness*, 191, 378, 561–2, 567, 608–9.

the sufferer of that evil. All the more is it impermissible to cause or permit a *horror* to be suffered by one person in order to bestow a pure benefit on another.

Even so, this is not sufficient to show that *horrors* can never be permitted for the good of another because sometimes the good attained is one that is not purely beneficial but rather harm-averting. The parents in Case D permit one child's suffering in order to avert greater suffering for another child. They seem clearly justified in this. It is true that God would not allow me to suffer *horrors* for the pure benefit of another, but Stump's blanket condition that God would never allow me to suffer for the sake of another fails to respect the asymmetries not only between *horrors* and non-*horrendous evils* but also between goods that are purely beneficial and those that avert greater harms.[106] Thankfully, for those who, like me, consider this an overly stringent condition, it can be left to one side when assessing Stump's approach.

My next two disagreements are with claims not made in "The Problem of Evil" but that emerge in *Wandering in Darkness*. The first is Stump's qualification that the *defense* presented in *Wandering in Darkness* is intended to cover only the suffering of "mentally fully functional adult human beings."[107] I worry that, with this qualification, even if Stump's project is completely successful, it does little to advance the projects of *defense* or theodicy, since no reason is given for thinking that the sort of world in which God coexists with suffering that befalls only mentally high-functioning adult human beings could be the sort of world in which God coexists with the kinds of suffering that are of greatest concern to contributors to the problem of evil literature.[108] I am therefore interested in assessing whether Stump's approach is *structurally promising* when this qualification is removed and even the most severe forms of suffering are taken into account.

The second claim that emerges in *Wandering in Darkness* and, to my mind, weakens the structure of Stump's approach is that the suffering of those already united to God is justified not because it is preventative of greater harm but because it procures pure benefits. For those who are already reconciled to God, God allows suffering not to avert hell but because it is "therapeutic for deepened union among persons."[109] This raises a structural concern because God is understood as permitting at least some *horrors* for pure benefit, making the structure of Stump's approach in *Wandering in Darkness* Type B rather than Type D. Stump recognizes that in order for this approach to be plausible, she needs for consent to play a significant role in justifying all kinds of suffering to which mentally fully

---

[106] Stump has highlighted the moral significance of the distinction between harm-averting and non-harm-averting benefits in Stump, "Saadia Gaon on the Problem of Evil," *Faith and Philosophy* 14 (1997), 533.

[107] See Stump, *Wandering in Darkness*, 4–5, 378, 476.

[108] Stump makes a similar point in "The Problem of Evil" when she writes, "Any attempt to solve the problem of evil must try to provide some understanding of the suffering of children" (410).

[109] Stump, *Wandering in Darkness*, 22.

functional adult human beings can be subject. But when we focus our attention on genuinely *horrendous* suffering rather than on running up hills for the purpose of athletic training, it seems clear that many committed Christians have not consented to that type of suffering.

Indeed, it is doubtful that many committed Christians *would* have consented had they been asked for prospective consent. Human persons tend to weight temporally near effects over temporally distant effects and the aversion of harm over the procuring of greater goods.[110] If *horrendous* suffering is the price to pay for first row heavenly seats, I suspect many would conclude that the view from the balcony is awesome enough. Moreover, if heaven is conceived of as a pretty egalitarian place, then likely this will further diminish one's motivation for consenting to suffering.[111]

Finally, it is plausible that in many cases of *horrendous* suffering the sufferers *could not* have given competent consent. Because competency in consenting to an outcome generally relies on having a reasonably accurate understanding of that outcome, and the badness of *horrendous* suffering often exceeds human capabilities of understanding, there is reason to think that many *horror* sufferers could not have given competent consent to their suffering. If the consent given is not competent consent, then this negates its moral import.

So with respect to at least some of the suffering of Christians, I believe that the sufferers have not consented, would not have consented, and even could not have (competently) consented. I think there is too little attention to this objection in *Wandering in Darkness*, and in general too little attention to the very worst forms of actual suffering. Stump admits there are far worse sufferings than what she treats explicitly.[112] While I affirm and deeply respect her commitment not to dishonor those who have suffered most severely by parading the details of their suffering as philosophical examples,[113] the ethics of the very worst forms of suffering is markedly different from the ethics of other forms of suffering. If theodicy or *defense* is to be successful, it must find some way—whether through the use of examples from literature or through the general description of suffering-types—of considering the moral implications of cases of the worst forms of actual human suffering.

To the specific objection I have raised to Stump's use of consent, Stump could respond that suffering bad enough to undermine the justificatory contribution of consent is also suffering bad enough to impair the mental functioning of adult human persons, and thereby falls outside the scope of her project.[114] But, firstly, I find even the more modest claim that committed Christians have consented to

---

[110] Compare Stump's related reasoning in *Wandering in Darkness*, 606–7, n. 3; 618, n. 71.
[111] I thank Tim Mawson for this point.
[112] Stump, *Wandering in Darkness*, 375.    [113] Stump, *Wandering in Darkness*, 16.
[114] Cf. Stump, *Wandering in Darkness*, 140.

suffer anything that does not impair their mental functioning very implausible. Parental suffering resulting from the murder of one's child, for instance, can be more than severe enough to call any morally significant form of consent into question, despite not always resulting in less than full mental functioning on the part of the parent. Secondly, excluding this class of sufferings would further attenuate the significance of Stump's *defense*.

Another way Stump could respond is by dropping her focus on consent altogether and instead claiming—in consonance with her earlier reflections in "The Problem of Evil"—that all suffering is harm-preventing. Stump assumes that once someone is united to God in loving relationship, suffering can no longer be hell preventing. But that is not clearly the case. She could say instead that, even for those currently united to God, suffering best enables them to avoid falling out of union with God and thus to avoid hell. In fact, Stump already suggests in her discussion of Abraham that lapses in faith are possible even after one has previously shown "whole-hearted trust in God's promises,"[115] and in another place she suggests that "a particular case of suffering that might have contributed to a sufferer's sanctification can, as it were, refold into a suffering contributing to the sufferer's justification if the sufferer reacts to the suffering by turning away from God and goodness."[116] In the next chapter, I will raise some doubts about Stump's use of harm prevention, but, given that she is already committed to it for the suffering of some, I see no insurmountable obstacle to extending its use to the justification of the suffering of those already in union with God, thereby negating the need for consent to play a justificatory role.

This move would allow for a structural return to the Type D approach outlined in "The Problem of Evil," and I believe this approach is *prima facie structurally promising*. It assumes that God has created from a permissible position of risk; he then permits *horrors* because doing so gives him the best chance of averting the greatest amount of *horrendous* suffering all told. For those apart from God, *horrors* motivate them to turn to God. For those reconciled to God, *horrors* motivate them to remain with God. Turning to God and remaining with God both avert the worst form of suffering. God is in a position similar to van Inwagen's doctor, but his patients are utterly helpless to avert greater harm on their own. In such a case, God seems morally justified and to be acting in ways consistent with ideal love.

In a passage that highlights the analogy between this approach and Case D, Stump likens God to the parents of a child with a terminal brain disease. The parents are informed by reliable doctors that there are treatments which may cure their child completely, but they are painful and their success is not guaranteed. Stump is surely right in claiming that the parents in this hypothetical situation are morally justified in choosing to subject their child to the recommended

---

[115] Stump, *Wandering in Darkness*, 303–4.    [116] Stump, *Wandering in Darkness*, 405.

treatments. All the more, she claims, is God justified in attempting to cure his children who are all suffering from "the spiritual equivalent of a terminal disease,"[117] one that if left uncured will "consign them to a living death in hell."[118] For "the loss inflicted by [*this*] disease and the benefits of *its* cure are infinitely greater" than those in the human analogue.[119]

This passage also highlights, however, the fact that Stump is not consistently sensitive to the distinction between causing and permitting.[120] Perhaps this is because she does not focus on *horrendous evils*. In her analogy, the parents are justified in *causing* harm in the life of their child in order to avert a still greater harm. It is nowhere assumed, however, that the harm caused by the parents is *horrendous*. Such an assumption would complicate the analogy. Would the parents in question be justified in causing their child to suffer *horrendously* in order to rescue him from suffering even more *horrendously*? This is a difficult question. The causation of some *horrors* is reasonably taken to be morally prohibited no matter what their intended or probable consequences. Similarly, a theodicy claiming that God directly *causes horrors* in order to avert still greater harm might be harder—though I suspect not completely unfeasible—to defend than one in which God merely *permits* all *horrendous evil*.[121]

Nevertheless, Stump's *defense* remains *prima facie structurally promising*. That the parents in Stump's analogy *cause horrors* happens to be disanalogous in this respect to her theodicy, at least as it is outlined in "The Problem of Evil." There, in affirming a historical and catastrophic fall of humanity by which even natural evil entered the world, Stump is plausibly interpreted as identifying non-divine agents as the *causers* of all *horrors*. God is understood only to *permit horrors* as a type of rescue operation. Thus, the causing/permitting distinction does seem to be doing justificatory work in Stump's Type D Theodicy—one in which God permits *horrors* only for the aversion of greater harm.

One remaining distinction between Case D and Type D Theodicy is that whereas the parents in Case D are not responsible for the system of torture they find themselves confronted with, God is the system creator. This raises questions about whether God's initial risk of the fall was justified and whether there are further difficulties raised by postulating a hell worse than earthly *horrors*. I consider these sub-structural concerns along with whether Stump's theodicy is otherwise plausible in the next chapter.

---

[117] Stump, "The Problem of Evil," 411.    [118] Stump, "The Problem of Evil," 411.

[119] Stump, "The Problem of Evil," 411 (italics mine).

[120] Stump does put this distinction to work in "Suffering for Redemption: A Reply to Smith," *Faith and Philosophy* 2 (1985), 433–4.

[121] Stump flirts with this more vulnerable position in "Sanctification, Hardening of the Heart, and Frankfurt's Concept of Free Will," *The Journal of Philosophy* 85 (1988), 418: "[I]t may be that in the case of a desperately evil man, *giving him* the strength to have as wicked a will as he wants is hazarding a last shot at reforming him" (italics mine).

# 5

# High Fall Theodicy

I have judged that Theodicy Types A and B fail structurally; they do not depict God as an ethically perfect being. I have identified *prima facie structural promise* in theodicy of Types C and D, the former partially developed by Peter van Inwagen and the latter emerging from the work of Eleonore Stump. According to these approaches, God takes a reasonable risk in creating and then either is morally bound not to cancel ensuing *horrors* or else permits them as the lesser of two evils. These theodicies share a reliance on the fall of humanity and its consequences in order to deny that God is *causing horrendous evils* and to depict God as averting greater harm (rather than merely securing pure benefit) by permitting *horrendous evils*.

Thus far, I have only motioned toward Marilyn Adams's arguments against fall-based theodicy. If I am right about the immorality of causing and permitting *horrors* for pure benefit and she is right about the deficiencies of fall approaches, the project of theodicy is in serious trouble. I now argue that theodicy is in this predicament.

## The *Structurally Promising* Theodicies

According to van Inwagen's theodicy, the first human persons had impressive preternatural powers including an awareness of potential evil keen enough to keep them free from all suffering. Hurricanes and tornados existed, but the first generation knew unfailingly not to be in the wrong place at the wrong time. Van Inwagen suggests that

> this awareness was somehow connected with the subject's ordinary sensory awareness of physical objects (which endure and move and have their being in God). I expect that the way in which I am aware of "invisible" thoughts and emotions of others through their faces and voices provides some sort of analogy. I expect that the way the natural world looked to unfallen humanity and the way it looks to me are as similar and as different as the way a page of Chinese calligraphy looks to a literate Chinese and to me. But whatever the nature of our primordial awareness of God, we have largely lost it.[1]

---

[1] Van Inwagen, "Non Est Hick," 198.

*Non-Identity Theodicy: A Grace-Based Response to the Problem of Evil.* Vince R. Vitale, Oxford University Press (2020).
© Vince R. Vitale.
DOI: 10.1093/oso/9780198864226.003.0005

In exercising their freedom, the first human persons "turned away from God…and ruined themselves. In fact, they ruined not only themselves but their posterity, for the separation from God that they achieved was somehow hereditary."[2] Van Inwagen says he finds the following analogy of the fall helpful: "Imagine a great modern city—New York, say—that has been lifted several yards into the air by the hand of some vast giant and then simply let fall. The city is now a ruin…We are all ruins, in a sense very closely analogous to the sense in which the Parthenon is a ruin."[3]

All of this is consonant with and a natural elaboration of Eleonore Stump's theodicy. She does not say as much about the fall, but she suggests in "The Problem of Evil" that at least all earthly evil suffered by persons can be traced back to it.[4] She proposes that moral evil originated with the sin of Adam and that "natural evil entered the world as a result of Adam's fall."[5]

## Blame-Shift by High Fall

The shared underpinning of the *structurally promising* theodicies I have identified is their attempt to shift the blame for evil off of God and onto new intervening agents—the first human persons. For this shift to be ethically plausible, the fall of these persons must be "high" in at least two respects. Firstly, the fall must be from a state that would not have been *horror* producing if not for the fall. If human persons would have been subject to *horrors* regardless of whether they had fallen, then God would cause *horrors* rather than permit them. Secondly, the persons who fell would need to be cognitively and morally robust enough beings to bear significant moral responsibility for the *horrendous* consequences of the fall. If they were immature beings tossed about by evolutionary impulses, then primary moral responsibility would remain with the system creator—God—in the same way that primary moral responsibility for the consequences of firing a gun would remain with me if I handed the loaded gun to a child or to an observably psychologically unstable person in a crowded street. A High Fall Theodicy is one that attempts to shift blame off of God by means of a high fall.

The emergence of high fall theory in Christian theology can be traced back to Tertullian (c.160–c.220) and was more thoroughly developed by Athanasius (c.296–373) and Ambrose (c.340–397).[6] Athanasius credits Adam with a

---

[2] Van Inwagen, "Non Est Hick," 196.   [3] Van Inwagen, "Non Est Hick," 197.
[4] Stump, "The Problem of Evil," 405.   [5] Stump, "The Problem of Evil," 398.
[6] Useful discussions of many of the early Christian writings referenced in this chapter can be found in J. N. D. Kelly, *Early Christian Doctrines*, 5th ed. (London and New York: Continuum, 1977) and in N. P. Williams, *The Ideas of the Fall and of Original Sin* (New York: Longmans, Green and Co. Ltd., 1927).

supernatural blessedness comprised of the highest intellectual, moral, and spiritual powers.[7] Ambrose went further still, referring to the paradisal Adam as a "heavenly being"[8] likened unto an angel.[9] Adam breathed "ethereal air,"[10] was free from the cares and weariness of life,[11] spoke face-to-face with God,[12] and enjoyed the perfect ordering of reason, will, and appetite.[13]

Bishop Augustine of Hippo—expanding on the thoughts of Athanasius and Ambrose before him—popularized and cemented this doctrine of high fall into the Christian theological tradition.[14] According to Augustine, human persons were originally highly impressive beings who lived in perfect harmony with God, each other, and their natural environment. The first persons had colossal intellectual powers[15] and were exceptionally morally robust (*posse non peccare*[16]). These qualities manifested themselves in a perfect control over their appetites[17] and a steadfast character of the utmost virtue.[18] Adam and Eve experienced neither suffering nor death in this original state.[19] Augustine describes their privileged state in Eden as "a condition mysteriously maintained by nourishment from the tree of life, which would have been able to preserve them from sickness and from the aging process."[20] Prior to the fall, God acted supernaturally to prevent all evils, but the effect of Adam's sin was to stop God intervening in this way and also for a proneness to sin to be transmitted *by nature* (that is, by some genetic means rather than merely by bad example) to all subsequent generations. Augustine concludes, therefore, that the "wanton will" of the first human person "is the cause of all evil."[21]

---

[7] Athanasius, *Contra gentes*, 2–3; *De incarnatione*, 3–4.

[8] Ambrose, *Expositio Psalmi cxviii*, 15.36. The following list of qualities ascribed by Ambrose to Adam is compiled in Williams, *The Ideas of the Fall and of Original Sin*, 301.

[9] Ambrose, *De paradiso*, 9.42.   [10] Ambrose, *Expositio Psalmi cxviii*, 4.5.

[11] Ambrose, *Expositio Psalmi cxviii*, 4.5.

[12] Ambrose, *Enarrationes in xii. Psalmos Davidicos*, 43.75.

[13] Ambrose, *Expositio evangelii secundum Lucam*, 7.142.

[14] Michael Murray speaks to the extent of this popularization when he claims that "for almost every major Christian thinker reflecting on evil, the Fall has played a central role in explaining both the origin and persistence of evil in the universe" (*Nature Red in Tooth and Claw: Theism and the Problem of Animal Suffering* (Oxford: Oxford University Press, 2008), 74).

[15] Augustine, *Opus imperfectum contra Julianum*, 5.1.

[16] Augustine, *De correptione et gratia*, 33.

[17] Augustine, *De nuptiis et concupiscentia*, 1.6–8, 2.30.

[18] Augustine, *Opus imperfectum contra Julianum*, 5.61; *De peccatorum meritis et remissione et de baptismo parvulorum*, 2.36.

[19] Augustine, *De civitate Dei*, 14.1, 14.10, 14.26. See also *De civitate Dei*, 12.21, *De libero arbitrio*, 3.18.52, and *De Genesi contra Manichaeos*, 2.8.

[20] Augustine, *De Genesi ad litteram* (New York: Paulist Press, 1982), 164 (11.32).

[21] Augustine, *De libero arbitrio*, in *On the Free Choice of the Will, on Grace and Free Choice, and Other Writings*, ed. Peter King (Cambridge: Cambridge University Press, 2010), 107 (3.17.48). Cf. *De vera religione*, 12.23, 20.39.

## Challenges to Broadly Augustinian Accounts

One fairly unproblematic tenet of the Augustinian account of the fall is that there was a historical origination of sin. Keith Ward claims that "[i]n the course of evolution, there must have been a first moment of conscious moral choice."[22] It is controversial whether considerations of vagueness tell against the claim that evolution would have produced a first moment of conscious moral choice; for that matter, given evolutionary assumptions, it might be arbitrary to select any one being as the first being with moral awareness.[23] But nonetheless a range of time in which moral choice appeared in an evolutionary process seems sufficient to speak meaningfully of a historic fall. With these qualifications, one holding to a Darwinian account of speciation could affirm the following account of the fall given by Swinburne:

> At some stage in the history of the world, there appeared the first creature with hominoid body who had some understanding of the difference between the morally obligatory, the morally permissible (i.e. right), and the morally wrong; and an ability freely to choose the morally right. So much is obvious; since on modern evolutionary views, as well as on all views held in Christian tradition, once upon a time there were no such creatures and now there are some, there must have been a first one. It seems reasonable to consider such a creature the first man; and we may follow biblical tradition and call him 'Adam'. (The Hebrew word means 'man'.)...Given [evolutionary assumptions], it seems highly plausible to suppose...that the first man was also the first subjective sinner—such would be the force of the desires inherited from his ape-like ancestors in one who alone dimly perceives moral obligations which run contrary to it.[24]

But while Augustine is correct that sin entered the world historically through the moral choices of the first human persons (whether one takes them to have been modern humans or Neanderthals), many believe it is implausible to suppose with those who followed Augustine that these first human persons originated suffering by their sin, were responsible for all subsequent human generations inheriting a nature prone to sin, and had supernatural defenses against evil until they sinned. These claims are judged by many to be in tension with modern scientific theory.

---

[22] Keith Ward, *God, Faith, and the New Millennium: Christian Belief in an Age of Science* (Oxford: Oneworld Publications, 1998), 42.

[23] For a useful discussion of these issues, see Williams, *The Ideas of the Fall and of Original Sin*, 514–17.

[24] Swinburne, *Responsibility and Atonement*, 141–2.

## Science Against High Fall

Consider firstly the claim that the sinful choices of the first human persons originated suffering and death. Augustine's views appear to be more subtle than this. In some places, he suggests that animal predation, disease, and death existed before the fall.[25] But many of those who continued on the Augustinian trajectory of elevating antelapsarian conditions came to understand not only human persons but creation in its entirety as immune to pre-fall suffering. It will be instructive to consider this fully developed high fall theory, but it faces serious challenges.

To begin with, on any broadly evolutionary approach to biology, suffering and death have been around far longer than human beings.[26] Sentient animals predate human beings by hundreds of millions of years, and trillions of them suffered as natural selection chose against them. If this is so, human choice cannot have originated these evils. Christopher Southgate puts it this way:

> Predation, violence, parasitism, suffering, and extinction were integral parts of the natural order long before *Homo sapiens*. As every T-Rex-loving six-year-old knows, there is evidence of these natural dynamics from the age of dinosaurs, which came to an end some 65 million years ago. Even the longest estimate of the time for which creatures that might be recognized as human have existed is no more than a million years at the very outside.[27]

This depends on what you mean by "human." *Homo erectus*—a tool user—is estimated to be hundreds of thousands of years older than that. But, in any case, it is very safe on evolutionary assumptions to say that no human ever saw a T-Rex.

The high fall theory of the origination of suffering is rejected not only by the majority of leading scientists, but also by many leading scientist-theologians, for example John Polkinghorne and Arthur Peacocke. Peacocke claims for death what he would apply equally to suffering:

> Biological death can no longer be regarded as in any way the *consequence* of anything human beings might have been supposed to have done in the past for evolutionary history shows it to be the very *means* whereby they appear, and so, for the theist, are created by God. The traditional interpretation of the third

---

[25] Augustine, *De Genesi ad litteram*, 8.10, 11.32.

[26] Even if one accepted Descartes's controversial claim that animals are automata incapable of suffering for some animals, this is implausible for animals with more sophisticated brains such as dolphins and gorillas.

[27] Christopher Southgate, *The Groaning of Creation: God, Evolution, and the Problem of Evil* (Louisville: Westminster John Knox Press, 2008), 29. Keith Ward confirms the point: "[W]hen humans first came into being, they were already locked into a world in which competition and death were fundamental to their very existence" (Keith Ward, *Religion and Human Nature* (Oxford: Oxford University Press, 1998), 161).

chapter of *Genesis* that there was a historical 'Fall,' an action by our human progenitors that is the explanation of biological death, has to be rejected… There was no golden age, no perfect past.[28]

Next, consider the Augustinian thesis that the first human persons are morally responsible for the transmission by nature of proneness to moral evil. On evolutionary assumptions, this too may be deemed implausible, firstly because the original human persons—as evolutionary products of natural selection— already would have been set up for sin.[29] Acknowledging that there is reasonable disagreement about how much selfishness is required by natural selection and about the relationship between altruism and evolutionary processes, we nevertheless can say with confidence that if the first human persons were produced by a gradual evolutionary process, they would have had only a dim awareness of morality and would have been under great temptation. The processes by which they came to be would have produced in them at least some selfish instincts and desires aimed at survival, and without training in or developed social expectations of resisting temptation. Against the Augustinian account, evolutionary theory suggests that acting rightly consistently is not what would have been built into the first human persons,[30] diminishing their ability to be primarily morally responsible for the consequences of their actions.

One could postulate that it was not the sin of these first morally dull humans that does the blame-shifting work for theodicy, but rather a fall of later humans who had developed sufficient moral awareness to bear significant responsibility for the consequences of their actions. Whether humans could ever develop to such a degree as to bear primary responsibility for *horrors* is a question I will return to later in this chapter. Even if they could, there are problems with this move. In particular, it aggravates concerns about antelapsarian suffering because, on the assumption of gradual evolutionary development, it would take many generations for it to be in any way plausible that humans had reached sufficient moral awareness. As a result, there would be numerous generations of human suffering prior to the point when blame could be shifted. The high fall theodicist wants to say that you have the sort of suffering that needs a theodicy right at the point when the sort of being exists that you can shift blame onto. He wants to identify

---

[28] Arthur Peacocke, *Theology for a Scientific Age: Being and Becoming—Natural, Divine and Human*, enlarged ed. (London: SCM Press Ltd, 1993), 222–3.

[29] Note also that moral responsibility for this transmission could not lie with a single individual or pair of individuals unless we are all descended from a single pair and that pair was the first with moral awareness. This is in tension with the evolutionary assumption that generations of humans or pre-humans were geographically spread out prior to the development of moral awareness. For a further discussion of this point, see Williams, *The Ideas of the Fall and of Original Sin*, 516.

[30] In fact, on the assumptions of some (especially Protestant) theologians such as Martin Luther, Philipp Melanchthon, Friedrich Schleiermacher, and Paul Tillich, these selfish desires already count as sin, making it still less plausible that the first human persons could be substantially morally responsible for originating a proneness to sin.

someone late enough in the process to bear primary responsibility but early enough in the process for there not to be prior suffering requiring justification. But that's implausible on evolutionary assumptions about *Homo sapiens* origination. On those assumptions, there is no creature who could at all plausibly bear the blame until much later than the point at which there is very serious human suffering to be accounted for.

Secondly, an evolutionary account of human origins suggests that any proneness to sin passed on from the first human persons to subsequent generations is unlikely to have been passed on *by nature*. Adam's descendants did inherit his proneness to sin, but—as Swinburne explains—

> given modern evolutionary and genetic theory, what was genetically inherited was not caused by Adam, for two reasons. The first is that, neo-Darwinian orthodoxy assures us, changes in genes are quite unaffected by changes in other parts of the body and so (contrary Lamarck's supposition) there is no inheritance of acquired characteristics. God could, it is true, have overruled normal genetic processes on this unique occasion. But against that supposition stands the second and stronger consideration that the desires which cause all the trouble are there in the monkeys and the apes as well. The desires are not caused in us by Adam's sin. Indeed, as we have noted, they must have been already there in Adam himself.
>
> Adam's responsibility for our sinfulness is confined to a responsibility for beginning the social transmission of morality (as such a good thing) which made sin possible, but a morality which, as a result of his own sinful example and perhaps false moral beliefs, was no doubt a corrupt morality and so made it easier for our genetically inherited proneness to sin to work in Adam's successors... [Responsibility for sin] belongs to the first man Adam peculiarly in this sense, that he began the process to which so many of us have subsequently contributed.[31]

On an evolutionary picture, the heritability of tendencies to sin is plausible. Instincts suited for sin are inherited genetically, and human culture passes on sinful habits by teaching people to fulfill roles that demand them. But, against Augustine, what was inherited genetically would not have been characteristics firstly acquired by Adam and for which Adam was primarily morally responsible.

As for Augustine's third supposition, it seems implausible evolutionarily that the first human persons enjoyed preternatural defenses against suffering since— as Swinburne reminds—modern evolutionary theory "suggests a very gradual evolution of man from more primitive creatures with a very gradual development

---

[31] Swinburne, *Responsibility and Atonement*, 143.

of his various capacities."[32] The presumption is that we didn't start better and get worse, but evolved from less intelligent and less resourceful things.

One might object that newer models of evolution suggest that there are lots of (relatively) big steps in the evolutionary process. But even if the evolutionary process is not universally "very gradual," it does suggest a process of progress more than one of radical elevation and decline. Even if there were a significant evolutionary step between humans and their pre-human ancestors, this would have to account for an enormous difference for blame-shift to be possible, on a scale that even the most liberal models of punctuated equilibrium would hold to be exceedingly improbable.

For the sorts of reasons detailed above, many believe that modern evolutionary biology disconfirms the belief that some fundamental genetic change in humans was caused by primeval sin, nor do they consider it plausible that such sin affected either human persons or the natural world in such a radical way as for it to be the cause of all suffering, or even of all *horrendous* suffering. High Fall Theodicy has significant plausibility challenges to overcome. Some will think these scientific considerations should be overruled by authoritative religious tradition or revelation. The next two sections explore this line of thought.

## Theological Tradition Against High Fall

A theist might reasonably think the judgments of science should be received with caution when they contradict well-established theological tradition. However, the Christian theological tradition may be interpreted as less than clearly in favor of an Augustinian approach to the fall. The Augustinian high fall became standard in the early medieval West, was adopted and expanded by Aquinas, Bonaventure, and Scotus, and came to dominate the Reformed creeds. But there was a variety of views on these topics among Christians of the first four centuries.[33]

Writing between the years 170 and 180, Tatian suggests that man was created not good but rather with the capacity for goodness,[34] and Theophilus goes further to say that man in his unfallen state was infantile and undeveloped, having been created not perfect but rather with "a starting point for progress."[35] It is on account of Adam's childlike status that Theophilus explains the divine prohibition against him acquiring knowledge in Genesis 3. Theophilus explains that while knowledge in itself is good, some kinds of knowledge are undesirable for children.

---

[32] Swinburne, *Responsibility and Atonement*, 141–2.

[33] Another view favored by a few of the early Christian theologians was to understand the Genesis fall story as a mythical representation of the state of each human person. Gregory of Nyssa, for example, writes of Moses as "placing doctrines before us in the form of a story" (*Oratio catechetica magna*, 5; quoted in Swinburne, *Providence and the Problem of Evil*, 41).

[34] Tatian, *Oratio contra Graecos*, 7.   [35] Theophilus, *Apologia ad Autolycum*, 2.24–25, 2.27.

Irenaeus (130–202) develops these views more comprehensively. "Man was a child," he writes, "not yet having his understanding perfected. Wherefore he was easily led astray by the deceiver."[36] He argues that, due to being a creature, Adam was necessarily infinitely removed from the divine perfection.[37] Even in Paradise, therefore, he was morally, spiritually, and intellectually a child.[38] Because of his strong passions and weak will, his sin was unsurprising,[39] and therefore God is more inclined to pity than to condemn the first persons on account of their low fall.[40]

Clement (c.150–c.215),[41] Methodius (d.311),[42] and Lactantius (c.250–325)[43] all make claims consonant with the Irenaean view, and even as late as Gregory of Nazianzus (c.329–c.390) the first human person is spoken of as

> midway between greatness and lowliness…naked in his simplicity and in his inartificial way of life, and devoid of any covering or defence; for such it was fitting that the original man should be…Now the Tree [of Knowledge] was Contemplation (as I see the matter), which can be safely climbed only by those who are of a more perfect and settled character; but it is not good for those who are simple-minded and of a somewhat greedy appetite, just as perfect (i.e. solid) nourishment is not profitable for those who are yet tender and stand in need of milk.[44]

Summarizing this predominantly Hellenic approach to the fall, N. P. Williams writes that

> it gives us a picture of primitive man as frail, imperfect, and child-like—a picture which is on the whole unaffected by the Rabbinical figment of Adam's 'Original Righteousness,' and is by no means incapable of harmonization with the facts revealed by the science of to-day. It exaggerates neither the height from which, not the depth to which, the first men are alleged to have fallen.[45]

---

[36] Irenaeus, *Demonstration of the Apostolic Preaching*, 12; quoted in Williams, *The Ideas of the Fall and of Original Sin*, 194.

[37] Irenaeus, *Adversus haereses*, 4.38.1–3, 4.62, 4.63.1.

[38] Irenaeus, *Demonstration of the Apostolic Preaching*, 12: "The lord (of the earth), that is, man, was but small; for he was a child; and it was necessary that he should grow, and so come to his perfection"; quoted in Williams, *The Ideas of the Fall and of Original Sin*, 194. See also Irenaeus, *Adversus haereses*, 4.64.1.

[39] Irenaeus, *Demonstration of the Apostolic Preaching*, 16.

[40] Irenaeus, *Adversus haereses*, 3.25.2 and 4.66.2.

[41] Clement, *Stromata*, 6.12.96: "[The first man] was not created perfect in constitution, but suitable for acquiring virtue"; quoted in Kelly, *Early Christian Doctrine*, 179. See also Clement, *Protrepticus*, 11; *Stromata*, 2.22.

[42] Methodius, *Symposium*, 3.5.     [43] Lactantius, *De ira Dei*, 100.15.

[44] Gregory of Nazianzus, *Oration xlv (In sanctum Pascha)*, 7–8; quoted in Williams, *The Ideas of the Fall and of Original Sin*, 283–4.

[45] Williams, *The Ideas of the Fall and of Original Sin*, 200.

From the Council of Ephesus in 431 down to the Great Schism of 1054, the Augustinian approach came to dominate in the West, but it did not take the same firm hold in the East. The Eastern Orthodox tradition remained unconvinced of original righteousness, and even as late as the fourteenth century Gregory Palamas describes the first persons as "being still in an imperfect and intermediate state—that is to say, easily influenced, whether for good or evil." Like Theophilus, he claims that as children they were not prepared for the superior knowledge attained by eating from the tree of the knowledge of good and evil. Instead, they ought "to have acquired more practice and so to speak, schooling in simple, genuine goodness."[46]

Especially when the Darwinian influence of the last one and a half centuries is added to the corpus of Christian theological reflection, it seems unjustified to claim that the tradition has ruled one way or another regarding the kind of persons the first human persons were.

## Scripture Against High Fall

This ambivalence in the theological tradition is unsurprising when one recognizes that the Bible is also less than perspicuous on this point.

There is little if any high fall tradition in the Old Testament. Commenting on aspects of a supposed original righteousness, Claus Westermann writes that "[i]t is of the utmost significance that the Old Testament knows nothing of such an idea of paradise."[47] Quite to the contrary, even in the Garden of Eden "there is a background echo of a distant past when humans and beasts were closer to each other."[48] Hermann Gunkel joins Westermann in hearing this echo at least faintly in the suggestion by the Yahwistic author of the possibility that mere animals could be man's "helper."[49] Additionally, Gunkel argues that "The knowledge and ignorance treated [in Genesis 2–3] concern,...in the first instance, the difference between the sexes. The model for these elements is clearly the state of children who are not yet ashamed—a state one can observe in every lane in the East, where the children go naked."[50] Consonant with this, he notes, are the Israelite attestations that children "do not know about good and evil" (Deuteronomy 1:39) and "do not know to choose good and avoid evil" (Isaiah 7:15–16).

---

[46] Gregory Palamas, *Topics in Natural and Theological Science*, in *Philokalia* iv, ed. and trans. G.E.H. Palmer, P. Sherrard, and K. Ware (Faber and Faber, 1995), 369–70; quoted in Swinburne, *Providence and the Problem of Evil*, 39.

[47] Claus Westermann, *Genesis 1–11: A Continental Commentary* (Minneapolis: Fortress Press, 1994), 220.

[48] Westermann, *Genesis 1–11: A Continental Commentary*, 226.

[49] Hermann Gunkel, *Genesis* (Macon, Georgia: Mercer University Press, 1997), 12.

[50] Gunkel, *Genesis*, 14. See also 29–30.

Whether one finds the positive textual arguments for the child-like condition of Adam and Eve plausible or not, what is clear is that the Genesis story does not contain anything like the full-blown Augustinian account of original righteousness. Nor is there strong support for the origination of a physically-inherited original sinfulness or for suffering having come into the world as a result of the primeval sin. As for the latter point, note that it has already been "not good for the man to be alone" (Genesis 2:18) and, while the Hebrew text of Genesis 3:16 can be reasonably translated into English in a number of ways, the common translation that the woman's pain was "greatly increased" certainly does not close the door to the possibility of her having suffered even prior to her sin.

Moreover, descriptions of talking—as opposed to our normal hissing—serpents and trees "of life and . . . of the knowledge of good and evil"[51]—as opposed to oaks or pines—as well as the personal names Man and Life[52]—as opposed to Vince and Joanna—at least lend themselves naturally to a mythical reading, as does the similarity in raw material between the Genesis creation accounts and other ancient near eastern myths.[53]

Turning to the New Testament, support for the high fall position is similarly sparse. There is no reference to the fall in the Gospels or in the Johannine corpus. Paul says nothing of original righteousness. Romans 5:12–21, for example, is used by Augustine in support of his high fall doctrine, but Paul does not here mention Adam's sin as the cause of later suffering, only of death and sin. We have seen that not all theories of the relationship between Adam's sin and subsequent sin commit us to a high fall, and, similarly, "death" could be taken to imply spiritual death—the moral estrangement from God that was initiated by the sin of the first human persons—as it seems to in several other Pauline and possibly-Pauline passages including Romans 6 and Ephesians 2. Ward notes that "[t]he Greek fathers usually interpreted 'death' primarily, though admittedly not exclusively, as spiritual death, as estrangement from God and lack of the divine spirit. In that sense, death is the consequence of sin."[54] One can accept this interpretation without accepting that physical death is the result of a cosmic fall of the first human persons. Commenting on the relevant Pauline texts, Williams writes that "[t]he Rabbinical fictions which represent Adam as surpassing the angels in glory, intellectual power, and conscious holiness are totally absent from his pages."[55]

High Fall Theodicy relies on the *height* of the fall to make plausible that suffering wasn't already in the natural course of divine design and that the first human

---

[51] Genesis 2:9.

[52] The literal renderings of the Hebrew words translated "Adam" and "Eve."

[53] These include *The Epic of Gilgamesh, Enuma Elish,* and *The Legend of Adapa.* See William W. Hallo and K. Lawson Younger (eds.), *The Context of Scripture: Canonical Compositions from the Biblical World,* vol. 1 (Leiden and New York: Brill, 1997).

[54] Ward, *Religion and Human Nature,* 184.

[55] Williams, *The Ideas of the Fall and of Original Sin,* 163.

persons could have had the competency to bear primary responsibility for the results of their sin. Many conclude, however, that the overall data of science, tradition, and scripture recommends Williams's conclusion about the initial condition of the first human persons:

> Man, at his first appearance on this planet, was in moral and intellectual stature a babe, created frail, imperfect, ignorant and non-moral, but endowed with self-consciousness and the power of self-determination, which constituted…a starting-point for progress and upward evolution.[56]

## In Defense of High Fall

The above reasons suggest that the biblical case for an Augustinian interpretation of the state of the first human persons is underwhelming. However, it would be wrong to say there is no biblical support for a high fall. For instance, 1 Corinthians 15—which states that "death came through a man" and that "in Adam all die"[57]— is perhaps most naturally read as implying that physical death (even if not hereditary sinfulness) was the result of Adam's sin.

Many people assume that current evolutionary science obliges the rational person to deny the claim that there was in history a literal Adam and Eve who fell from a cognitively and morally elevated state into sin. But this assumption can be called into question for at least two reasons. Firstly, most scientific theories once judged by the majority to be true are now taken to be false. Science is constantly finding new evidence that requires its theories to be revised. That does not mean that currently accepted theories do not contain important truths, but it does mean that a conflict between current science and a theological claim is not always incontrovertible evidence against that theological claim. This is especially the case if you take the theological claim to be endorsed by the Bible and you take the Bible to be an authoritative communication from God.

Darwin's theory of evolution itself has undergone significant changes. The very gradual emergence of species through the accumulation of small hereditary differences that it predicted—termed *phyletic gradualism*—was not present in the fossil record of Darwin's day. This troubled Darwin, but he supposed that intermediate species would surface once more of the earth's surface had been mined for fossils. Today at least one hundred times more fossils have been discovered than in Darwin's day, but there are still very few if any conclusive examples of intermediates. Brian Goodwin, who helped to found the fields of biomathematics

---

[56] Williams, *The Ideas of the Fall and of Original Sin*, 453.   [57] 1 Corinthians 15:21–22.

and theoretical biology, quotes with approval the conclusion of Ernst Mayr—one of the most honored evolutionary biologists of the twentieth century who remained a leader in the field into the twenty-first century: "[There is] no clear evidence…for the gradual emergence of any evolutionary novelty."[58] One way to account for this is a theory of punctuated equilibrium, according to which most species spend most of their existence in a state of stasis, undergoing little evolutionary change, until certain environmental conditions cause smaller isolated populations to undergo rapid (geologically speaking) speciation. This is one attempt to square the lack of intermediates in the fossil record with the assumption that the diversity we find in the biological world is *fully* explained by the dual factors of natural selection and random mutation.

However, some people, van Inwagen for instance, though maintaining that natural selection and random mutation are important parts of the explanation of biological diversity and complexity, are less confident that these two factors comprise the whole explanation. Van Inwagen is not at all sure that all of the supposed intermediates missing from the fossil record are "anatomically and physiologically possible" results of the types of incremental changes that could be made solely by random mutations and the pressures of natural selection from one generation to the next.[59] He writes, "I doubt whether there is any path in logical space from [a fish] to [an amphibian] that proceeds by changing a small number of genes at each step: every path you try will (I suspect) eventually run up against organs and systems that are no longer coordinated."[60] Van Inwagen does not see what reason we have for assuming that natural selection and random mutation do all of the evolutionary work, and, if other factors contribute to the workload, he takes it to be an open question whether those other factors are natural or supernatural ones.

We have seen that the Bible does not flesh out the history of human origination in full detail, but for one holding to a divinely inspired and authoritative biblical text the 1 Corinthians 15-suggestion that Adam's sin resulted in human susceptibility to physical death could carry a lot of weight and could lend itself, especially when combined with a recognition of the fallibility and still-maturing nature of modern science, to belief in a pre-fall preternatural state. Alongside this, while theological tradition may not rule definitively in favor of a high fall, there is plenty in the tradition to suggest that high fall theories are worthy of serious consideration. Moreover, if a high fall is the only *structurally promising* way to maintain the goodness of God in the face of evil and suffering, and if you take

[58] Brian Goodwin, *How the Leopard Changed Its Spots: The Evolution of Complexity* (Princeton: Princeton University Press, 2001), xii.

[59] Peter van Inwagen, "Doubts About Darwinism" in *Darwinism: Science or Philosophy?*, eds. Jon Buell and Virginia Hearn (Richardson, TX: Foundation for Thought and Ethics, 1994), 183.

[60] Peter van Inwagen, "Genesis and Evolution" in *God, Knowledge, and Mystery: Essays in Philosophical Theology* (Ithaca and London: Cornell University Press, 1995), 150.

yourself to have independently strong reasons to believe in the goodness of God, then this too could give you reason to believe in a high fall.

Perhaps these reasons could justify belief in a high fall even without a working hypothesis about how the first persons in their high fall state could have had supernatural defenses against evil until they sinned, played a significant role in originating suffering, and been responsible for all subsequent human generations inheriting a nature prone to sin while also being consistent with modern evolutionary theory. And yet, some progress can be made even toward such a hypothesis. Augustine, for instance, can be interpreted as believing there was animal suffering before human sin but that human sin initiated human suffering. On this rendering, a high fall could acknowledge that suffering and death were intrinsic to the evolutionary process. Human persons were not immune to suffering and death in the natural course of things but rather God supernaturally protected the first human persons in a specifically designated garden. This would leave (at least pre-fall) animal suffering unexplained (more on this in Chapter 6), but nevertheless providing a good explanation for all human suffering would be plenty reason for High Fall Theodicy to celebrate.

Van Inwagen endorses a broadly Augustinian narrative of this sort, whereby at some stage in an evolutionary process God miraculously elevated some primates to a morally auspicious human status. Surely that is within the scope of omnipotence. It is consistent with the findings of science, especially considering the discontinuities present in the fossil record. Perhaps it is also a fitting method of creation for a God hoping that human persons will find value in the natural processes discoverable by science while also not forgetting that their very existence depends on his miraculous provision.

Perhaps the toughest element of a high fall to square with modern science is the idea that the first two human persons were responsible for all subsequent human generations inheriting a nature prone to sin. But even here possibilities present themselves. Swinburne concedes that "God could, it is true, have overruled normal genetic processes on this unique occasion."[61] Plantinga fleshes this out a bit further, claiming that, contrary to popular opinion, "it certainly seems that there is no conflict between current science and a literal Adam and Eve who fell into sin."[62] As Plantinga writes,

> Some scientists speak of a bottleneck (perhaps 160,000 to 200,000 years ago) in the line leading to current humans, when the relevant population dwindled to 10,000 to 12,000 individuals. Here's a possible scenario. At that time God

[61] Swinburne, *Responsibility and Atonement*, 143.
[62] Alvin Plantinga, "Historical Adam: One Possible Scenario," *Think Christian* (blog), February 14, 2013, http://thinkchristian.reframemedia.com/historical-adam-one-possible-scenario.

selected a pair of these individuals, bestowing on them a property in virtue of which they are rightly said to be made in the image of God. This pair was wholly innocent, with properly directed affections. Nevertheless, they fell into sin, which in some way altered their natures (original sin). Furthermore, both the image of God and original sin were heritable, and also dominant in the sense that if either parent has either of these properties, their offspring will also have those properties. In this way both properties spread through the whole population, so that at present all human beings are descendants of this original pair, and all human being possess both the image of God and original sin.[63]

I am not saying you should accept this specific account of humanity's origin, nor am I saying that I do, but it is not irrational to believe that it is both consistent with current mainstream views in evolutionary science and within the capability of an omnipotent God. The same could be said of a scenario that differs from Plantinga's in that, rather than being selected from already existing beings, Adam and Eve were made directly by God in a special act of creation. If God is omnipotent, he can be pretty resourceful and creative.

All of this suggests that a starting point for considering the relations between evolution and the problem of evil should be caution with respect to two widely held assumptions: firstly, that current majority positions in science are definitive and, secondly, that there is an obvious conflict between current majority positions in science and there having been a high fall.

However, even if a high fall can be made more plausible that often supposed, there are at least two reasons why it will be advantageous for the theist to develop a theodicy that does not depend on a high fall. Firstly, many people are deeply committed to the belief that evolutionary assumptions rule out a high fall; it would be beneficial, therefore, to be able to deploy a theodicy that does not rely on changing this belief. Secondly (and more damagingly for High Fall Theodicy), even if a high fall can be made plausible, there are additional plausibility and substructural problems with the High Fall Theodicies identified in Chapter 4 as having *prima facie structural promise*. I now turn to these problems.

---

[63] Plantinga, "Historical Adam: One Possible Scenario." For an alternative approach to reconciling the fall of Adam and Eve with modern evolutionary science, see Hud Hudson, *The Fall and Hypertime* (Oxford: Oxford University Press, 2014). There Hudson argues that, on certain epistemically possible assumptions about the metaphysics of time, Genesis could literally describe what happens in some universe up until roughly the fall. Then Adam and Eve could be transplanted into our universe at a specific point in hominoid development that would allow them to become the progenitors of all of humankind. While Hudson is not endorsing the truth of this theory, he takes it to be an epistemic possibility and to have "the extraordinary and delightful feature of being thoroughly consistent with the reigning scientific orthodoxy and with the current deliverances of astronomy, physics, geology, paleoanthropology, genetics, and evolutionary biology" (13).

## Additional Plausibility Problems for the *Structurally Promising* Theodicies

Despite the ways in which it can be challenged, a belief that the sin of the first human persons is responsible for all subsequent moral and natural evil (at least that suffered by human persons) remains not uncommon, not merely at the popular level but among professional philosophers and theologians.

We have observed this in the way Types C and D Theodicy emerge from the thought of Peter van Inwagen and Eleonore Stump. Because of the way these approaches rely on a high fall, they are vulnerable to many of the general objections just enumerated. I'll now recapitulate these two *structurally promising* theodicies and raise additional plausibility problems particular to each.

### Peter van Inwagen's Type C Theodicy

In Chapter 4, I summarized van Inwagen's theodicy in four claims:

(1) Necessarily, only beings with sin in their possibility of choice are capable of freely loving God. Human beings are among these beings, and freely loving God is of great value.

(2) Necessarily, the natural consequences of human beings' sin are catastrophic and horrendous. These consequences account for all of the human suffering in the world.

(3) Necessarily, because God is *ex hypothesi* not a deceiver, he must permit much of the natural consequences of human sin.

(4) The horrors of this world are a necessary postlapsarian condition of the great good of God's plan of atonement, and the expected overall value of God's plan of atonement for human persons—given potential horrors—is highly positive.

I noted that (4) is ambiguous between

(4a) The horrors of this world are a necessary postlapsarian condition of the great good of God's plan of atonement, the expected overall value of God's plan of atonement for human persons—given potential horrors—is highly positive, and the expected good of God's plan of atonement *averts still worse harm.*

and

(4b) The horrors of this world are a necessary postlapsarian condition of the great good of God's plan of atonement, the expected overall value of

> God's plan of atonement for human persons—given potential horrors—
> is highly positive, and the expected good of God's plan of atonement
> *bestows pure benefit.*

and I claimed that for van Inwagen's theodicy to be *structurally promising*, he needs the truth—together with (1) and (2)—of either (3) and (4b) or (4a) on its own. In the former case as van Inwagen fills it out, God takes a permissible risk of *horrors* in creating human persons, and is morally obligated to permit *horrors* when they occur in order to avoid the charge of having been deceptive. In the latter case as van Inwagen presents it, God again takes a permissible risk in creating, and then is justified in permitting *horrors* because they are the best means to averting still greater harm. If both (3) and (4a) are true, then God's justification for permitting *horrors* is overdetermined.

## Plausibility Problems with (1)

I am sympathetic to van Inwagen's (1), but there are serious objections to it. For one, if God is essentially perfectly good, freedom to love does not seem to be incompatible with essential goodness. Why, then, is our ability to sin necessary for our ability to freely love God? And even if it is, what makes the value of our freely loving God greater than that of our having an otherwise rationally self-determined love for him, perhaps as those in heaven do? A thorough discussion of (1) would take us too far afield and I find the objections to (2)–(4) more damaging to van Inwagen's account, so I will move on.

## Plausibility Problems with (2)

As detailed in Chapter 4, by claiming that these consequences are "natural," van Inwagen means to imply that God could not have made it such that the natural consequences of human separation from God were not *horrendous*. Without supernatural protection, a radical vulnerability to the magnitude, duration, and distribution of evil is the unavoidable cost of creating human beings in a "structurally and nomologically coherent world complex enough to contain [them]."[64]

To make such a claim compelling, van Inwagen will need to say a good deal more about what it is for a consequence to be natural. At times, van Inwagen sounds as if a consequence's being natural is simply its being made probable by physical laws. For instance, he seems to use "natural causes" synonymously with "non-miraculous causes" when he contrasts the belief that the weather at Dunkirk

---

[64] Van Inwagen, "The Magnitude, Duration, and Distribution of Evil," 119.

during Operation Dynamo[65] had "purely natural causes" with the belief that it was brought about by "a specific and local divine action."[66] But if that is what van Inwagen means by natural, then couldn't God have set up the system so that different consequences would have been the *natural* result of living in the world as sinful persons?

My intuition aligns with Swinburne's that God would have significant control over the relations holding between physical laws and production of evil. It does seem "logically possible to have disease, even incurable disease, without agonizing pain,"[67] and "it was surely not beyond the power of God to make medicines which could not poison, and food in which we felt no inclination to indulge immoderately."[68] Similarly, the hydration benefits of water for humans may be dependent on the threat of drowning "if water and humans are made as they are. But it seems to me far from evident that there could not be a different system of chemistry (deriving from a different system of physical laws), such that there was a substance which played the beneficial role of water without embodied rational creatures being at risk of death by drowning in it."[69]

If we take van Inwagen's natural consequences to be synonymous with non-miraculous consequences, reflection on the contingency of the miraculous makes his (2) implausible. And it is still more implausible when applied to *horrors* in particular. Given that the possibility of suffering *horrendous evil* is largely a function of one's conceptual capabilities under duress and one's pain threshold, and given that these things are already greatly limited in human persons, it seems likely that they could be further naturally limited in embodied, rational beings to a point that evil suffered by those beings would not be *horrendous*.

But perhaps when van Inwagen claims that the natural consequences of human sin are *horrendous* he is relying on a more Aristotelian understanding of "natural." Perhaps he is thinking that each natural kind has a metaphysically necessary nature that determines the active and passive causal powers of that kind, and that *human* nature entails that, unaided by miracles, human beings cannot exist in a *horror*-free world any more than water can act as a drying mechanism.

There are a couple of places in "The Magnitude, Duration, and Distribution of Evil" where van Inwagen seems to have something like an Aristotelian essentialism about natures in mind. For instance, he imagines God saying,

---

[65] This was the evacuation operation which, aided by bad weather that greatly limited the ability of German aircraft to bombard Dunkirk, rescued 338,000 men in late May and early June of 1940.

[66] Van Inwagen, *The Problem of Evil*, 92–3.

[67] Swinburne, *Providence and the Problem of Evil*, 43.

[68] Swinburne, *Providence and the Problem of Evil*, 43.

[69] Swinburne, *Providence and the Problem of Evil*, 44.

Even I can't make a world which is suitable for human beings but which contains no phenomena that would harm human beings *if* they were in the wrong place at the wrong time. The reasons for this are complicated, but they turn on the fact that the molecular bonds that hold you human beings together must be weaker by many orders of magnitude than the disruptive potential of the surges of energy that must happen here and there in a structurally and nomologically coherent world complex enough to contain you.[70]

This could be interpreted to imply that the natural kind *Homo sapiens*—unaided by supernatural gifts—necessarily has the passive power of being vulnerable to *horrendous* suffering. What, if any, vulnerability to evil is entailed by the identity conditions of human persons is a very interesting question. I will return to it in Chapter 6.

But if something along these lines is what van Inwagen once had in mind, he doesn't seem to anymore. In his more recent treatment of evil in *The Problem of Evil*, he drops talk of what is natural *for human beings* and defends only the more general claim that "(at least for all we know), only in a universe very much like ours could intelligent life, or indeed life of any sort, develop by the operation of the laws of nature, unsupplemented by miracles."[71] As discussed above, I think this too greatly limits the scope of omnipotence to be plausible.

On top of the difficulty establishing any relation of necessity holding between the natural consequences of this world and its being inhabited by human or other embodied rational beings, the origination of evil as van Inwagen describes it is not even in keeping with this-worldly consequences. In their review of van Inwagen's theodicy, Frances and Daniel Howard-Snyder point out that van Inwagen's claim

> that wickedness is *somehow hereditary* is puzzling, especially if we think of it as genetic. It is not a *natural consequence* of a parent's free choice that her child be genetically disposed to behave similarly. To this, van Inwagen replies that "it is possible to construct models of the Fall according to which its hereditary aspect is due to the effects of unaltered genes operating under conditions for which they were not 'designed'—namely, conditions attendant upon separation from God." Unfortunately, he leaves this tantalizing suggestion undeveloped.[72]

---

[70] Van Inwagen, "The Magnitude, Duration, and Distribution of Evil," 119. See also van Inwagen, *The Problem of Evil*, 118–19 and the rest of Lecture 7.

[71] Van Inwagen, *The Problem of Evil*, 119.

[72] Frances and Daniel Howard-Snyder, "Review of *God, Knowledge and Mystery: Essays in Philosophical Theology*, by Peter van Inwagen," in *Faith and Philosophy* 16 (1999), 128. The quotation from van Inwagen is from "The Magnitude, Duration, and Distribution of Evil," 100.

In *The Problem of Evil*, van Inwagen explains that "[t]he inherited genes that produced these baleful effects had been harmless as long as human beings had still had constantly before their minds a representation of perfect love in the Beatific Vision."[73] It seems the genetic inheritance van Inwagen has in mind is simply our animal heredity unaltered by the fall. But if that is all that van Inwagen means by saying that the consequences of the fall were hereditary, then he has said little more than that God chose not only to remove the Beatific Vision from those who willfully rejected him but to deny it to all of their descendants as well. This does more to raise questions of divine fairness and love than to provide further resources for theodicy.

There are significant plausibility problems with (2). But even if we granted van Inwagen that the natural state of human beings in particular or embodied rational beings in general is a radical vulnerability to *horrendous evil*, other plausibility problems abound. For one, the question remains: What is so valuable about living in a *natural* state? Van Inwagen's answer to this is his (3) and (4).

## Plausibility Problems with (3)

As a reminder from last chapter, van Inwagen supports (3) with an analogue of two brothers who quarrel violently and come to hate one another. Their mother then prays to God and asks him to immediately restore the love between her sons. Van Inwagen claims that this immediate restoration would involve at least deleting all memory of what happened just before the quarreling began, and that God would not grant such a request because "as Descartes has pointed out, God is not a deceiver."[74] Analogously, van Inwagen concludes, God would not always miraculously cancel the effects of sin. To do so would be to "engender an illusion with the following propositional content: It is possible for human beings to live apart from God and not be subject to destruction by chance."[75]

I think van Inwagen's (3) is problematic on at least four counts. Firstly, it is implausible that allowing *horrors* is the only way for God to avoid deceiving human persons about their ruined state. Divine resourcefulness must be creative enough and powerful enough to make us understand our ruined state by other means as well. God could have let us live with significantly bad—though not *horrendous*—consequences, for example. He then could have given us detailed seminars on how the human body works and what the full natural consequences of our sin would be if he allowed them. He could have coupled these seminars

[73]  Van Inwagen, *The Problem of Evil*, 86–7.
[74]  Van Inwagen, "The Magnitude, Duration, and Distribution of Evil," 108.
[75]  Van Inwagen, "The Magnitude, Duration, and Distribution of Evil," 117–18. See also 108.

with the most vivid of dreams showing us what it would be like to live with these natural consequences.

Writing in a different context, van Inwagen makes a similar suggestion:

> It is not at all evident that an omnipotent creator would need to allow people to experience *any* pain or grief or sorrow or adversity or illness to enable them to appreciate the good things in life. An omnipotent being would certainly be able to provide the knowledge of evil that human beings in fact acquire by bitter experience of real events in some other way. An omnipotent being could, for example, so arrange matters that at a certain point in each person's life—for a few years during his adolescence, say—that person have very vivid and absolutely convincing *nightmares* in which he is a prisoner in a concentration camp or dies of some horrible disease or watches his loved ones being raped by soldiers bent on ethnic cleansing…The general point this example is intended to illustrate is simply that the resources of an omnipotent being are unlimited—or are limited only by what is intrinsically possible—and that a defense must take account of these unlimited resources.[76]

Van Inwagen neglects his own suggestion when he claims that the *horrendous* experience of "real events" is necessary in order for God to be honest with human persons about their postlapsarian state.

Moreover, the problems with this claim are compounded by van Inwagen's account of the antelapsarian human condition. In this condition, God supernaturally guarded human persons from their *horror*-prone natural state "by endowing [them] with the power never to be in the wrong place at the wrong time, a power [they] lost when [they] ruined [them]selves by turning away from [God]."[77] Either this aboriginal state was itself deceptive, or else in that aboriginal state God had some non-deceptive means other than the actual experience of *horrendous evils* of making us aware that our natural state is *horror*-prone. If the former, van Inwagen is already committed to divine deception. If the latter, why wouldn't God use this same means of communication in our postlapsarian state?

In sum, through various forms of possible divine communication, God could make us appreciate the natural consequences of our sin without subjecting us to *horrors*. This is precisely what the mother should do in van Inwagen's example. She should impress upon her children the natural consequences of their quarrelling, but she should also try to prevent and minimize those consequences. All the more so where *horrors* are involved.

A second problem with (3) arises because van Inwagen is insensitive to an ethically significant distinction between giving someone reason to believe a

---

[76] Van Inwagen, *The Problem of Evil*, 69–70.
[77] Van Inwagen, "The Magnitude, Duration, and Distribution of Evil," 119.

falsehood and deceiving someone. Motive is relevant to deceit. If a lawyer walks into a brothel where one of his clients was previously abused in order to ask questions or drop off legal documents, he may give bystanders reason to think that he is a customer of the brothel. But it would be very odd, given his motive, to say that he deceived these bystanders, and it would be odder still to *accuse* him of deception. The same is true in the God case. If God curbs the *horrendous* consequences of our sin not in order to mislead us but with the good motive of looking out for our welfare, it seems natural to say he has not been deceptive.

Thirdly, even if van Inwagen were correct that canceling the natural consequences of our sin would be deceptive, isn't the avoidance of *horrors* worth—mightn't it even obligate!—the deception? If we build *horrors* into van Inwagen's example of the mother and her quarreling children, deceive is precisely what the mother should do. The mother being held with her child in a concentration camp is to be praised, not blamed, for her efforts to shield her child from the *horrendous* realities of their situation. Frances and Daniel Howard-Snyder agree when they ask us to

[t]hink of the matter this way: suppose that unbeknownst to us, God would prevent an all-out global nuclear war, even if a natural consequence of our fallen condition were an inability to do it. Should we accuse him of wrongful deception? No. We should fall to our knees and thank Him for His great kindness.[78]

Fourthly, van Inwagen himself says that if God did not step in miraculously often, the evil of our world would be much worse than it is. So if God already "deceives" (i.e., shields us from the natural consequences of our sin) to some extent, why would his shielding us from *horrors* be particularly problematic? We have already seen van Inwagen's response: God has to allow *much* of the natural consequences of our sin in order not to be a deceiver and, due to issues of vagueness, there is no precise amount of evil where God ought to draw the line. We therefore cannot fault him just as we cannot fault the government for imposing illegal-parking fines of $25.00 when $24.99 would have been just as effective.

But in this response, van Inwagen fails to make another ethically significant distinction, this time between *horrendous* and non-*horrendous evil*. What van Inwagen's considerations of vagueness show—if correct—is that we cannot fault God for allowing this or that particular evil, so long as roughly the amount and type of evil we have is justified. But what van Inwagen does not recognize is that where *horrors* are caused or permitted for life-enhancing pure benefit, the *type* of evil is not justified. Van Inwagen pleads that God has to stop somewhere, but he fails to see that the unique justificatory demands of *horrendous evils* make them an especially good place to stop.

I think this same concern about the justificatory asymmetry between *horrendous* and non-*horrendous evil* is what motivates the Howard-Snyders to use the example of genocide when responding to van Inwagen's reasoning. They object that

> even if, for the reasons mentioned, God must permit most of the natural conse-quences of our fallenness and hence a great deal of suffering, we cannot see why God must permit so much rather than a lot less. What would count as *a lot* less? Well, a world without genocide would do.[79]

Of the approaches to theodicy I have considered, only van Inwagen's (3) sug-gests a structure where God is morally obliged to permit *horrendous evils*. He risks them in setting up the system that he does, but when he sees them coming, his hands are tied. His divine nature as a non-deceiver necessitates that he not inter-vene to stop them. With (3) undercut, I am inclined to think any plausible risk theodicy is undercut. I have been unable to think of any other plausible reasons why God's hands would be tied.[80] God knows too much and has too much power to ever just be risking *horrendous evils*. He must at least be permitting them.

## Plausibility Problems with (4a) and (4b)

Even if (3) were plausible, van Inwagen would need either (4a) or (4b) to be plaus-ible in order for his theodicy to be plausible. Without (3), van Inwagen needs (4a). But both (4a) and (4b) rely on the assumption that living in a *horror*-prone world is the only motivationally plausible option for persuading human persons to return to and remain with God.

We have seen that in support of (4), van Inwagen claims, firstly, that to remove the suffering of this world would be to remove "the only motivation fallen human beings have for turning to [God],"[81] and secondly that the memory of how bad it is to live apart from God will ensure as perhaps nothing else could that those in heaven will remain freely united to God.[82]

---

[79] Howard-Snyder and Howard-Snyder, *"Review of God, Knowledge and Mystery,"* 129.

[80] One might surmise, in an Augustinian fashion, that because God is essentially just, he is morally bound to punish those who sin and refuse to opt into his plan of atonement. But to raise two initial objections to this possibility, I find it plausible that some *horrendous evils* are too cruel and degrading to ever be morally permissible punishments, and even if they could act as just punishments for sin, I see no reason to think that they alone could play this role.

[81] Van Inwagen, "The Magnitude, Duration, and Distribution of Evil," 113.

[82] Van Inwagen, "The Magnitude, Duration, and Distribution of Evil," 112.

Once again, I think divine resourcefulness has not been given its due. A *vision* of hell was enough to motivate Teresa of Avila to turn to God. I'm inclined to think the same would be the case for many of us. Reframing events come in many different forms—from the death of a loved one, to sunrise atop Mount Kilimanjaro, to the birth of a child, to the marriage of dear friends—and they cause us to brush into the sacred in ways that convince us the world is not limited to the frame we thought it was. Priorities shift; we realize what is most important in life and turn in a new direction.

If reconciliation is the goal, *horrendous evil* is not the only motivationally plausible option. *Horrendous evil* is not the only motivationally plausible option even in non-divine analogues. In van Inwagen's example of mother and quarreling children, seeing their mother weep with sorrow at their estrangement or being reminded of a happy memory that they share is as likely as a threat of punishment to motivate the children to reconcile. Still more so must various expressions of *divine* love be enough to motivate us to return to God and to stay united to him apart from our living in misery.[83] Van Inwagen seems incorrect that the *horrendous* natural consequences of our sin are the "only" motivation we could have to return to God, regardless of whether that returning is conceived of as purely beneficial or as harm averting.

The plausibility problems with van Inwagen's theodicy are substantial. Van Inwagen's own standard of success for his response to the problem of evil is that it be a "very real possibility,"[84] one that will elicit the following reaction from his audience: "Given that God exists, the rest of the story might well be true. I can't see any reason to rule it out."[85] I believe the reasons I have given here are sufficient to show that such a reaction would be unjustified.

## Eleonore Stump's Type D Theodicy: *Very* Tough Love

Even if we read van Inwagen's (4) as (4a), van Inwagen's theodicy does not commit him to belief in a traditional form of hell. It is consistent with his approach that the hideousness of our current state of separation from God (and the growing hideousness of this state correlated with its duration) is the harm that *horror* allowance seeks to avert.

---

[83] Moreover, it is not even clear that threats of previously experienced misery are particularly effective deterrents where something as natural to us as sin is concerned. Former drug addicts can remember how horrible it was to detox, and yet it is often easy for them to slip back into drug use.

[84] Van Inwagen, *The Problem of Evil*, 66.

[85] Van Inwagen, *The Problem of Evil*, 66. Van Inwagen makes a similar claim later in the same work: "I contend that, in the present state of human knowledge, we could have no reason for thinking that the story was false unless we had some reason—a reason other than the existence of evil—for thinking that there was no God" (Van Inwagen, *The Problem of Evil*, 90).

Now, you might think this world is not bad enough to justify the harm-averting tactics. By putting a traditional doctrine of hell to work in her theodicy, Eleonore Stump suggests a harm bad enough to enhance the *structural promise* of her harm-averting approach. She suggests that God permits the *horrendous* consequences of human sin because those consequences provide a fitting environment for rescuing fallen human persons from hell, which she describes as "perpetual living death."[86] The *prima facie* ruin of some human lives is permitted in an attempt to avoid the *ultima facie* ruin of human lives.

Central to Stump's theodicy—detailed at greater length in Chapter 4—are the beliefs that "Adam fell, natural evil entered the world as a result of Adam's fall, and after death, depending on their state at the time of their death, either a. human beings go to heaven or b. they go to hell."[87] She claims that "all human beings since Adam's fall have been defective in their free wills," and that "it is not possible for human beings in that condition to go to heaven."[88] Because coercion would negate rather than fix a *free* will, the only way the condition can be fixed, according to Stump, is if a person freely wills for God to fix her will. But God can instigate this process by designing an environment that is "most conducive to bringing about both the initial human willing of help and also the subsequent process of sanctification."[89]

Stump proposes that we live in such an environment, one that makes us dissatisfied with our own evil and desirous of a better state, and she claims that this may be "the only effective means"[90] of motivating human persons to freely ask God to rescue them from hell. As evidence for this claim, Stump notes that it is among the oppressed that Christianity has flourished most.[91]

To the charge that God's rescue operation is a failure because so many people die without turning to God, Stump claims that "it is not incompatible with Christian doctrine to speculate that in the process of their dying...God offers them a last chance to choose."[92] It may be, therefore, that many avert hell due to near-death conversions.

## Plausibility Problems

I have discussed how modern science and to some extent theological tradition raise concerns about Stump's claims that human persons were once in a superior moral state and that natural evil entered the world as a result of the sin of the first

---

[86] Stump, "The Problem of Evil," 415.  
[88] Stump, "The Problem of Evil," 406.  
[90] Stump, "The Problem of Evil," 409.  
[92] Stump, "The Problem of Evil," 412.  
[87] Stump, "The Problem of Evil," 398.  
[89] Stump, "The Problem of Evil," 409.  
[91] Stump, "The Problem of Evil," 410.

human persons.[93] Even if these concerns can be abated, Stump's approach suffers from more specific plausibility problems as well.

The first of these problems relates to Stump's use of hell. Stump offers hell as the harm that *horror* allowance seeks to avert. On one level, this is *structurally promising*. Horrors are only *prima facie* life-ruinous whereas hell—understood as "perpetual living death"—is definitively so. But the problem is, once you conceive of a hell more *horrendous* than this-worldly *horrors*, then you have also conceived of a hell *horrendous* enough to call into serious question the goodness of the system creator. (I'll discuss this claim further in the next section of this chapter.)

A second problem with Stump's account is that she echoes van Inwagen's claim that evil is the *only* effective means at God's disposal to motivate people to turn back to him and thereby avert hell. I see no reason to grant this claim greater plausibility in Stump's account than in van Inwagen's. As before, the motivational possibilities of divine love and resourcefulness should get more credit. In human relationships, expressions of love are often as motivationally effective as threats of harm. Even more so must this be the case when the motivating lover is perfect in all respects.

Perhaps Stump is right that God cannot restore us to union with himself by forcing our *free* will to be other than it is. If union with God consists in freely willing to live with him and coercion negates freedom, then coercion could not fix the problem. But I see no reason to think that motivating expressions of love must be any more coercive than threats of harm. If anything, the threat of harm seems more inclined to produce coercion. Loaded guns tend to be coercive in a way that gift-wrapped roses are not, and roses tend to contribute to meaningful personal unions in a way that guns do not. Given the motivational power of expressions of love and the resourcefulness of omnipotence (a resourcefulness so great on Stump's view that God can make every instance of (non-voluntary and undeserved) actual suffering primarily to the sufferer's benefit), there is good reason to deny that God would ever need to resort to the use of *horrendous evil* to get people to freely will to be united with him. If this denial is correct, then a divine policy of motivation through suffering is an alarming form of very tough love.

Thirdly, leaving alone the thought that *horrendous evil* is God's *only* effective means to motivate us, I doubt it is an effective means at all. Even if Stump is correct that Christianity has tended to flourish among the oppressed (a controversial claim in itself),[94] has it tended to flourish among *horror* sufferers in particular? This is the more relevant question to ask when evaluating her theodicy, especially

---

[93] Stump, "The Problem of Evil." 403–4. As one example of what this moral change might have looked like, Stump cites the Thomistic theory whereby "[t]he original inclination of the will to will the good proposed by reason has been lost and replaced by an inclination to will what is sought as good by the appetites" (404).

[94] In England, for instance, both historically and at present, there has been a great deal of lower-class alienation from Christianity.

given her caveat that any suffering must benefit the one who suffers it,[95] and it is a much more difficult question to answer affirmatively.

Van Inwagen and Stump—like Hick before them—assume that people tend to benefit psychologically from *horrors*. I find this assumption highly dubious. For those who turn to God as a result of *horrendous* suffering, there are many others who either come to hate God or have their agency so utterly debilitated that they are not even capable of willing God's help. As David Lewis reflects,

> An omnipotent God could be expected to convert resisters by other means—displays of magnificence, for example. If it is suggested that these are not guaranteed to do the trick, that the resistance may persist, then it should also be noted that, under the conditions of incompatibilist freedom, punishment also comes without any guarantee of repentance. Why should sticks work better than carrots?[96]

It is not plausible to think that *horrors* tend to act as catalysts for right willing.[97]

For Stump, the way to maximize the chance that we will freely avoid the worst evil is to permit *horrendous evil*. I have claimed that reflection on human behavior and psychology gives strong reason to think that for an all-loving and all-powerful God, there must be a better way. Perhaps the reason Stump disagrees is because she chooses not to reflect philosophically on the realities of the most *horrendous evils*. With respect to an evil as *horrendous* as the Holocaust, Stump suggests that "since we are all members of the species which perpetrated that evil, since we are in some sense siblings of the evil doers, perhaps the only seemly response is one like Job's (cf. Job 40:4–5 and 42:2–3): silence in the face of something beyond our capacities to understand, in recognition of our unworthiness to judge."[98] As for trying to account for an evil of this sort within her approach to theodicy, she says, "I do not even want to try."[99]

I sympathize with Stump's concern; such evils are unspeakable in the sense that we cannot come even close to giving them an adequate description, and there certainly are indecent ways of talking about them. But I am also concerned that

---

[95] As noted in Chapter 4, Stump makes the particularist claim that a good God "must govern the evil resulting from the misuse of that significant freedom in such a way that the sufferings of any particular person are outweighed by the good which the suffering produces *for that person*; otherwise, we might justifiably expect a good God somehow to prevent that *particular suffering*" (Stump, "The Problem of Evil," 411).

[96] David Lewis (published posthumously with Philip Kitcher), "Divine Evil," in *Philosophers Without Gods: Meditations on Atheism and the Secular Life*, ed. Louis M. Antony (Oxford: Oxford University Press, 2007), 235.

[97] Simone Weil endorses the same point in her own terminology when she writes that "affliction is not suffering. Affliction is something quite distinct from a divine educational method" (Weil, "The Love of God and Affliction," 181).

[98] Stump, "Suffering for Redemption: A Reply to Smith," 434.

[99] Stump, "Suffering for Redemption: A Reply to Smith," 435.

systematically avoiding philosophical reflection on the ethical distinctiveness of the very worst evils leads to the at best implausible and at worst highly offensive belief that *horror* participation is psychologically beneficial.

Fourthly, as for deathbed conversions, it is an enormous argumentative leap from "not incompatible to speculate" to "plausibility."[100] Compatibility may be enough for a logical *defense* in the Plantingean sense, but it is not enough for the "successful solution to the problem of evil"[101] that Stump explicitly aims for in "The Problem of Evil." If what motivates these deathbed conversions is the evil of this world, then shouldn't we see more of them? If it is something other than the evil of this world that motivates the near-death conversions, then why does God need this-worldly evil as well? These and other questions would require addressing before the plausibility of Stump's final speculation could be adequately assessed.

## Can High Fall Theodicies Maintain Their Claim to *Structural Promise*?

Even if the theodicies of van Inwagen and Stump are *structurally promising*, their plausibility faces serious challenges. I now question whether High Fall Theodicies such as these could maintain their *structural promise* even if they were otherwise plausible.

In Chapter 4, I argued that a high fall approach to theodicy is promising with respect to the ethical framework I have constructed. That framework is constructed out of two primary variables: whether *horrendous evils* are caused, permitted, or risked, and whether they are done so for pure benefit or for the aversion of greater harm. However, useful as this structure is, it does not exhaust the ethically relevant structural variables.

I now argue that High Fall Theodicies are structurally vulnerable on grounds other than those highlighted by my taxonomy. Harm aversion may be sufficient to justify God's allowance of evils *given the justification of some system where there is greater harm to be averted*. But if God is responsible for the system itself, then the *structural* question remains: Would a perfectly good God create the harm-threatening systems that harm-averting theodicies rely on?

The use of harm aversion makes High Fall Theodicy more plausible on one level because it allows for the justification of some suffering as harm-preventing, and, generally, harm prevention has significantly greater justificatory power than improvement of an already good situation. But on a more fundamental level, the divine creation and sustenance of a system that includes the potential for harm so

---

bad that even *horrendous* earthly suffering is harm-preventing brings with it its own problems. That the amputation of a patient's leg prevents greater harm overall may justify a doctor in performing the procedure, but it will not justify anything he did to contribute to his patient being in need of an amputation in the first place. Likewise, any subsequent policies of harm prevention will not justify (on their own) the divine production of a hell-prone system in which harm prevention is required. God didn't have to create the *horror*-prone system he created; he didn't have to create at all. On Augustinian assumptions about a high fall, did God take a justifiable risk in setting up the system he did?

## Cognitive Limitations Limit Moral Responsibility

In response to this objection, Stump concedes that her *defense* is committed to the claim that "the human propensity to moral wrongdoing is not the fault of an omnipotent, omniscient, perfectly good God."[102] Her thought seems to be that because on Aquinas's view God is goodness itself,[103] morally wrong choices are also choices against God. And because hell just is being in the state of resisting God, clearing God of responsibility for human moral wrongdoing will go at least some significant way toward clearing him of responsibility for the existence of hell. But Stump then leaves believers in a perfect God to generate their own explanation for the human propensity to moral wrongdoing, and she assumes that "whatever explanation [is given]…it will not assign responsibility for this propensity to God."[104]

I find it difficult to think of an explanation that will meet this condition of exempting God from responsibility. The best shot is perhaps to deploy a causing/permitting distinction whereby an agent is responsible for the things she does in a way she is not responsible for those states of affairs she merely permits or allows. Stump affirms the significance of this distinction in several places[105] and makes use of it in the one explanation for the human propensity to moral wrongdoing that she does offer—that of original sin resulting from the fall of the first human persons.[106] On this scenario, creatures (human persons and perhaps angels before them) rather than God are supposed responsible for the human propensity to sin: "[E]vil is first introduced into a good world created by a good God through the misuse of free will on the part of the creatures created good by God."[107] Blame for *horrors* is shifted off of God and onto new intervening agents.

[102] Stump, *Wandering in Darkness*, 377.    [103] Stump, *Wandering in Darkness*, 164.
[104] Stump, *Wandering in Darkness*, 153.
[105] See Stump, *Wandering in Darkness*, 208, 385, and 393.
[106] Stump, *Wandering in Darkness*, 153.    [107] Stump, *Wandering in Darkness*, 385.

144 NON-IDENTITY THEODICY

Marilyn Adams challenges this approach by arguing that human persons could not be fully responsible for *horrors*. In summarizing her view, Adams writes that

> the *necessary* disproportion between human agency and horrendous evils makes it impossible for humans to bear full responsibility for their occurrence. For we cannot bear full responsibility for something to the extent that—through no fault of our own—"we know not what we do." But (as noted above) where horrendous suffering is concerned, our ability to produce it radically and inevitably exceeds our ability to experience and thus adequately to conceive how really bad it is. It follows that we cannot be fully responsible for those dimensions of horrendous evil that are inevitably inadequately conceivable by us. Insofar as culpability is directly proportional to responsibility, we cannot be fully to blame either.[108]

One might object; even if Adams is correct that incorrigible "ignorance diminishes the voluntary,"[109] human persons who have suffered *horrors* are not ignorant of them. If *horror*-sufferers can conceive of the consequences of *horrors*, perhaps they can be fully responsible for them.

There are several reasons to doubt this conclusion. Firstly, due to the agency wrecking effects of *horrors*, even those who have experienced *horrors* cannot fully conceive of their consequences. Quite to the contrary, those who have experienced *horrors* are often particularly incapable of conceiving of their consequences. This is because, as Weil recognizes, *horrendous evils* have

> the power to seize the very souls of the innocent and to possess them as sovereign master. At the very best, he who is branded by affliction will only keep half his soul. As for those who have been struck the kind of blow which leaves the victim writhing on the ground like a half-crushed worm, they have no words to describe what is happening to them.[110]

Weil gives reason to think that conceiving of *horrendous evils* is impossible for human persons. We can't conceive of the experience of suffering *horrors* outside of that experience. But equally, in the experience of suffering *horrors*, our conceptual frameworks are exploded. Weil's conclusion: "The knowledge of affliction

---

[108] Adams, *Horrendous Evils and the Goodness of God*, 38. Simone Weil comments that "those who have never had contact with affliction in its true sense can have no idea what it is, even though they may have known much suffering" (172).

[109] Adams, *Christ and Horrors*, 229.

[110] Weil, "The Love of God and Affliction," 172. Weil's category of affliction is importantly different from Adams's category of the *horrendous*, but not in ways that affect the use I am making of Weil here.

[is] by nature impossible both to those who have experienced it and to those who have not."[111]

Secondly, even if prior experience of *horrors* were sufficient for bearing full moral responsibility for producing *horrors*, anyone who has already suffered *horrors* will come too late in the explanatory story to bear responsibility for why there are *horrors* in the first place. *Ex hypothesi*, the Adam and Eve of High Fall Theodicy haven't suffered *horrors* in their antelapsarian state; they are postulated in order to explain *horror* origination.

Finally, even if souped-up antelapsarian human persons had psychic capacities capable of conceiving of *some horrendous* suffering, I doubt they would be capable of conceiving of *all horrors*. Where suffering is concerned, capacity to conceive follows capacity to experience. For this reason, Adams is correct in noting that "Pol Pot's psychic capacity was not large enough to suffer each and all of the tortures he inflicted on millions."[112] I doubt that anything recognizably human could have a psychic capacity large enough to suffer each and all of the *horrors* resulting from a high fall.

The first human persons are not plausible candidates for bearing full responsibility for *horrors* because the badness of *horrors* inevitably outstrips human conceptual capacities. On evolutionary assumptions, the first human persons would have been intellectually infantile, having only the dimmest ability to appreciate the future consequences of their sin. On high fall assumptions, they would have had "no experience at all of evil or suffering."[113] Either way, they likely lacked the conceptual ability necessary for bearing full responsibility for all ensuing *horrors*.

Would it be more plausible to posit an angelic fall in order to shift blame for *horrors* onto angels rather than onto human persons? We don't know much about angelic nature, but there could be some very remarkable beings that God has the power to create. Perhaps angels could have conceptual abilities great enough to conceive of all *horrendous* human suffering.[114] Or, if one angel could not, perhaps we could posit the fall of a great host of angels, each capable of conceiving of some instance of *horrendous* suffering for which he is responsible. Against this

---

[111]  Weil, "The Love of God and Affliction," 189.       [112]  Adams, *Christ and Horrors*, 35.
[113]  Adams, *Horrendous Evils and the Goodness of God*, 38.
[114]  It is an interesting question whether even God could have the psychic capacity to be fully responsible for *horrendous evil*. This may depend on whether God has suffered *horrendous evils*, and whether he has done so in a form that allowed him to maintain the highest conceptual sensitivities throughout that suffering. Perhaps certain theories of the incarnation and passion of Jesus Christ lend themselves to making a case in favor of the possibility of full divine responsibility for *horrors*. But even then, Jesus lived only one human life, and it is not clear that even a *divine* human person could experience *horrors* to the extent necessary to be able to conceive of the consequences of all *horrors* throughout history. Perhaps some penal substitution theories of atonement would lend themselves to the thought that the Christian God could be fully responsible for *horrendous evil*. But even if the badness of *horrendous evils* necessarily outstrips responsibility for them, the overall argument of this chapter is unaffected. Due to his superior powers of imagination and prediction, God can be much more responsible for *horrendous evils* than anyone else, and as system-creator he is in fact ultimately responsible for the *horrendous evils* of the actual world.

move are the facts that there is no scientific evidence favoring the existence of angels and that the theological tradition has generally given angels only a modest role in theodicy.[115] But still, perhaps angels could be cognitively better-placed than the first human persons to take responsibility for *horrors*.

However, even bracketing concerns about cognitive limitations, attempts to shift responsibility—whether to human or angelic agents—falter for the following additional reason: Responsibility need not be either/or. The addition of new intervening responsible agents does not necessarily diminish the responsibility of any other agents. Specifically, it does not follow from upping the blame of proximate causes that the ultimate cause is less responsible. This can be the case, for example, when a politician encourages his staff to do something illegal or when a murderer bribes or otherwise manipulates a new intervening agent to carry out his crime. As discussed in Chapter 4, both traditional views about divine agency—occasionalism and concurrentism—understand divine actions to be so interwoven with human actions as to give God ultimate authority in all matters. For responsibility for *horrors* to be shifted off of God, it's not enough to posit additional agents who are culpable for all *horrors*. It also has to be the case that God, in his position of authority, has not acted wrongly by setting up and continuing the system that allows for them. This gives additional reason to doubt that a causing/permitting distinction will do significant responsibility-diminishing work when God is the agent in question.

## From Responsibility to Blame

Even if a high fall resulting in either human or angelic persons being significantly to blame for *horrendous evils* were otherwise plausible, there are good reasons to doubt that creating a system with high fall potential would be a morally permissible risk for God to take. The usual justification given for the creation of the system is that God values human responsibility and respects our free choices to use it for better or for worse. Indeed, being given responsibility over the well-being of others can be a very good thing. When someone gives responsibility to you, they honor you by putting their trust in you and they give you opportunities to be of use and to achieve valuable ends.

But would a good God value these pure benefits so greatly that he would let the introduction of all *horrendous evil* hang on a single creaturely choice? Adams reminds us that the "most causally salient features of human nature and the environment lie outside the creature's control and are produced by God instead."[116] Even if a high fall were otherwise plausible, its structure is one where the sin of

---

[115] For a discussion of this point, see Swinburne, *Providence and the Problem of Evil*, 107–8.
[116] Adams, *Horrendous Evils and the Goodness of God*, 39.

one person ramifies into *horrors* for millions or more, and what causes this ramification is the frame God produced.

I register my agreement with Richard Swinburne and Marilyn Adams that while human responsibility is a good thing, it cannot suffice as the primary justification for creating a system where whether billions of subsequent humans will suffer *horrendously* is based on a single choice of a single human person—even a preternaturally empowered one.[117] Adams helpfully encapsulates the point:

> Classical free fall approaches make human agency so robust as to stand between God and evil; the dignity of human nature and its self-determining action are taken to be so great as to outweigh or defeat any evil side-effects or means. In my judgment, these estimates should not survive sober consideration of human entrenchment in horrors.[118]

Moreover, though angels may fare better as blame-shifting intervening agents in terms of their conceptual capabilities, they fare worse here because, plausibly, it is more suspect to give responsibility over the suffering of others to those who are not in significant forms of relationship with those who will suffer. Human persons have meaningful social relationships that require us being able to act against one another's desires, but human persons do not tend to have relationships at all with angels.

Admittedly, it is a reasonable, if controversial, belief that it can be good for human persons to govern the suffering of lower animals even when we are not in significant social relationships with them, and despite the fact that we often cause them serious and unnecessary suffering. But *horrors* change things. It would be worse for my actions to risk *horrors* in the lives of some extraterrestrial persons I have never had any contact with than in the lives of those with whom I am in meaningful social relationships of mutual dependence. Similarly, granting responsibility over all *horrors* throughout human history to angels seems even more dubious than granting it to the first generation of human persons.

And, relatedly, why wouldn't God revoke this angelic power once he sees where it is headed? A good manager is not just going to give unmonitored reign, and all the more so when important social frameworks are not involved. Human persons exist in social frameworks that depend on policies of responsibility being sustained. Even if a mother is not treating her child well, it is often as bad for the child to be separated from his mother's rule as to continue in it. Our meaning-making systems are caught up in the responsibility we have over one another. But apart from relationships of mutuality, this is not as clearly the case. It may be good for a farmer to entrust care of the chickens to a child, but if the kid is

[117] See Swinburne, *Providence and the Problem of Evil*, 110.
[118] Adams, *Horrendous Evils and the Goodness of God*, 36.

wringing the chickens' necks day after day, it's time to step in and revoke his authority. Likewise, if responsibility for this world has been devolved to angelic beings, haven't they messed us up to the point that a good and loving God would step in?

All of this suggests that much responsibility must remain with the system creator. If we reject Augustinian original righteousness in favor of an evolutionary understanding of the first human persons, then an attempt to shift responsibility will be challenged by what Adams refers to as

> *The Stove Analogy:* Suppose a parent introduces a three-year-old into a room which contains gas that is not harmful to breathe but will explode if ignited and also contains a stove with brightly colored nobs which if turned will light the burners and ignite the gas. Suppose further that the parent warns the child not to turn the nobs and then leaves the room. If the child turns the nobs and ignites the gas, blowing up the room, surely the child is at most marginally to blame, even though it knew enough to obey the parent, while the parent is both primarily responsible and highly culpable.[119]

If we instead carve out a middle ground according to which the first human persons were what we would typically think of as competent human adults—neither the feeble creatures of evolutionary theory nor the supernatural beings of original righteousness—then attempts to shift blame will have to deal with what Adams names

> *The Terrorist Analogy:* Suppose a terrorist announces his intention to kill one hundred citizens if anyone in a certain village wears a red shirt on Tuesday. The village takes the threat seriously, and everyone is well informed. If some adult citizen slips up and wears his favorite red shirt on Tuesday, he will be responsible and culpable, indeed seriously so. But the terrorist, who set up the situation, will be far more responsible and culpable.[120]

Finally, even if we accept Augustinian original righteousness, the structural lack of integrity of a blame-shifting approach will be exposed by what could be termed

---

[119] Adams, *Horrendous Evils and the Goodness of God*, 39. In a similar passage, Pierre Bayle considers a mother who consents to her daughter attending a ball without a chaperone. If the daughter is seduced at the ball, the mother may be excused if she had reason to think her daughter was strong enough to resist the seduction, but not if the daughter was inexperienced and her seduction was no surprise. This analogy by Bayle is discussed in Thomas M. Lennon and Michael Hickson, "Pierre Bayle," in *The Stanford Encyclopedia of Philosophy* (Spring 2009 Edition), 23 Aug 2011, http://plato.stanford.edu/entries/bayle/.

[120] Adams, *Horrendous Evils and the Goodness of God*, 39.

*The Superhero Analogy:* Suppose a terrorist announces his intention to kill one hundred citizens if Superman wears a red shirt on Tuesday. Superman takes the threat seriously, is well informed, and is preeminently likely not to slip up. If Superman has a super bad day and wears his favorite red shirt on Tuesday, he will be gravely responsible and highly culpable. But the terrorist, who set up the situation, will still be far more responsible and culpable.

Adams has articulated the ironic result for fall approaches to theodicy: "Turning the appeal to *novus agens interveniens* on its head, there is another, fully competent and independent agent whose actions in setting up the world 'intervene' between created free choices and their *horrendous* consequences. And this agent is none other than God!"[121] High fall approaches depict God worryingly similar to the parent who threatens *horrendous* abuse if his children behave badly, and then follows through on his threat.

I began this chapter by discussing plausibility vulnerabilities of high fall theory grounded in modern science and theological tradition. I next called attention to more specific plausibility vulnerabilities in the High Fall Theodicies of van Inwagen and Stump. I have now suggested that High Fall Theodicies are structurally problematic as well. Cases C and D rely for their *structural promise* on the fact that the parents' decisions are made within a system that they are not responsible for. But High Fall Theodicies are disanalogous in this crucial respect. These theodicies depict God as merely risking or permitting *horrors* in order to attempt to shift blame for them, but they are vulnerable because of what they must admit God has *caused*—the system itself.

## The Evolutionary Problem of Evil

That a high fall is incapable of absolving God from the charges brought forward by the problem of *horrendous evil* does not make it unhistorical. However, for those who reject a high fall and even for some who accept a high fall but deny that it originated natural evil, theodicy must find an alternative explanation for animal suffering, including many prehistoric years of (what has been termed) evolutionary evil.

Non-human animals certainly experience acute pain, and studies show physiological evidence of distress in some hunted animals.[122] Non-human animals suffer, especially ones with complex brains processing information from pain-detection systems. Without a very high fall, human persons can't originate this suffering.

---

[121] Adams, *Horrendous Evils and the Goodness of God*, 39.
[122] See Southgate, *The Groaning of Creation*, 4.

Indeed, on evolutionary assumptions, it's precisely by this suffering that human persons have come to exist.

Charles Darwin was aware of this evolutionary challenge to theism when he wrote to J. D. Hooker, "What a book a devil's chaplain might write on the clumsy, wasteful, blundering, low and horridly cruel works of nature!"[123] If God exists, has he allowed millions of years of animal suffering that is seemingly unrelated to human free will and human well-being? And moreover—in seemingly sharpest contrast to the biblical exaltation of laying down one's life for one's friends[124]—if God exists, has he set up a system where progress occurs through natural selection, through the merciless self-preservation of the strong at the expense of the weak?

Earlier I considered a variety of arguments both against and in favor of a high fall. But irrespective of your judgment on that matter, a theodicy will be in a stronger position if it can defend the goodness of God—and to the point at hand offer a plausible explanation for animal suffering—without relying on the veracity of a high fall. In the next three chapters, I suggest that Non-Identity Theodicy is uniquely positioned to meet this challenge.

## Conclusions of Part I

Conjoining the results of the last few chapters, the problem of *horrendous evils* appears intractable. It both demands and problematizes shifting responsibility for evil off of God. Things don't look good for theodicy:

- Theodicy Types A and B (according to which God causes or permits *horrors* for pure benefit) are *structurally unpromising*.

- Theodicy Types B, C, and D (according to which God permits *horrors* for pure benefit, risks *horrors* for pure benefit, and permits *horrors* in order to avert greater harm, respectively) tend to rely on a high fall. Resultingly, they face a variety of plausibility challenges motivated by modern science and theological tradition, and they are sub-structurally problematic (due to the fact that God set up the *horror*-prone system). Additionally, there are considerable plausibility

---

[123] Southgate, *The Groaning of Creation*, 1. It is also this challenge that Darwin seemed to have in mind when he wrote to the American naturalist Asa Gray (May 22, 1860), "I cannot persuade myself that a beneficent and omnipotent God would have designedly created the Ichneumonidae with the express intention of their feeding within the living bodies of Caterpillars"; quoted in Southgate, *The Groaning of Creation*, 10. However, this quote is less to the point given the fact that it is not clear that caterpillars suffer. Quentin Smith explores thoughts similar to Darwin's in "An Atheological Argument from Evil Natural Laws," *International Journal for Philosophy of Religion* 29 (1991): 159–74.

[124] John 15:13.

problems particular to each of the most influential contemporary philosophical attempts at theodicy of these types.

• If a high fall is rejected as an explanation for the origination of natural evil, then the theodicist will need to propose an alternative response to (so called) evolutionary problems of evil. In particular, for a theodicy to be fully successful, it will need to offer a plausible justification for animal suffering, including any pre-human animal suffering.

# PART II
# BEYOND THE FRAMEWORK

Part I argued that the most commonly cited theodicies are in trouble. Those that rely on justification by pure benefits are *structurally unpromising*, and those that rely on justification by harm aversion are both implausible and sub-structurally problematic. In Part II, I develop and defend a theodicy that seeks justification for evil allowance neither in pure benefits nor in harm aversion, but rather in the good of worthwhile human lives lived by people who otherwise would not have existed.

It is controversial whether being made to exist can come to one as a benefit. On my account of benefit, it cannot. This is because it does not make someone better-off than they were temporally or counterfactually; prior to and without being brought into existence, there is no one to be made better-off.

Perhaps my account of benefit should be amended so that coming to exist with a worthwhile life counts as a benefit. I am sympathetic to this suggestion, though I won't follow it in this project. I prefer to refer to coming to exist with a worthwhile life more broadly as a non-harm-averting good in order to emphasize its distinctiveness from typical pure benefits.

Whether you classify coming to exist with a worthwhile life as a benefit or not, what's important for my project is the less controversial claim that it can be a good for the one who comes to exist. It is a good for him because he is made the subject of a good state of affairs (even if not of a better state of affairs). As such, it reasonably can be taken to be a candidate-good for harm justification.

Since Derek Parfit's *Reasons and Persons*, there has been a growing literature in the ethics of procreation and in intergenerational ethics reflecting on the following question: Does it matter morally whether or not the people harmed or benefited by an action would have existed had that action not been performed? Parfit terms cases where the affected people are not identical with anyone who would have existed otherwise cases of *non-identity*.[1]

---

[1] Early discussions of this question were also published by Robert Merrihew Adams (see n. 5, this section), Thomas Schwartz ("Obligations to Posterity," in *Obligations to Future Generations*, ed. R. I. Sikora and Brian Barry (Philadelphia: Temple University Press, 1978)), and Gregory Kavka ("The Paradox of Future Individuals," *Philosophy and Public Affairs* 11.2 (1982): 93–112). There have been many important publications focused on this question since the publication of *Reasons and Persons*.

Non-identity considerations also feature in the literature on "moral luck," in particular with respect to what Thomas Nagel and Bernard Williams call "constitutive luck"—broadly, luck in who one is.[2] Nicholas Rescher, for instance, writes that

> a person can be fortunate to have a good disposition or a talent for mathematics, but she cannot be *lucky* in these regards, because chance is not involved. Her disposition and talents are part of what makes her the individual she is; it is not something that chance happens to bring along and superadd to a preexisting identity...It is not as though there were some world-external, fertilization-preceding version of oneself who has the luck to draw a good assignment.[3]

Daniel Statman reasons similarly:

> Suppose somebody says, "Oh, how lucky I am to have such parents!" The natural response to this seems to be, "Well, had you had different parents, you wouldn't have been the same person." That is, luck necessarily presupposes the existence of some subject who is affected by it. Because luck in the very constitution of an agent cannot be luck for anyone, the idea of one being lucky in the kind of person one is sounds incoherent.[4]

Theodicy is also concerned with evaluating actions that determine who will live, but with a couple of exceptions, and one very notable exception in Robert Adams, sustained reflection on non-identity has been absent from contemporary work on the problem of evil.[5]

---

Among them are James Woodward, "The Non-Identity Problem," *Ethics* 96.4 (1986): 804–31; Matthew Hanser, "Harming Future People," *Philosophy and Public Affairs* 19.1 (1990): 47–70; Seana Valentine Shiffrin, "Wrongful Life, Procreative Responsibility, and the Significance of Harm," *Legal Theory* 5 (1999): 117–48; and Elizabeth Harman, "Can We Harm and Benefit in Creating?," *Philosophical Perspectives* 18.1 (2004): 89–113.

[2] See Thomas Nagel, *Mortal Questions* (Cambridge: Cambridge University Press, 1979) and Bernard Williams, *Moral Luck* (Cambridge: Cambridge University Press, 1981).

[3] Nicholas Rescher, *Luck: The Brilliant Randomness of Everyday Life* (New York: Farrar, Straus & Giroux, 1995), 30–1.

[4] Daniel Statman, Introduction to *Moral Luck*, ed. Daniel Statman (Albany: State University of New York Press, 1993), 12.

[5] Robert Merrihew Adams considers the relevance of non-identity considerations to theodicy in "Must God Create the Best?," *The Philosophical Review* 81 (1972): 317–32; "Existence, Self-Interest, and the Problem of Evil," (originally published in *Noûs* in 1979 but reprinted with corrections) in Robert Merrihew Adams, *The Virtue of Faith and Other Essays in Philosophical Theology* (Oxford: Oxford University Press, 1987); and "Love and the Problem of Evil," *Philosophia* 34.3 (2006): 243–51. Tim Mawson also considers the relevance of non-identity considerations to theodicy, in particular to the prospects for theodicy on the assumption that determinism is true, in "The Problem of Evil and Moral Indifference," *Religious Studies* 35.3 (1999): 323–45.

Part II addresses this lack in three chapters. Chapter 6 develops two versions of Non-Identity Theodicy—that is, theodicy that takes as its primary claim the position that our existence as the individuals that we are depends on God's policy of evil allowance—and defends them against objections to their *plausibility* and their depiction of divine *character*. Chapter 7 considers how significant a difference the fact that a case is a non-identity case can make to the *moral* status of harm-inducing actions, and ultimately advocates a favorable overall evaluation of Non-Identity Theodicy. Chapter 8 takes a step back to consider the place of Non-Identity Theodicy in the contemporary theodicy literature and to highlight some of Non-Identity Theodicy's more general recommendations.

# 6

# Non-Identity Theodicy

A number of celebrated Christian theologians—among them Duns Scotus, Karl Barth, and Gottfried Leibniz—have attempted to make sense of the biblical idea that God has chosen human persons individually prior to their conception.[1] In his *Confessio Philosophi*, Leibniz appropriates this idea for theodicy. He considers whether we should be indignant that God did not respond to Adam and Eve's fall by replacing them with better creatures who would not have transmitted sin and its consequent suffering down through the generations. Leibniz answers that

> if God had done that, sin having been taken away, an entirely different series of things, entirely different combinations of circumstances, persons, and marriages, and entirely different persons would have been produced and, consequently, sin having been taken away or extinguished, they themselves would not have existed. They therefore have no reason to be indignant that Adam and Eve sinned and, much less, that God permitted sin to occur, since they must rather credit their own existence to God's tolerance of those very sins.[2]

Leibniz goes on to compare those who hold such indignation with a half-noble son who is "irritated with his father because he had married a woman unequal in rank…not thinking that if his father had married someone else, not he, but some other man, would have come into the world."[3]

This line of thought follows from Leibniz's belief that every possible individual exists in only one possible world.[4] Because any difference in events constitutes a different possible world, it follows that none of us who actually exist could have

---

[1] Verses of the Bible that could be taken to imply this include Jeremiah 1:4–5 ("The word of the LORD came to me, saying, 'Before I formed you in the womb I knew you, before you were born I set you apart; I appointed you as a prophet to the nations.'"), Ephesians 1:4–5 ("For [God] chose us in him before the creation of the world to be holy and blameless in his sight. In love he predestined us to be adopted as his sons through Jesus Christ, in accordance with his pleasure and will."), and Psalm 139:16 ("Your eyes saw my unformed body; all the days ordained for me were written in your book before one of them came to be.").

[2] Gottfried Wilhelm Leibniz, "The Confession of a Philosopher," in *G.W. Leibniz, Confessio philosophi: Papers Concerning the Problem of Evil, 1671–1678*, ed. and trans. Robert C. Sleigh Jr., with contributions from Brandon Look and James Stam (New Haven and London: Yale University Press, 2005), 107.

[3] Leibniz, "The Confession of a Philosopher," 107.

[4] See Adams, "Existence, Self-Interest, and the Problem of Evil," 65.

*Non-Identity Theodicy: A Grace-Based Response to the Problem of Evil.* Vince R. Vitale, Oxford University Press (2020).
© Vince R. Vitale.
DOI: 10.1093/oso/9780198864226.003.0006

existed if anything—including any actual evil—had been in any way different. Otherwise put, God's choice to actualize the actual world is a non-identity case. If we add to these assumptions that we are offered lives that are very worthwhile for us all things considered, then this complicates the question of who, if anyone, God has wronged in actualizing the actual world.

While Robert Adams thinks Leibniz's theory of personal identity is implausible, he also thinks that the Leibniz quotes above are true on more modest and plausible assumptions about personal identity, and that reflection on the fact that we owe both our existence and the content of our lives to great and various evils can take us at least some way toward constructing a successful theodicy.

Adams suggests that evil preceding our existence may be justified because we owe our existence to it and that evil within our lives may be justified because it is the result of an ongoing policy that is good for us on the whole. Further, Adams suggests that reflection on what lives it would be rational for us to wish for can supplement these justifications. Finally, Adams suggests that God is motivated to allow the evil he does in order to create and love a specific community of individual persons, and that this motivation is in keeping with the character of an ethically perfect being.

Adams makes these suggestions across a number of different works published primarily in the 1970s, and he says that his work in this area does not constitute a full theodicy.[5] I am optimistic that Adams's insights can be organized and added to in order to yield a full theodicy, and in the next two chapters I write with this aim.

The Non-Identity Theodicy I will develop can be summarized in three primary claims:

(1) Those who come to exist could not have come to exist without God's policy of evil and suffering allowance.
(2) God offers a great life all things considered to everyone who comes to exist.
(3) God is motivated in creating and sustaining the universe by a desire to love those who come to exist.

---

[5] Richard Gale says (Richard Gale, "R. M. Adams's Theodicy of Grace," *Philo: A Journal of Philosophy* 1 (1998): 36–44) that in "Must God Create the Best?" (1972) Adams puts forth a theodicy, but that is not precise. "Must God Create the Best?" considers whether God could be justified in creating a less than best world; it does not suggest justifying reasons for creating the actual world. Adams comes closer to presenting a theodicy in "Existence, Self-Interest, and the Problem of Evil" (1979), but even there he is explicit in his judgment that non-identity "does not yield a complete theodicy" (66). Likewise, when discussing Adams's work in this area, William Hasker says that "the argument cannot bear the weight of 'positive theodicy'—that is, of the task of explaining *why* evil exists or why it is appropriate that God should allow it to exist" (*Providence, Evil and the Openness of God* (New York: Routledge, 2004), 19).

I clamed in Chapter 1 that a successful theodicy must meet two primary conditions: Firstly, it should show that God has not wronged anyone by allowing evil and suffering, and, secondly, it should show that God's allowance of evil and suffering is motivated by virtue rather than by some flaw in character. Non-Identity Theodicy suggests that these two conditions can be met if (1), (2), and (3) are true.[6]

I will discuss (2) most briefly. While some may not accept the offer, I assume that God offers to every person a life that would be a great good to them all things considered. Among Christians, and theists more generally, there are a variety of views about how and when God makes this offer. The reader can fill in these details concerning condition (2) in a manner that she takes to be consonant with the actions of a perfect being. Additionally, some believe that a perfect God must not only offer but guarantee a great life for every person. The reader who takes this view can amend (2) to read "God ensures a great life all things considered for everyone who comes to exist."

I take it that the plausibility of (2) will depend on or at least be greatly aided by the potential for worthwhile life after death. There are interesting questions about how God can make it the case that a person in the afterlife will be the same person as me. Perhaps all that is necessary for some post-mortem person to be me is that he uniquely seems to remember being me and shares core aspects of my personality and interests. Perhaps, in addition to this, God needs to bring together enough of the physical matter that constituted me at some point in my life in a similar enough arrangement. Perhaps I am an immaterial soul and God only needs to ensure that this immaterial soul exists in the afterlife, or that it is connected to some physical body in the afterlife.

I assume (along with the vast majority of theodicies) that divine omnipotence is capable of meeting the challenge of allowing people who have died on earth to exist eternally, either continuously or through being brought back to life. I accept van Inwagen's contention that at the very least God could do this in the following way: "[A]t the moment of each man's death, God removes his corpse and replaces it with a simulacrum which is what is burned or rots. Or perhaps God is not quite so wholesale as this: perhaps He removes for 'safekeeping' only the 'core person'— the brain and central nervous system—or even some special part of it."[7] Perhaps God could accomplish life after death in other ways as well, but van Inwagen's story is sufficient to show that "resurrection is a feat an almighty God *could*

---

[6] I am not claiming that these three conditions are necessary or sufficient for divine ethical perfection. Perhaps God can be ethically perfect even if each person is offered a merely worthwhile life rather than a great one. Perhaps God could be less than ethically perfect even if he meets these three conditions, for example if he has lied or deceived without justification. Nevertheless, I take it that if these three conditions can be met, the believer in an ethically perfect God will be in a strong position to offer a reasonable explanation for the variety and intensity of evil and suffering that occur in the actual world.

[7] Peter van Inwagen, "The Possibility of Resurrection," *International Journal for Philosophy of Religion* 9.2 (1978), 121.

accomplish."[8] I also assume that the goods present in the afterlife can be great enough and exist for long enough to outweigh even the greatest evils of the present age.

## Evils Preceding Our Existence

(1) is the distinctive claim of Non-Identity Theodicy. Adams argues for (1) in two steps—one for evil preceding our existence and one for evil in our lifetimes. Drawing on Kripkean identity theory,[9] Adams holds that the evil preceding our existence—more or less—is a metaphysically necessary condition of our existence. He writes,

> I do not think it would have been possible, in the metaphysical or broadly logical sense that is relevant here, for me to exist in a world[10] that differed much from the actual world in the evils occurring in the parts of history that contain my roots...My identity is established by my beginning. It has been suggested [by Kripke, according to Adams] that no one who was not produced from the same individual egg and sperm cells as I was could have been me...If so, the identity of those gametes presumably depends in turn on their beginnings and on the identity of my parents, which depends on the identity of the gametes from which they came, and so on.[11]

If our identities are established by our beginnings, Adams takes it that "[a] multiplicity of interacting chances, including evils great and small, affect which people mate, which gametes find each other, and which children come into being."[12]

It does not take much to affect procreation history. Any events that have a significant effect on the movement of matter will, given enough time, have an effect on who comes to exist. This is because over time a "butterfly effect"—which can be readily demonstrated in our best weather prediction models—will exponentially multiply the amount of matter that has its movements and thus locations changed by even very slight variations in initial conditions, and eventually this will affect the movement of people enough to influence who conceives with whom, when they conceive, and therefore by which sperm and egg they conceive, and thus who subsequently comes to exist.

---

[8]   Van Inwagen, "The Possibility of Resurrection," 121.
[9]   Adams references Saul A. Kripke, "Naming and Necessity," in *Semantics of Natural Language*, ed. Donald Davidson and Gilbert Harman (Dordrecht: Reidel, 1972), 312–14.
[10]   "World" is used here, as elsewhere, in the technical sense of a maximal state of affairs. Nothing that Adams or I say implies that God could not transfer persons to a very different environment at some future time. Cf. n. 14, this chapter.
[11]   Adams, "Existence, Self-Interest, and the Problem of Evil," 67–8.
[12]   Adams, "Existence, Self-Interest, and the Problem of Evil," 66.

"The farther we go back in history," writes Adams,

> the larger the proportion of evils to which we owe our being; for the causal
> nexus relevant to our individual genesis widens as we go back in time. We
> almost certainly would never have existed had there not been just about the
> same evils as actually occurred in a large part of human history.[13]

This causal nexus will include both moral evils (lying, stealing, cheating, and killing) and so-called natural evils (earthquakes, tornadoes, diseases, and droughts).
It also will include the history relevant to the coming to be of the human race,
together with any pre-human evolutionary evil. The truth of any hypothesis about
human origins—the gradual emergence of full humanity through evolutionary
means, the miraculous raising of hominoids to full humanity, or the direct divine
creation of the original humans—would have a major effect on the causal history
of the world and therefore on the procreative history of the world. Whatever the
truth about human origins, it is likely that none of us could have existed had the
truth about human origins been significantly different.[14] Adams concludes that
"[i]f we have lives that are worth living on the whole, we cannot have been
wronged by the creation of a natural and historical order that has [evil] features;
for we could not have existed without them."[15]

Mark Wynn objects to this conclusion, suggesting that

> God could have allowed cosmic history to take its course until 'Adam and Eve'
> (or whoever the first human beings may be) appeared. He could then miracu-
> lously have removed appropriate sperm and eggs from them and miraculously
> have caused them to be united, and so on for further generations, in such a way
> as to bring into being the very individuals who have in fact come to be. On this
> scenario, it seems we do have some reason to suppose that it is the very individ-
> uals who have existed in our world who would come to be, and not merely indi-
> viduals like them.[16]

Against this objection is the fact that sperm is not produced in male humans until
years after birth. Why think that the very same sperm that is produced by a
human person after years of living in an evil-prone world could be produced by a
human person after years of living in an evil-free world? One reason not to think

---

[13] Adams, "Existence, Self-Interest, and the Problem of Evil," 66.

[14] None of this implies that we cannot one day live in an eternal state where there will be "no more
death or mourning or crying or pain" (Revelation 21:4). It is an individual's *origin* that establishes his
identity. Once he comes to exist, however, his *future* can take many different forms (including living in
very different environments) while maintaining personal identity.

[15] Adams, "Existence, Self-Interest, and the Problem of Evil," 67.

[16] Mark Wynn, *God and Goodness: A Natural Theological Perspective* (London: Routledge,
1999), 87.

this is that the atoms that make up our bodies (and therefore any physical things produced by our bodies) at any given time depend on the conditions of our natural environment, which would be radically different in an evil-free world. So I believe Wynn's objection can be resisted. That said, Wynn is right to press Adams's ambitious claim of a metaphysical necessity holding between an individual's existence and the evil preceding his coming to be. I will challenge and defend this claim in greater detail later in this chapter.

## Evils in Our Lifetimes

But even if this claim can be defended, Adams recognizes that we may still ask "why God does not intervene in the natural and historical process *in our lifetime* to protect us."[17] In addition to each act of creating individuals, the theodicist must account for God's allowance of evils (and especially of *horrendous evils*) in the context of each individual's life, and you might think that an ethically perfect being would prioritize the well-being of actual individuals over any desire to actualize merely possible individuals in the future.

This highlights that even if Non-Identity Theodicy can claim that people *could* not exist without the evils prior to their existence, it can only claim that they *would* not exist without the evils in their lifetimes. The reason they would not exist is because God's general policy of evil allowance would be different and this would have serious effects on who comes to be. For the fact that someone would not exist without them to plausibly play a significant role in justifying evils, however, it must be that the person would not exist *for good reason*. If there were no good reason that the person should not exist without the evils they suffer, then we could expect that a good God would create the person without the evils. Justification based on the fact that one would not exist relies on there being some good reason for God's general policy of evil allowance.

In response, Adams firstly points out that we do not always prioritize the well-being of those who exist over possible future goods in our moral assessments.[18] Many of us believe that one generation could act permissibly by taking steps to ensure that the human race does not die out, that future generations have access to the same natural resources that they do, or that a free society or a particular culture endures, even when those steps increase the suffering of those who currently exist and alter who will exist in the future. Similarly, perhaps God— especially in light of his unique ability to make good on suffering in the end—can justify imposing significant costs on actual individuals in order to aim for possible future individuals.

---

[17]   Adams, "Existence, Self-Interest, and the Problem of Evil," 67 (italics mine).
[18]   Adams, "Existence, Self-Interest, and the Problem of Evil," 69–70.

Moreover, Adams suggests that no person or generation has the right to special pleading.[19] It does not

> seem to be a demand of fairness that God should end the policy that has bene-
> fited us, and cease pursuing whatever goals he has been pursuing in the way he
> has been pursuing them, once it becomes convenient for our generation that he
> should change. This is a reason for thinking, not only that we are not wronged
> by prior evils that were necessary for our coming to be, but also that God is not
> unfair to us in letting evils befall us in our own lifetime.[20]

By enabling our existence, God's policy of evil allowance has been good for us on the whole; this is true even of those who bear the heaviest burden of the policy. And so—as long as God has good reasons for continuing the policy—morality does not seem to require that in our lifetimes it should be discontinued.[21]

## The *Self-Interest Relation*

Adams believes that reflection on our self-interest can fortify Non-Identity Theodicy's justification of evil occurring within our lives. What we value in a reasonable self-interest, Adams contends, is not just our metaphysical identity but "a treasure of meaning that is inextricably bound up with details of our actual personal histories."[22] Our lives as we experience and understand them are fundamentally shaped by "projects, friendships, and at least some of the most important features of our personal history and character."[23]

Adams suggests—where $S$ is a subject, $L'$ is a possible life that $S$ could have lived other than $S$'s actual life, and $t$ is a time—that

> $S$ bears a self-interest relation to $L'$ at $t$ to the extent that, at $t$, it should matter to
> $S$ that $L'$ could have been $S$'s life.[24]

According to Adams, one bears no *self-interest relation* to a possible life if it "contains so little of the concrete content that [one] care[s] about in [her] actual life

[19] Adams, "Existence, Self-Interest, and the Problem of Evil," 70–1.
[20] Adams, "Existence, Self-Interest, and the Problem of Evil," 71.
[21] William Hasker affirms a similar point on page 19 of *Providence, Evil and the Openness of God.*
[22] Adams, "Love and the Problem of Evil," 246.
[23] Adams, "Existence, Self-Interest, and the Problem of Evil," 74.
[24] Adams actually speaks of the self-interest relation as a relation between lives rather than between a person at a time and a possible life. As a relation between lives, it can be formalized thus: Where $S$ is a subject, $t$ is a time, $L$ is $S$'s actual life, and $L'$ is a life $S$ could have lived other than $L$, $L$ bears a self-interest relation to $L'$ at $t$ to the extent that, at $t$, it should matter to $S$ that $L'$ could have been $S$'s life.

that it should not matter to [her] that it could, metaphysically, have been [hers]."[25] By "*should not* matter to her," I take Adams to be saying that it would not be rational for it to matter to her.

Adams believes the *self-interest relation* can provide supplementary justification for allowing the evils occurring within our lifetimes. He firstly considers evil occurring in the early stages of one's life, and cites Helen Keller as an example: "Take the blindness and deafness out of her life-history, and most of the concrete content that she actually cared about would go with it. To wish that away would be disturbingly like wishing that she—the person she had *become*—had never existed."[26] Whatever the advantages of sight and hearing would have been, "such a life would not have had a single day in it that would have been much like any day in her actual life after the first 19 months. The two lives would not only differ at every moment in the sensory qualities of experience. They would differ in what she loved."[27]

With evils occurring early enough in one's life, one may bear no *self-interest relation* to lives without those evils at any time at which one is capable of considering the question, and Adams thinks this lack of conscious self-interest helps with the justification of such evils. One reason for thinking this is because one of the key bad-making features of much evil—that it creates a rift between a subject's will for his life and his experience of it—is absent in cases where there is no *self-interest relation*.

Remaining are evils occurring in one's life after the point at which one is capable of considering her self-interest. With respect to these evils, one *will* have a conscious self-interest in lives not including them, at least initially. Still, the further removed we become from any given evil, the greater the effect of its inclusion in our lives on the concrete content of our lives, and therefore the weaker our self-interest in lives devoid of that evil. As Adams explains,

> You may still think...that the life you had planned or hoped for before an evil befell you ten years ago would have been better than your actual life. Yet you may be so attached to actual projects, friendships, and experiences that would not have been part of that other life that you would *not* now wish to have had it instead of your actual life. There is some self-interest relation between the other life and your actual life up to the present, but it may not be strong enough to give you sufficient reason now to prefer the one you judge to be better. Ten years ago, however, the life you hoped for bore the strongest possible self-interest relation to your actual life up to then, and you had no reason not to prefer it to the life you have now actually had.[28]

[25] Adams, "Existence, Self-Interest, and the Problem of Evil," 74.
[26] Adams, "Love and the Problem of Evil," 246.
[27] Adams, "Love and the Problem of Evil," 246.
[28] Adams, "Existence, Self-Interest, and the Problem of Evil," 74.

To this I would add that if an eternal life awaits us and will be a great good for us on the whole,[29] then, from the perspective of eternity, any significant evil experienced during our earthly careers—and *a fortiori* any *horrendous evil*—may be far enough back in the causal nexus of our all-things-told life histories to make it the case that ultimately we will not be self-interested in lives that do not include that evil.[30] In fact, if our earthly careers compose only the earliest fraction of our entire existence, the vast majority of our lives will be spent having no *self-interest relation* to lives differing significantly in their evil content from our actual lives.[31]

Adams thinks that this "retrospective point of view is not irrelevant to God's goodness."[32] Even with respect to evil befalling us after we are aware of our self-interest, that we will spend the vast majority of our lives having no self-interest in lives not including that evil "complicates the question whether it is better for *you* that this or that evil happened."[33]

Adams has argued that God does not wrong us by the evil preceding our existence because we could not have existed without it, nor by the evil within our lives because God's policy of evil allowance has been to our advantage overall. Self-interest considerations supplement these justifications by highlighting that at no point will we rationally wish away significant evil in the early stages of our lives, and that for most of our eternal existence we will not rationally wish away significant evils occurring later in our earthly careers.

## Considerations of Character

This brings us to condition (3) of Non-Identity Theodicy. Even if God does not *wrong* anyone by allowing evil to occur, whether creating and sustaining an evil-producing universe reveals a defect in character is another question. To again cite Adams's explanation of this,

> It may be thought that the creation of a world inferior to the best that he could make would manifest a defect in the creator's character even if no one were

---

[29] Adams thinks the theist should believe that "our existence will be a great good to us on the whole (except perhaps by our own fault)" (Adams, "Existence, Self-Interest, and the Problem of Evil," 70).

[30] Consonantly, Adams writes, "The retrospective preferability of our actual lives to even better ones is based, as we have seen, on our attachment to actual projects, friendships, experiences, and other features of our actual lives. Alas, not everyone is able now to love his life in this way. But it is clear that love for projects, experiences, and friendships that one is engaged in is highly correlated with happiness. So to the extent that the theist believes we shall all be happy in the end, he may well believe we shall all have reason to prefer our actual lives to others we could have had" (Adams, "Existence, Self-Interest, and the Problem of Evil," 75).

[31] I may retain a rational self-interest in infinitely many possible lives other than my actual life, for example in the life which differs from my actual life only in that I wore green instead of black socks this morning, but these lives don't contain significantly less evil than my actual life.

[32] Adams, "Existence, Self-Interest, and the Problem of Evil," 74.

[33] Adams, "Existence, Self-Interest, and the Problem of Evil," 74.

thereby wronged or treated unkindly. For the perfectly good moral agent must not only be kind and refrain from violating the rights of others, but must also have other virtues. For instance, He must be noble, generous, high-minded, and free from envy. He must satisfy the moral ideal.[34]

Perhaps in creating a universe that includes great evil and suffering God displays a vice.[35] Perhaps, for instance, his motivation for creating an evil-prone universe is so that he can play hero, or because he finds violence entertaining: "As flies to wanton boys are we to th' gods. They kill us for their sport."[36]

Following Adams, Non-Identity Theodicy resists this suggestion by proposing that one of God's motivations in actualizing the actual world is to create and love a specific group of creatures, and that

> A good person accepts significant costs—and sometimes, where he has a right to, imposes them on others—for the sake of what he loves [or desires to love], and not only for the sake of what is best.[37]

Reflecting on this, Adams suggests that an ethically perfect God could be motivated to create a specific community of people even if the individuals that make up that community would suffer less in other possible worlds. As support for this conclusion, Adams offers the following:

> [T]he desire to create and love *all of a certain group of possible creatures* (assuming that all of them would have satisfying lives on the whole) might be an adequate ground for a perfectly good God to create them, even if His creating *all* of them must have the result that some of them are less happy than they might otherwise have been. And they need not be the best of all possible creatures, or included in the best of all possible worlds, in order for this qualification of His kindness to be consistent with His perfect goodness. The desire to create *those* creatures is as legitimate a ground for Him to qualify His kindness toward some, as the desire to create the best of all possible worlds. This suggestion seems to me to be in keeping with the aspect of the Judeo-Christian [*sic*] moral ideal which will be discussed.[38]

---

[34]   Adams, "Must God Create the Best?," 323.

[35]   Adams notes ("Must God Create the Best?," 323) that Plato suggests the vice of envy in *Timaeus* 29E-30A.

[36]   William Shakespeare, *King Lear*, Act 4, scene 1.

[37]   Adams, "Existence, Self-Interest, and the Problem of Evil," 72 (brackets mine).

[38]   Adams, "Must God Create the Best?," 322–3 (italics mine). Relatedly, Guy Kahane argues that "*history couldn't have realistically been jointly better for all of the people who had existed.* History could have been better at one point in history, or at another, but that's it. There is no way to 'add up' various local person-centred improvements to get even better alternative histories. Actual history is depressing enough but it is sobering to realize that, realistically, things just *couldn't* have been a lot better, at least not in the ways that most matter to us" ("History and Persons," *Philosophy and Phenomenological Research* 99.1 (2019), 179).

The aspect of the moral ideal that Adams alludes to is the virtue of grace. A gracious person, according to Adams, is one with "a disposition to love which is not dependent on the merit of the person loved," one who "sees what is valuable in the person he loves, and does not worry about whether it is more or less valuable than what could be found in someone else he might have loved."[39] Therefore, "A God who is gracious with respect to creating might well choose to create and love less excellent creatures than He could have chosen."[40]

While the virtue of grace may be foreign to some ethical sensitivities (to those of Plato and Leibniz, for instance), understanding God as gracious in this way is consonant with the tendency of religious worshippers to express gratitude to God for taking a particular interest in them despite their comparative deficiencies—"What are human beings that you are mindful of them, mortals that you care for them?"[41] Religious worshippers tend to thank God not for his wisdom in creating beings as objectively valuable as them, but rather for their lives as if for "an underserved personal favor."[42]

By these moves, Adams likens God's decision to create our universe to Adams's own unabashed preference for "the preservation of the human race...to its ultimate replacement by a more excellent species,"[43] to human parents preferring to procreate a normal child rather than a genetically enhanced super-child, to an activist's preference for a free society even if a totalitarian one would be better overall, and to a man breeding goldfish rather than more excellent beings. All of these examples are most naturally construed as including preferences not aimed at maximizing value, and the first three examples can be naturally construed as including preferences not aimed at minimizing suffering. Intuitions are controversial here, but I join Adams in not thinking that he, the parents, the activist, or the goldfish breeder have—under otherwise normal circumstances—displayed a vice. And God is in a still more favorable position than they because only he has the omnipotence to offer all created persons lives that are great goods to them all things considered.

God's primary creative choice, according to Non-Identity Theodicy, is of a group of particular persons whom God finds loveable. Because God is gracious, his desire to love us is not on the condition that we are more valuable than other creatures he could have created or that our existence allows for the maximization of overall world value. On the contrary, reflection on the virtue of grace suggests that desiring to create and love persons vulnerable to significant evil can be just as

[39] Adams, "Must God Create the Best?," 323–4.
[40] Adams, "Must God Create the Best?," 324.
[41] Psalm 8:4 (NRSV). Adams uses this verse to make a related point in "Must God Create the Best?," 324–5.
[42] Adams, "Must God Create the Best?," 324.
[43] Adams, "Existence, Self-Interest, and the Problem of Evil," 71.

fitting with the abundance of divine generosity as desiring to create and love the most valuable, most useful, or most well-off persons God could create.

## Summary

Conjoining Adams's belief that God has not wronged those he has created with his claim that God's world choice is motivated by the virtue of grace rather than by any defect in character, we have the outline of a full theodicy: In sum, God's policy of evil and suffering allowance does not wrong those he creates because this policy enables their existence (condition (1)) and God offers them lives that are great goods all things considered (condition (2)). God displays praiseworthy character because his actions are motivated by a desire to love those who come to exist (condition (3)).[44]

The postulated justifying goods of Non-Identity Theodicy are individual human persons, and accepting evil and suffering as an inevitable consequence of attaining these goods is consistent with divine morality and virtue so long as the human persons are objects of divine love, otherwise could not have existed, and are offered very worthwhile lives. Uniquely, these goods are not states that human persons are or will be in, but the very subjects required for the actualization of any such states. Likewise, this justification is neither a harm-averting benefit nor a pure benefit. It is not a benefit of any sort because existence is presupposed for all benefits.

*Horrendous evils* render the lives of those who suffer them *prima facie* not worth living. They are so bad that they resist divine justification by both harm aversion and pure benefit bestowal. Non-Identity Theodicy suggests that one alternative justification for *horror* allowance is a life that is *ultima facie* worth living lived by someone who could not have existed otherwise.

## Objections

For a theodicy to be successful, I hold it must depict God as not wronging anyone and as having an otherwise flawless character, and it must not be implausible on other grounds. According to Non-Identity Theodicy, no one is wronged by God's creative choice of this universe. Those who never come to exist are not wronged because non-existent beings cannot be wronged. Those who do come to exist are

---

[44] Because I claim that God is motivated in creating by a *desire* to love individuals rather than by love for them per se, I am not committed to the possibility of loving non-existent objects. William Hasker raises a concern about this when he writes, "Prior to [God] making the decision, there *are no* creatures for God to love; there is only a set of abstract possibilities" (*The Triumph of God over Evil: Theodicy for a World of Suffering* (Downers Grove, Ill: IVP Academic, 2008), 84).

not wronged because they could not have existed otherwise and are offered great lives overall.[45] Focusing on the moral distinctiveness of the value-engulfing badness of *horrors* calls this conclusion into question. I will bracket this concern for now; Chapter 7 will return to consider it at length. I now defend Non-Identity Theodicy against an array of character-based and plausibility objections. One of these objections motivates me to develop a second form of Non-Identity Theodicy.

## Character-Based Objections to Non-Identity Theodicy

### C1. Is God Irrational?

Some who accept that on the assumptions of Non-Identity Theodicy God has not wronged anyone and is motivated virtuously may, nevertheless, have a lingering worry that there is something ethically problematic or irrational about deliberately choosing to bring about a worse state of affairs involving a great deal of suffering and injustice in preference to a better state of affairs. Isn't the God of Non-Identity Theodicy like a person who—given a choice between many mortgage packages—wastes his money by choosing one considerably worse than the best?[46]

Non-Identity Theodicy suggests that a preference for the best becomes less evident when choosing the best will not be better for anyone.[47] No one who exists in the actual world would be there to be bettered by the best world. Non-Identity Theodicy also suggests that God acts as a lover of particular individuals, and further that a lover can have significant reasons for acting, in virtue of being a lover, other than those that impartially maximize general value. Perhaps government officials have no place making bureaucratic decisions based on love for particular individuals. But God is no bureaucrat, according to Non-Identity Theodicy, and he makes some of his most significant decisions—including decisions about which type of universe to create—based on love for particular individuals.

---

[45]  Adams writes, "Perhaps I can have a right to something which would not benefit me (e.g., if it has been promised to me). But if there are such non-beneficial rights, I do not see any plausible reason for supposing that a right not to be created could be among them" (Adams, "Must God Create the Best?," 320).

[46]  This raises the question of whether there is a best possible world. I am inclined to believe there is not—for any possible world, something of value could be added to that world to make a better possible world. If there is no best possible world, then God cannot be morally obligated to actualize a best possible world. However, even if there were a best possible world, I do not believe, for reasons I will go on to discuss, that God would be obligated to actualize it.

[47]  Guy Kahane makes this point well: "Although it's natural to think that we should wish that things had gone as best as they could have, such a preference becomes less obvious if what counts as best *won't be better for anyone*. This is because…on the impersonal perspective, the course of history we should most prefer is also one that contains none of the people who had actually lived. Everyone would be erased. So no one could benefit from this rewriting of history" ("History and Persons," 171).

Underlying this approach to theodicy is a resistance to invoking value-maximization as the ethical or rational ideal,[48] and also to approaches to decision-making that weight the instrumental and comparative value of persons over valuing those persons and relationships with those persons for their own sakes. Whether we are instrumentally necessary for the *best* world God could have created (as Leibniz would have it), for a world *better* than many others (as Plantinga would have it), or for *greater* goods such as meaningful free will and being of use (as Swinburne would have it) is not of primary importance.[49] If creation is primarily an act of love, then evaluating that act primarily on comparisons of value is a category mistake. According to Non-Identity Theodicy, God is not just after benefits *for* objects of love, but rather he is after the individuals who *are* the objects of love. He is after them because he finds them loveable, and loveableness as a quality is very different from a measurement of value. An economic model—whereby costs are evaluated solely for their instrumental use in acquiring greater goods—may be useful when buying a home, but I agree with Adams that "[i]n some areas of human life…and particularly where certain kinds of personal relationship are concerned, the economic model is grossly inadequate for an understanding of what is involved in being good to people."[50] Guy Kahane worries, similarly, that an impersonal approach to ethics "regards persons merely as dispensable receptacles for value…merely extras in a drama whose real subject matter is the fluctuation of accumulated overall value."[51]

Ideal love is an essential component of ethical perfection, and ideal love is particular in that it prizes its objects for their own sakes, not merely or primarily as a way of obtaining further ends.[52] This particularity of ideal love supports the conclusion that there can be rational preferences for situations that are less good on the whole than others one could aim for. One who has a genuine love for truthfulness, for instance, will at least sometimes prefer not to lie even when his honesty is not instrumental for a greater good and results in a comparatively worse state of affairs. Similarly, those who love one another sometimes have rational preferences to be worse off together rather than better-off apart. I read the "for better *or* for worse" in many marriage vows in this way. Far from being reproachable, I take

---

[48]  Adams writes, "I do not think it is best, or an inescapable part of the ethical ideal, always to prefer what is best" (Robert Merrihew Adams, *Finite and Infinite Goods* (Oxford: Oxford University Press, 2002), 133).

[49]  Adams wrote "Must God Create the Best?" (1972)—his first article with direct import for Non-Identity Theodicy—at a time when it was common for philosophers to assume a God who created would have to create a best of all possible worlds. Writing in 1969, for instance, Roderick Chisholm says, "We may assume that if an omnipotent, omniscient, and benevolent deity were to create a world, then that world would be at least as good as any other possible world" ("The Defeat of Good and Evil," *Proceedings and Addresses of the American Philosophical Association* 42 (1969), 36).

[50]  Adams, *Finite and Infinite Goods*, 143.       [51]  Guy Kahane, "History and Persons," 173.

[52]  Adams concurs when he writes, "Some measure of such a noninstrumental relational interest seems to me to be part of anything that would be recognized as a paradigm of *love* of any sort" (Adams, *Finite and Infinite Goods*, 139).

preferences of this sort to be closely related to some of the best forms of human relationship.

When I married my wife, Jo, I did this because I love her for her own sake and I love our relationship for its own sake. It wasn't just that I decided life would be *better* with her than without her; it wasn't just that I decided she compared favorably with others of her general type; it wasn't just that I judged her to be instrumentally useful for attaining further ends. The most relevant affections are more particular than these assessments. I love her and our relationship as ends in themselves.[53] I desire *life-together* with her, for better *or* for worse. If I were not willing to accept any loss of overall value for the sake of my relationship with Jo, this would call into serious question the genuineness of my love for her.[54] Non-Identity Theodicy can be understood as exploring the related idea that God created out of a loving desire for life-together with a community of individuals, and that he accepts evil as the metaphysically necessary cost of realizing that desire in relationship with us.

Interestingly, this emphasis on the particularity of love is not only alien to but explicitly at odds with the ethical assumptions underlying much contemporary theodicy. Swinburne is explicit that he takes the primary assessments relevant to theodicy to be ones of comparative value, for instance when he writes that "the issue of whether the goods are great enough to justify the bad states which make them possible is the crux of the problem of evil."[55] In fact, Swinburne goes so far as to claim that "[a] perfectly good being will never allow any morally bad state to occur if he can prevent it—except for the sake of a greater good."[56] In doing so, he fails to appreciate that some of the most powerful expressions of love are those that accept bad states for the sake of particular people and particular relationships as ends in themselves, rather than for the sake of bringing about greater goods.

Moreover—setting aside concerns about the *sake* for which a bad state is allowed—it does not even seem to be a requirement of ethical or rational perfection to only allow bad states that are likely to be counterbalanced by greater goods. If one is not willing to make the sacrifices necessary to support a friend unless the overall expected value of making the sacrifice is positive, then it is doubtful that one genuinely loves the relationship or the person one is related to.

---

[53] Adams affirms this line of thought in an insightful passage: "Comparative reasons have something unappreciative about them...optimization and maximization are enemies of appreciation; and appreciation is part of the soul of love. This may seem paradoxical to our competitive souls, which sometimes feel most appreciated when we are favorably compared with others. But in truth, being placed on a scale, even at the top of it, is as such quite different from being loved or appreciated for oneself" (Adams, *Finite and Infinite Goods*, 169).

[54] Cf. Adams, *Finite and Infinite Goods*, 151ff.

[55] Swinburne, *Providence and the Problem of Evil*, 239.

[56] Swinburne, *Providence and the Problem of Evil*, 13. Later in the same work Swinburne puts it this way: It must be the case that "the expected value of allowing the bad states to occur is positive, i.e. roughly that the goods which they make possible are at least a tiny bit better than the bad states necessary for them are bad" (223).

It is in keeping with ideal love to sometimes be willing to make sacrifices for those you love when the goodness of the goods attained by those sacrifices is incommensurate with or even less than the badness of the sacrifices.

Not only is Swinburne's condition not a necessary condition of perfect goodness as he claims it is, but I take it to be sufficient on at least two counts for less-than-perfect goodness.[57] Stump likewise seems to underappreciate the justificatory possibilities of relationships loved for their own sakes when she assumes that divinely permitted evils can only be justified if they are "outweighed" by the resultant goods,[58] and William Rowe does the same when he assumes that a God "would prevent the occurrence of any intense suffering it could, unless it could not do so without thereby losing some greater good or permitting some evil equally bad or worse."[59]

A greater-goods condition is almost universally assumed in the contemporary literature on the problem of evil, and most follow Rowe in assuming that evils not leading to greater goods are appropriately termed "pointless evils."[60] But, as I have been suggesting, it is far from obvious that evils leading to lesser or incommensurate goods valued for their own sakes are necessarily pointless.

There are important ethical differences between house mortgages and human persons; they are valued in very different ways. Contemporary analytic theodicy has generally been conducted along an economic ethical paradigm that uses a metric to weigh the moral value of consequences. As such, it has underemphasized the valuing of people and relationships for their own sakes which is essential to ideal love. If ideal love is a significant component of divine rationality and ethical perfection, as I believe it is, Adams is correct to recommend a significant shift in emphasis away from the instrumentalism and comparativism of an economic model and toward love and grace, and his doing so does not depict God as irrational or unethical.[61]

Admittedly, even in the area of human relationships, people are sometimes rightly accused of irrationality or foolishness in entering into and remaining in certain relationships. But this reaction is typically motivated by reasons for thinking that, in the context of the relationship in question, one person is likely to unjustifiably harm the other. In contrast to typical human relationships, God (on

---

[57] Another concern about Swinburne's condition is that it does not seem to take into account that one may sometimes have an obligation to allow an evil even when it will not lead to a greater good. This can be the case, for instance, when one has promised not to interfere or when interference would be beyond one's rightful involvement. Perhaps Swinburne is thinking that God would not make such a promise and that nothing is outside of his rightful ruling.

[58] Stump, "The Problem of Evil," 410.

[59] William L. Rowe, "The Problem of Evil and Some Varieties of Atheism," *American Philosophical Quarterly* 16 (1979), 336.

[60] Rowe, "The Problem of Evil and Some Varieties of Atheism," 337.

[61] Guy Kahane recommends a related shift from an impersonal perspective on history to a person-centered one in "History and Persons."

the assumptions of Non-Identity Theodicy) does not harm unjustifiably and, if he can be harmed, is uniquely capable of sustaining psychological health when harmed.

As a final response to this charge of irrationality, note that Non-Identity Theodicy is consistent with God bringing into existence creatures other than those we are aware of. Even if you think it would be irrational to aim solely for the inhabitants of earth in creating, Non-Identity Theodicy is consistent with God creating far more excellent creatures, either in other universes or in other parts of our universe.[62] If God has created a range of good creatures—and among them some of the most excellent—then he is still less vulnerable to the charge that he has been irrational in not creating better beings or beings who suffer less; for all we know, he has.[63]

## C2. Does God Lack Appropriate Regret?

It is plausible to suppose that anyone perfect in character would have to deeply regret much of the suffering we find in the actual world. But if God accepts each and every evil in order to achieve his desired end of giving life to a specific community of individuals, wouldn't he lack this appropriate regret?

It is worth pointing out, to begin with, that this is not a problem unique to Non-Identity Theodicy. Any theodicy wanting to hold onto divine omniscience and omnipotence will have to say that God accepts every evil for ends he deems worth aiming for all things considered.

But to answer the question, wouldn't God lack appropriate regret? Not necessarily. In a more recent article, "Love and the Problem of Evil" (2006), Adams reflects on the fact that God would not be alone in having a sort of ambivalence about much of the evil of the actual world. For all of us who love, "What we prize concretely in our loving presupposes evil as well as good."[64] Without World War I, it is plausible to suppose that my grandparents never would have met, and, as a result, that my parents never would have existed. But it doesn't follow from my being happy that my parents exist and recognizing the dependence of their existence on World War I that I lack an appropriate regret regarding World War I. To maintain an appropriate regret, it seems enough for me to regret that my parents' existence is dependent on World War I. It's enough for me to wish they could

---

[62] In fact, the principle of plentitude—according to which all possible kinds of being would be created—had significant philosophical influence from ancient times until the eighteenth century. A. O. Lovejoy documents the history of this principle in his *The Great Chain of Being* (Cambridge, Massachusetts and London: Harvard University Press, 1936).

[63] In fact, for all we know, God could have created all universes above a certain threshold of value, or all universes of positive value, thus accommodating the intuitions of even the best-possible-world theorist.

[64] Adams, "Love and the Problem of Evil," 246.

have existed without that war, even if the conditions of their existence cause me to have some ambivalence about the war all things considered.

Procreation suggests another example. I intended to procreate a child despite knowing that doing so would mean that my child will suffer physical death. Reflecting on the inevitability of death may complicate our views about the ethics of procreation, but I suspect many will nevertheless join me in my judgment that fully reflective procreation does not entail an ethically objectionable lack of regret about the death of one's child. Similarly, we can imagine God making a fully informed choice to actualize the actual world while maintaining a deep localized regret about the evils it contains.[65]

The primary reason we regret past evil is because of the harm done to the victims of that evil, and the badness of such harm is grounded in the value of the victims. There is a tension, then, in saying that appropriate regret of evil requires a desire to erase the victims of evil from history. Kahane likens such reasoning to "using a guillotine to stop a headache."[66]

## C3. A Divine Depleter?

The responses to the first two objections provide resources for responding to a related objection by analogy. Even if, in creating, God does not wrong anyone, by creating a universe with more suffering than other universes God could have created, hasn't God shown a defect in character similar to the defect we show when, by depleting resources now, we knowingly cause the existence of future people who suffer more than those who would have existed had we not depleted?

It might seem so initially, but there are relevant disanalogies. It is true that the predictable result that we will cause to exist persons who suffer more gives us and God some *prima facie* reason against depleting resources and against creating a world with greater suffering. However, according to Adams, God is able to weigh that reason against another reason in favor—his desire to love and bestow grace upon specific individuals. As human depleters, we cannot appeal to this counter-reason.[67] Our choice for future generations is constrained by our greatly limited predictive ability. The result is that we are too epistemologically challenged to know enough about the persons that will result from our depletion to cite our desire to be gracious to them as a depletion-justifying motivation.[68] Moreover, in

---

[65] This is one way of understanding biblical passages implying that God regretted having created human persons, for example Genesis 6:6. This is also related to the Nietzschean demand for eternal recurrence—the view that our precise lives will repeat infinitely—to be accepted and loved (*amor fati*).

[66] Guy Kahane, "History and Persons," 173.

[67] Shortly, I will discuss whether even God can take this way out.

[68] To cast this in the language of harming and benefiting (if it were assumed that being made to exist could come as a benefit), human depletion is a case of harming but not of benefiting future

practice, it simply never is the case that we are motivated in this way, and our choice for future generations is further constrained by the fact that we can only be gracious to future generations by leaving them the planet earth in a habitable form.[69]

In addition to lacking this potentially justifying divine motivation for our decisions to deplete, in depleting, we also manifest a vice that God does not—the vice of selfishness. When we deplete excessively, it is often because we care much more about our own well-being than that of others. But this vice is not easily transferable to God, who is most commonly understood to lack nothing in himself. God does not create for his benefit. In fact, from some Christian perspectives, God creates the actual community of human persons knowing that this will result in him sacrificing something of his own.

But these are controversial issues. It might still seem selfish of God to prioritize the satisfaction of his desire to get a specific community of actual persons when *horrendous evils* are the cost of that satisfaction. Doesn't this depict God with an excessive concern for his own satisfaction?

This form of the objection can be avoided, I think, by shifting the emphasis of God's reason for creating. According to Adams, God creates because he desires to love us. But this can be interpreted with two different emphases. On the first, the emphasis is on the fact that God creates in order to fulfill this desire of his. That the desire is to *love us* is of only secondary importance. On the second interpretation, however, God creates not primarily in order to fulfill a desire of his but *out of love for us*. Here we have an important distinction between acting in order to obtain some relational value and acting out of the motives involved in having that relational value. On the latter, it is not the selfish satisfaction of his own desire that God is after in creating, but rather the good of those he creates. That God *desires* to love us remains relevant to his decision, but the primary motivation for his decision is other-centered rather than self-centered. He is motivated to create so that others will be loved.

So long as we interpret Adams's approach in this latter way, I believe it avoids accusations of divine selfishness. And, importantly, a maximal being would be loving and powerful enough to offer for any lives that are shattered by *horrors* to be put back together and be, from the vantage point of eternity, great goods on the whole to those who live them.

While it is true that both divine creation and human resource depletion could result in the existence of generations worse off than others that could have existed, the analogy is not strong enough to undermine Non-Identity Theodicy.

---

generations because the intention to benefit is necessary for benefiting whereas the intent to harm is not necessary for harming.

[69] Gregory Kavka makes similar points in his "The Paradox of Future Individuals," *Philosophy and Public Affairs* 11 (1981), 103.

## Plausibility Objections to Non-Identity Theodicy

### P1. Conditions of Personal Identity

Non-Identity Theodicy relies on the claim that particular persons could not have existed had the evil preceding their physical origination been much different because even slight variations would have affected procreation history, and our biological parentage is essential to who we are. But some don't share the intuition that our biological parents are essential to who we are as strongly as Adams and Kripke, and, once it is denied, the question of whether omnipotence would allow God to get the very same individuals in possible worlds of significantly less evil is reopened.

Seemingly still worse for Non-Identity Theodicy, there is one theory of personal identity that is both popular among theists and rejects *any* connection between personal identity and physical origination. This is a theory according to which human persons are immaterial souls (sometimes referred to as Cartesian egos) that exist logically (and in some versions temporally) prior to their embodiment. This *creationist* theory of the soul has been endorsed in various forms by Plato, René Descartes, Joseph Butler, Thomas Reid, Roderick Chisholm, and Richard Swinburne, among many others. On some versions of this view, not only is the immaterial soul the individuating feature of persons, but God can join any soul to any or no lump of matter as he likes, in any universe that he chooses to create. If a theory of this sort is correct, then it is not true that suffering (let alone the precise suffering of the actual world) is essential for the existence of the specific community of actual-world human inhabitants (nor, for that matter, for the existence of any other human persons God could have created); God could have gotten the very same individuals in possible worlds with significantly less evil and suffering, or even with no evil and suffering at all.[70]

It is worth noting that this disconnection between physical origination and personal identity is not representative of theories of the soul in general. Many who believe in human souls *do* accept the claim that physical origination affects personal identity. This claim will be plausible to those who hold that a human person consists essentially of both a specific body and a specific soul. It may also be plausible to some who believe human persons *are* immaterial souls—for example, to some holding a traducian view (according to which the soul is generated from the specific souls of the parents during the reproductive process) or to

---

[70] If human persons are immaterial souls and souls are featureless—as they are sometimes thought to be—this threatens to undermine Non-Identity Theodicy in a second way because, if souls lack differentiating features, it is hard to see what reasons God could have for loving that would be particular to specific individuals. But, as I argue later in this chapter, God's creation-motivating love should be understood as tracking not merely bare metaphysical identity but at least some of the concrete content of a person's life.

some holding an emergent view (according to which the soul results in some way from the structure and/or functioning of the human organism). This claim may even be plausible to some who believe human persons are immaterial souls and hold creationist views of the soul. William Hasker notes that some "Thomists, for instance, hold that the soul, as a form, is individuated by the matter which it informs; the soul is created as the soul of *this particular body*."[71]

However, even those who accept a connection between physicality and personal identity might not accept the stronger claim that the specifics of our causal history, including our biological parentage, are essential to our personal identity. Some, including David Oderberg to take one example, suggest that transworld personal identity can be maintained despite radically different causal histories. Oderberg writes,

> [E]ven though a person could not have been born with a different genotype, and hence of different parents or gametes if this entailed that the person had a different original genotype, still the person might have had a radically different origin altogether from the normal human one. I share [the] intuition that Socrates might have popped into existence ex nihilo…[T]hat such a beginning might not have involved any human or animal generation, or even any physical process at all, is coherent and consistent with the essences not only of Socrates but of any material substance…For the essence of Socrates, as for any substance, is nothing more or less than the union of prime matter and substantial form.[72] The substance exists just in case the union is present. How the union is produced is another matter altogether, extraneous to the essence.[73]

One view (different from Oderberg's) that allows transworld identity to be maintained across very different causal histories, and on which God could have produced the same people who actually exist in a world with far less or no suffering, is the view that sameness of original matter and sameness of initial composition is sufficient for personal identity. On this view, all God needed to do is join the same microparticles into the same initial arrangements, and he could have done this as easily in a suffering-free world as in our suffering-prone world.

There are some reasons to be suspicious of any approach claiming that the combination of matter and configuration is sufficient for identity. Imagine a case

---

[71] Hasker, *Providence, Evil and the Openness of God*, 11.

[72] For Oderberg, "form *actualizes the potencies of matter* in the sense of being the principle that unites with matter to produce a finite individual with limited powers and an existence circumscribed by space and time. Together with matter, it composes the distinct individual substance. Hence all substances in the material world are true *compounds* of matter and form" (David Oderberg, *Real Essentialism* (New York: Routledge, 2007), 66).

[73] Oderberg, *Real Essentialism*, 175–6.

where a being can magically produce Socrates merely by waving an arm. If matter plus composition is sufficient for identifying the object produced, then this being should be able to produce Socrates by waving either of its arms. But what if this being waves both arms simultaneously, producing two qualitatively identical people? They can't both be Socrates, but on a matter-plus-configuration theory of identity they have an equal claim to being Socrates. Matter plus initial composition is not sufficient for individuating them, or for individuating any lumps of matter produced in this way.

Moreover, it seems possible for the same microparticles to wind up in the same configuration multiple times. The same matter that was configured in the initial state of my existence could be identically configured at a later time. Because the matter constituting our bodies changes over time, it could even be so configured outside of my body while I am still alive. However, the same person certainly can't begin to exist while already existing, so this again suggests that matter plus configuration is not sufficient for identity.[74]

All accounts of identity have costs, but here are three theories that are amenable to Non-Identity Theodicy's reliance on the sensitivity of procreation history:

*The Complete Causal History View:* On this view, an object is identified by its initial state and the complete causal history leading to its origination.[75] Attractions of this theory include its simplicity, its provision of a necessary and sufficient condition, and its avoidance of vagueness. This theory also deals well with the counterexamples to matter-plus-composition views raised above. On the complete causal history view, matter plus composition is not sufficient for identity; the history and mode of production must also be the same. This allows us to differentiate between the lumps of matter produced by waving one's right arm and one's left arm and between the objects produced by the same matter being identically configured at multiple times.

However, the complete causal history view also has costs. It requires denying Oderberg's intuition that God could have created Socrates *ex nihilo*. It also requires accepting what some will see as an overly strong origin essentialism. Many will think that identity could be maintained through some changes to the causal history, for example if the causal history were the same except that, on the night of conception, the same sperm and egg were united through consensual sex rather than rape.

*The Casual History View:* On this view, an object is again identified by its causal history and initial state, but identity can be maintained despite some variation in these factors. For a possible object to be me, its causal history and initial state must be *similar enough* to my actual causal history and initial state. This theory is

---

[74] I am indebted to Alexander Pruss for suggesting these counterexamples.
[75] Cf. Alexander Pruss and Joshua Rasmussen, *Necessary Existence* (Oxford: Oxford University Press, 2018), 23.

still conducive to Non-Identity Theodicy, so long as God is understood to be aiming for all (or, at any rate, many) of the individuals of the human race. The proponent of this theory can hold that while an individual's identity can be sustained through some variation in causal history, these variations have knock-on effects such that, over a long enough time span, even very marginal variations will affect the identities of future individuals.

One cost of this theory is that a level of vagueness is introduced. As a result, the theory is vulnerable to Chisholm's Paradox: Through a series of incremental changes (and assuming transitivity of transworld identity), two people—Adam and Noah, for instance—can swap all of their qualitative properties without changing their identities. Adam might be taller than Noah in the actual world, but there is a series of worlds through which Adam gets incrementally shorter and Noah gets incrementally taller until they have swapped heights while maintaining their identities. The same process could be repeated for every other qualitative difference between Adam and Noah. This leads to the paradoxical conclusion that Adam in one possible world could be identical with Noah in another possible world. As Quine puts it, "You can change anything to anything by easy stages through some connecting series of possible worlds."[76] Nevertheless, this might be judged to be an acceptable cost, given that very many philosophical accounts of various important concepts invoke some level of vagueness in the boundary conditions for the applicability of the concepts. Plus this theory also has advantages. Some will take it to get the more intuitive result that the same person could come to exist despite minor changes in his or her causal history of origination. It thereby can allay some concerns about an overly strong origin essentialism.

*Actualism and Thisness:* A third option for the Non-Identity Theodicist is to hold, with Robert Adams, that no purely qualitative facts are sufficient to individuate an object. Instead, according to Adams's haecceitism, an individual is individuated by a primitive non-qualitative thisness which "is the property of being a particular individual, or of being identical with that individual."[77] That this property is non-qualitative and primitive motivates Adams's actualist assumption that there are no nonactual individuals; thisnesses come into existence with actual individuals and only actual individuals have thisnesses. It follows that there is no way to distinguish a possibility as a possibility for a specific individual until that individual actually exists, analogous to the inability to individuate a dollar in your bank account until you withdraw it and hold the specific dollar in your hand. (It would be nonsensical, for instance, to withdraw a dollar from your account and then to accuse the bank teller of giving you the wrong dollar!) Therefore, the only worlds in which we (or God) have reason to think a specific individual exists are

---

[76] W. V. Quine, "Worlds Away," *The Journal of Philosophy* 73.22 (1976), 861.
[77] Robert Merrihew Adams, "Actualism and Thisness," *Synthese* 49 (1981), 4.

the worlds that include the actual history of the actual world up to the coming to be of that individual.

One cost of Adams's view is that it requires denying the existence of "possible but nonactual entities [that] can enter into relations and have properties," and therefore denying that possibilia can be "values of variables in the logic of predicates."[78] If the only facts about nonactual things are facts of suchness, not thisness, then, for example, prior to my existence there was no truth value to be assigned to the claim, "Possibly, Vince exists." One attraction of Adams's view is that it provides a clear reason for rejecting the identity of indiscernibles. The two qualitatively identical spheres making up the totality of Max Black's hypothesized world, for example, would be individuated by their thisnesses if that were the actual world.[79]

One worry for the non-identity theodicist is whether this view affirms too much. It affirms Non-Identity Theodicy's claim that only worlds with the history of the actual world up to the origin of an individual can guarantee that individual's existence, but the appeal to thisness also results in God not being able to aim for specific individuals in creating. On Adams's assumptions of actualism and primitive thisnesses, even actualizing the actual world did not guarantee my existence. God could withdraw a dollar from his account, but he could not specify which dollar he would receive; there is no way to fully individuate a specific individual until that individual exists.

Notwithstanding, Adams reminds us that "[t]o love a person...is not just to care about a bare metaphysical identity;" it is also to care for her "projects" and "aspirations," finding hope and value in particular "actions" and "experiences."[80] God can create out of love for individuals in valuing and bringing into existence the concrete content of their lives, even if he has to wait to meet the specific individuals who come to exist. This can be likened to human procreators, who can create out of love for future children prior to knowing which specific children they will bring into existence. If expectant human parents can create out of love, despite the many limitations on what they can know qualitatively about who their child will be, then God has a much greater claim to be able to create out of love.

---

[78] Adams, "Actualism and Thisness," 7. Another cost that might be proposed is having to accept the (what some will take to be counterintuitive) claim that it is possible for the history of the world to have been otherwise identical in every respect and yet for not you but a qualitatively identical doppelgänger of yours to have existed. This possibility might be thought to follow from the assumption that even God cannot decide what thisness an individual will have. But while this may be a cost of some haecceistic views, Adams assigns no clear meaning to this hypothesis. On his view, a thisness arises only from the existence of the individual whose thisness it is, and what thisness it is is determined, necessarily, by the existence of that individual and the logic of identity. Because your proposed doppelgänger—being nonactual—does not have a thisness, there simply is no truth value to be assigned to the claim that he could have been someone other than you. Otherwise put, it is not possible to specify the individual whose possible existence is being inquired about, and neither possibility nor impossibility can be assigned to the existence of an unspecified object. For further discussion of this proposed cost, see Graeme Forbes, *The Metaphysics of Possibility* (Oxford: Oxford University Press, 1985), 127–8.

[79] See Max Black, "The Identity of Indiscernibles," *Mind* 61 (1952): 153–64.

[80] Adams, "Love and the Problem of Evil," 246.

God's aim in creating can be much more precise; in fact, provided the actual world contains no qualitatively indiscernible persons, God even can aim for a person by way of a uniquely individuating comprehensive qualitative description of the form "the $x$ that will exist and will be such that $\varphi(x)$".[81] Therefore, a case can be made that on Adams's assumptions of actualism and primitive thisnesses God still can satisfy condition (3) of Non-Identity Theodicy and be virtuously motivated in creating. (I say more about this analogy between divine creation and human procreation in Chapter 7.)

All theories of identity are disputable and come with costs and benefits, but there are at least three serious views of identity on which Non-Identity Theodicy can meet its key condition (1). Moreover, even for those who don't accept condition (1), whether because they hold certain creationist views of the soul or because they hold to some other theory of identity that would allow God to create the same people in very different worlds, it may be that something akin to Non-Identity Theodicy can be sustained with the help of Adams's *self-interest relation*.

Earlier I introduced Adams's claim that our rational self-interest does not follow our bare metaphysical identities but rather "a treasure of meaning that is inextricably bound up with details of our actual personal histories."[82] Even if God could have created us in a very different universe with a very different physical origination, it is another question whether his doing so would have been good *for us*. What we value in life is not just our metaphysical identity but the specific projects, relationships, commitments, experiences, memories, hopes, and aspirations that constitute the concrete content of our lives and in which we have found meaning. Adams suggests that because of the way the potential for evil and suffering is inextricable from so much of what we value in life, a significant alteration in God's policy of evil allowance would have made our lives in such alternative universes radically and fundamentally different from our actual lives. It would have made our lives so different with respect to what we care about that, plausibly, we lack a rational self-interest in those alternative lives.[83]

Indeed, to wish for the idyllic lives that so often we are inclined to wish for may be akin to wishing ourselves out of existence. William Hasker reflects, on similar grounds, that if we are glad that we exist (or glad that those we love exist), then "preferring [an alternative] life to one's actual life might be nearly as difficult as preferring not to have lived at all."[84] Reflection on our rational self-interest raises questions about whether and to what extent God could have wronged us by his current policy of evil and suffering allowance if under a different policy the concrete content of our lives would have been so different that to wish for one of

---

[81] I am thankful to Robert Adams for apprising me of this point.

[82] Adams, "Love and the Problem of Evil," 246.

[83] See Adams, "Existence, Self-Interest, and the Problem of Evil," 74–5.

[84] Hasker, *Providence, Evil and the Openness of God*, 21. Hasker attributes this point to Robert Rosenthal.

those alternative lives is to wish away most of what we actually care about and are glad about.[85]

If Non-Identity Theodicy were forced to give up its claim that people could not exist without God's policy of evil and suffering allowance, would a lack of rational self-interest in the lives resulting from alternative policies be a sufficient substitute for Non-Identity Theodicy's condition (1)? Intuitions will differ here. I noted previously that Adams believes that God could not have wronged people by not giving them even better lives if those lives are ones that bear no *self-interest relation* to their actual lives at any time.[86] I am inclined to agree with this. But, of course, the problem of evil is concerned not merely with the fact that people have been given lives worse than other lives they might have lived but with the fact that people have suffered severe forms of harm. It is not clear to me whether a lack of self-interest in alternative lives is sufficient, even when combined with conditions (2) and (3) of Non-Identity Theodicy, to justify the *horrendous harm* of the actual world. However, I do think that the severity of harm often has a comparative component, that the comparative component of harm is significantly correlated with the extent to which a person's interests have been frustrated, and therefore that the severity of harm can be mitigated to some degree if the one harmed by a bad state does not have a rational self-interest in the objectively better states that were possible.

I believe this reasoning explains, at least in part, why in some cases it might be more objectionable to permanently relocate to a suffering-prone part of the world with a teenage child than to do so while pregnant. Clearly many factors could be morally relevant to such a situation, but among them is that a teenager might have a strength of self-interest in life as she has known it and invested in it that a not-yet-born child would lack. The teenage child is correct when she notes that the badness of the move for her is enhanced by the fact that she will have to leave all of her friends, start at a new school, and give up her dream of working in an industry that is peculiar to the country of her birth. Similarly, the harm resulting from a moderate ligament tear in one's shoulder may be much less severe for most people than for a professional baseball pitcher because most people do not have a particular self-interest in having ligaments that can withstand the physical strain of professional pitching.

There are several reasonable identity theories that are consistent with Non-Identity Theodicy. Moreover, even if the independence of personal identity from physical origination is affirmed and (1) is denied, a lack of self-interest (rather than a lack of existence) in alternative worlds can to some extent attenuate the

---

[85]   If those who exist could have come to exist in worlds of significantly less evil, it would follow that God has failed to benefit them, for they are counterfactually worse off than they might have been. But, generally speaking, failure to benefit is not sufficient for wrongdoing.

[86]   Adams, "Existence, Self-Interest, and the Problem of Evil," 74–5.

harm motivating the problem of evil and therefore, at minimum, contribute to a successful solution to that problem. This could be the case if a successful solution to the problem of evil is cumulative in nature, whereby a number of reasons for God's allowance of evil are individually morally insufficient but jointly morally sufficient. (I will have a bit more to say about the role that Non-Identity Theodicy can play in cumulative case theodicy in Chapter 8.)

## P2. Evil at the End

A second plausibility objection questions whether Non-Identity Theodicy can account for evils suffered in the *final* generation of persons. On Adams's view, God is motivated by his desire to love a specific community of future persons. Once the last member of this divinely ordained community has been procreated, however, subsequent evil can no longer be justified by citing its necessity for attaining that community. Even if the justification of evil in the final generation can be aided by the fact that, from the perspective of eternity, many who suffer evil in that generation will lack a *self-interest relation* to the lives they would have lived had evil been discontinued, is it plausible that this consideration alone could justify an *unchanged* policy of suffering allowance in the final generation?

Suppose you think not. What, then, should we make of evil in the final generation? Should we expect a substantial diminution of evil once the last divinely elected human person comes to exist?[87]

The defender of Non-Identity Theodicy has at least three responses available. One is to bite the bullet and hold that evil will undergo a significant change if not a complete annihilation after the birth of the last person in the community motivating God's creative decision. This is not an uncommon thought. Several major religious traditions do hold that life as we experience it will be radically shifted in end times.[88] Theists already eschatologically committed in this way might find in Non-Identity Theodicy a compelling way of justifying their belief that although in the present age evil serves God's purposes, there will come an age when, for all who accept God's offer, there will be no more tears.

As a second response, one could deny that there is going to be any final generation of persons. If the community God desires to love through his creative act is comprised of an infinite number of persons stretching forward for eternity, Non-Identity Theodicy is unperturbed. For any person anywhere along the historical

---

[87] That is not quite precise because evil causally connected to the origin of the last human person presumably would cease before that origin. But even so, the question remains whether there will be a short timeframe near the end of procreation history in which a radical diminution of evil will occur.

[88] It was a common report in medieval theology that once enough people were produced to repopulate heaven, the heavenly bodies would stop orbiting the earth and generation and corruption would end.

continuum, we can account for the evil in her life by citing future lives made possible by that evil.

Thirdly, the defender of Non-Identity Theodicy can suggest a justification for evils that is unique to the final generation. We are creatures habituated to live in a certain environment, and in general we do not do well with rapid ecological or psychological changes. Perhaps changing the system so radically in the final generation of persons would have severe negative effects.[89] If so, God might have reason to stay-the-course in the final generation even after his primary motivation to grace future generations with existence is no longer operative. If you are already attracted to a non-identity approach to theodicy, any of these moves seems to me a not implausible way of expanding it.

## P3. Empirically Falsifiable?

A third objection to the plausibility of Non-Identity Theodicy that I find interesting but unsuccessful claims that the theodicy as I have outlined it is empirically falsifiable. One way to go about falsifying it, this objection suggests, would be for one hermit to kill another hermit, and then kill himself. No hermit will be directly involved in the procreation of future persons, and because they are hermits you might think no one other than themselves is obviously affected by their actions. It's tempting to think this is a type of evil that cannot be accounted for by its necessity for producing certain future persons.

The mistake here is not looking past the *obvious* effects of an event. Even a very tempered commitment to sensitive dependence on initial conditions in chaos theory gives us reason to think the hermits' actions are more than significant enough to, in due course, affect the procreative history of the world. I would stay the same course if one suggested William Rowe's fawn as a still more extreme example of an evil seemingly irrelevant to procreation history.[90] Even the details of the suffering of a fawn in a forest fire will significantly affect the locations and movements of many atoms, which will in turn affect the environments in which human persons interact and the interactions they have in those environments, eventually leading to the altering of procreation history.

Moreover, it is worth noting that the challenge to account for these types of apparently pointless evils is not unique to Non-Identity Theodicy. For any theodicy to be plausible, it must have something to say about these sorts of cases. Non-Identity Theodicy can claim that if we take careful account of so-called butterfly effects, we should judge that even the suffering of Rowe's fawn alters the

---

[89] Though according to the Christian tradition this radical shift will occur at some point, it is significant that it will occur only in the presence of God.

[90] See Rowe, "The Problem of Evil and Some Varieties of Atheism," 337.

community of person who will exist in the future. Such suffering is a side-effect of the cosmic order needed to produce the individuals God intends.

To my mind, this is not only plausible, but it is significantly more plausible than most other attempts to link seemingly useless sufferings to justifying goods. Swinburne, for example, writes that "it is a good for the fawn caught in the thicket in the forest fire that his suffering provides knowledge for the deer and other animals who see it to avoid the fire and deter their other offspring from being caught in it."[91] But Rowe could easily stipulate that the suffering of his fawn is unobserved by any non-divine being. It seems likely that there are such unobserved sufferings in the actual world. That there are evils irrelevant to procreation history, however, is decidedly more controversial.

## P4. Understanding Grace

Richard Gale offers a final instructive but ultimately unconvincing plausibility objection to Non-Identity Theodicy. He argues that if Molinism is false, God cannot know enough for his creating to be motivated by grace in the manner suggested by Adams.

Gale begins to formulate this objection by asking whether it is only non-moral evils that the motivation of grace is supposed to explain, or moral evils as well. He suggests—rightly in my opinion—that the most natural reading of Adams is that both non-moral and moral evils are supposed to be explained by divine grace. God was inclined to create beings as diminutive as we are, both metaphysically and morally, simply because it was us that he longed to love. Gale believes this reading is suggested by Adams's understanding of "God's gracious creation of less perfect humans as a bestowal of 'an *undeserved* personal favor,' since questions of merit or desert concern the manner in which creatures employ their free will for good or evil."[92]

Gale next claims that "[s]ince God's creating people who are undeserving is an instance of salvific grace, it must be based upon what they will freely do after they are created."[93] Gale's underlying assumption is that people can receive grace with respect to moral evils only to the extent that they have already failed morally. "But," he asks, "can God know about this at the time of creation?"[94]

---

[91] Swinburne, *Providence and the Problem of Evil*, 103.

[92] Gale, "R. M. Adams's Theodicy of Grace," 37.

[93] Gale, "R. M. Adams's Theodicy of Grace," 38. Gale understands salvific grace as "grace in which [God] freely bestows some benefit, some aid towards sanctification, upon persons who have already proven themselves by their misuse of free will not to be meritorious" (38). As I make clear in my ensuing discussion, this is not the sense of grace Adams is working with.

[94] Gale, "R. M. Adams's Theodicy of Grace," 38.

Gale argues that without *middle knowledge*, "God's creation of free persons is a gamble [with respect to whether or not they will be deserving of the goods God bestows]…[I]t [therefore] precludes his granting salvific grace in his very act of creating free persons."[95] Gale concludes that "God cannot bestow salvific grace by creating a person."[96]

One question I have for Gale is, why think beings of our type could ever *deserve* the extent of the gifts God gives in creating us and (perhaps eternally) sustaining us in lives that are great goods to us all things considered? It seems reasonable to believe that even the most meritorious human person could not merit this much. God metaphysically outclasses us to an even greater degree than we outclass cats. Cats may do meritorious things, but a cat could never merit dining at the head of his owner's table on the best of his owner's food. Similarly, God's grace is undeserved because of what we are, regardless of our moral track record.[97] If this is correct, then God does not take the gamble assumed by Gale. In advance of his creating, God can know that human persons will be undeserving of the extent of the grace he bestows, even if he has to wait and see whether they will freely choose to act in meritorious or unmeritorious ways.

I also question one of Gale's analogies. To explain why he thinks God could bestow grace in creating if *middle knowledge* were had by God, Gale uses the analogy of parents who "leave cookies out for their children to eat upon their return from school even though they foreknow that the children will freely perform some bad acts at school."[98] But this is not a case of *middle knowledge*! This is simply a case of parents being able to predict the actions of their children with some significant reliability. If human parents can do this, and if—as Gale implies—this puts them in a robust enough epistemic position to bestow grace upon their children, then it seems likely that God can bestow grace in this manner as well, for his powers of sans-*middle-knowledge* prediction will be much more reliable than those of any human parents.

Even if my previous two criticisms could be resisted, the most fundamental criticism of Gale's position would remain. Gale's objection goes awry from the outset because Gale misunderstands the nature of grace. He assumes that grace can only be bestowed to undeserving persons. "[I]f God could be gracious to a deserving person, then Adams's theodicy is undercut," Gale thinks, "because the idea that it is especially valuable to give grace to an undeserving person would be undercut."[99]

---

[95] Gale, "R. M. Adams's Theodicy of Grace," 39.

[96] Gale, "R. M. Adams's Theodicy of Grace," 40.

[97] Writing after Gale's article was published, Adams endorses this response: "It is commonly and plausibly thought that the love of an infinite, transcendently good being for finite beings could not be anything but grace in this sense, on the ground that no finite excellence could *deserve* the love of such a transcendent being" (Adams, *Finite and Infinite Goods*, 151).

[98] Gale, "R. M. Adams's Theodicy of Grace," 40.

[99] Gale, "R. M. Adams's Theodicy of Grace," 44, n. 10.

This is mistaken. Adams does not claim that grace can only be bestowed on undeserving persons, nor that grace is especially valuable when bestowed on undeserving persons.[100] In fact, he explicitly contradicts this in "Must God Create the Best?" when he clarifies that his argument

> is not to suggest that grace in creation consists in a preference for imperfection as such. God could have chosen to create the best of all possible creatures, and still have been gracious in choosing them. God's graciousness in creation does not imply that the creatures He has chosen to create must be less excellent than the best possible. It implies, rather, that even if they are the best possible creatures, that is not the ground for His choosing them.[101]

Grace does not imply demerit for Adams. It is by definition a favorable attitude not based on merit or demerit. Therefore, that God's motivation in creating is a desire to bestow grace does not imply that he will create particularly undeserving persons. It implies only that he will create people without regard for whether or not they are deserving. When grace is understood in this way, Gale's objection dissolves. God does not need to know the future results of free will in order to be motivated by grace in creating.

## A Non-Identity Theodicy for Molinists and Determinists

While Gale's objection to Adams's approach is misguided in several respects, I do think he's on to something. His general concern is that God may not have the requisite knowledge to play the part Adams assigns him. I share this concern, though for a different reason than Gale. Adams has suggested that, in creating, God aims to bestow grace upon specific future persons. We have seen that, contra Gale, general grace policies do not require detailed knowledge of the future. However, I will now argue that intending to create a community of specific persons does.

As I have outlined Non-Identity Theodicy to this point, God aims to produce specific persons—more precisely, all of the specific persons who make up the community of inhabitants of the actual world. But for God to will a cosmic

---

[100]  Simone Weil is one who does make this latter claim. She suggests that "[w]e are what is furthest from God, situated at the extreme limit from which it is not absolutely impossible to come back to him" ("The Cross," in *Gravity and Grace*, ed. Gustave Thibon (London and New York: Routledge, 2002), 89. The reason for this: "So that the love may be as great as possible, the distance is as great as possible. That is why evil can extend to the extreme limit beyond which the very possibility of good disappears. Evil is permitted to touch this limit. It sometimes seems as though it overpassed it. This, in a sense, is exactly the opposite of what Leibniz thought. It is certainly more compatible with God's greatness, for if he had made the best of all possible worlds, it would mean that he could not do very much" ("The Cross," 90).

[101]  Adams, "Must God Create the Best?," 324.

system because it will produce these rather than those specific persons, God would have to have strong reason to believe in advance of creation that it will in fact produce these rather than those.

How could he have such knowledge? Given the extreme sensitivity of procreation history, God could only have such knowledge by deterministic (or very nearly deterministic) control or Molinist control. If the cosmic system includes only natural causes, then God could have the requisite knowledge by deterministically controlling the history of the world. If the system includes libertarian voluntary causes as well, then God would need *middle knowledge*; the combination of *middle knowledge* and a deterministic control of natural causes would allow God to guide the unfolding of history with the precision necessary to produce specific persons.

However, on libertarian non-Molinist assumptions (that is, the assumptions that we have undetermined free will and God does not have *middle knowledge*),[102] God could not know enough in advance about the future free and contingent choices of persons to ensure—or even make probable—that he would wind up with the specific community of human persons he was motivated to bestow grace upon in the first place.[103] Even seemingly trivial free choices—for example, to take the scenic route to work or to stop to pick up a piece of trash—are enough to significantly alter which sperm and eggs join in conception, when they do so, and the circumstances under which their joining proceeds.[104]

You might think God could determine procreation history in a non-deterministic, non-Molinist system by stepping in miraculously immediately prior to each conception of a human life. Couldn't he thereby create and conjoin the sperm and eggs he so desires, and by these miracles get whatever people he desires? On theories of identity amenable to Non-Identity Theodicy, the answer is "no." On some of these theories, sperm and eggs—like human persons—will be identified in part by the causal history leading to their origins. Sperm and eggs created miraculously by God, therefore, will be different sperm and eggs from even sperm and eggs qualitatively identical at the time of conception but created through natural processes, and this difference will substantially alter the casual history of origin and therefore the identity of the resulting human persons. On another

---

[102] Some think God does not have *middle knowledge* because there are no truths to be known about how someone would freely act in a given situation prior to their actually freely acting in that situation. See also Chapter 1, n. 21 on Molinism and *middle knowledge*.

[103] Even if (without deterministic or Molinist control) God could not have this knowledge *in advance*, it may be that he has this knowledge timelessly. Nevertheless, because this timeless knowledge would be logically posterior to the free human choices in question, this knowledge would not be of use to God in deciding which universe to create.

[104] If human persons are the first inhabitants of earth with non-Molinist free will, then maybe God still could have aimed individually for some of the first human persons. Even so, the suffering of countless subsequent generations could not be plausibly justified by God's intention to create a relatively small number of human individuals at the commencement of the species.

theory, sperm and eggs are individuated by primitive, non-qualitative thisnesses such that only the actual history of the actual world up to the coming to be of those sperm and eggs will ensure their existence.

Moreover, even if these theories are rejected, part of loving a person is finding value in much of the concrete content of her life. Even if God could aim for a specific group of people *metaphysically* through miraculous intervention at conception, aiming for them in the robust sense relevant to his motivating desire to *love* particular individuals would have to include a commitment to much of the concrete content of their lives.

On libertarian, non-Molinist assumptions about free will, then, God can't know enough to be motivated by grace in the way Non-Identity Theodicy depends on. We have seen that Adams himself affirms that

> Without middle knowledge, God must take real risks if he makes free creatures (thousands, millions, or trillions of risks, if each free creature makes thousands of morally significant free choices). No matter how shrewdly God acted in running so many risks, his winning on *every* risk would not be antecedently probable.[105]

But Non-Identity Theodicy seems to rely on just this sort of antecedent probability! This exposes that the version of Non-Identity Theodicy I have outlined to this point is logically committed to either theological determinism or Molinism, whereby God chooses at the point of creation among fully determinate possible worlds.[106] Only by deterministic or Molinist control could God know enough to be motivated in creating by a desire to love specific persons.

## A Non-Identity Theodicy for Non-Molinist Libertarians

If one has arguments that favor the existence of non-Molinist libertarian free will or thinks that theological determinism or even Molinism would make God too directly involved in the bringing about of evil for him to be perfectly good, then he or she will be inclined to reject the version of Non-Identity Theodicy I have

---

[105] Adams, "Middle Knowledge and the Problem of Evil," 125.

[106] This interpretation of Adams is confirmed by the fact that the question initially framing his theodicy-relevant thoughts is, must God create the best possible world (if there is one and he creates)? Adams could have spoken only of God creating the best possible initial-world-segment, one then subject to the future contingencies of non-Molinist libertarian free will. By speaking of God making a choice between worlds rather than between initial-world-segments, Adams implies that God has sufficient control to make the choice of a world up front; God doesn't have to wait and see which world he gets.

presented.[107] However, I believe Non-Identity Theodicy can be reformulated to be made plausible on non-Molinist libertarian assumptions about free will. If I am correct, some version of Non-Identity Theodicy will be available to the theist regardless of her assumptions about free will.

Without *middle knowledge* or deterministic control of the universe, God's motivation in creating cannot be desire for specific individuals. But even if (on non-Molinist libertarian assumptions) God cannot know (in advance of creation) enough about the future free and contingent choices of the persons he will create to aim for specific individuals, he can nonetheless aim for specific being-*types*, and perhaps this too can be a loving motivation consonant with having a flawless character and not wronging those he creates. Moreover, because plausibly the individuals who actually exist could not have originated as other being-types, this remains for God a non-identity choice—one that brings into existence people who otherwise could not have existed. Condition (1) of Non-Identity Theodicy is therefore satisfied.

Likewise, the assumption of non-Molinist libertarianism will not impede Non-Identity Theodicy's ability to meet condition (2). The denial of theological determinism may even make it easier for those who believe in certain theories of hell to maintain that condition (2) is satisfied.[108]

This leaves condition (3). On this second version of Non-Identity Theodicy, God can be likened to human procreators. Choices to procreate are non-identity choices. However, even in cases of well-informed and fully voluntary human procreation, parents cannot know enough about their future children to aim for specific individuals. Nevertheless, they can aim for a being of a certain type—for a human child or for their biological child—and intuitions suggest that there is a morally significant sense in which parents can procreate out of love for their future children despite only aiming for a being-type.

And this despite the fact that, as David Benatar details,

> Children cannot be brought into existence for their own sakes. People have children for other reasons, most of which serve their own interests. Parents satisfy biological desires to procreate. They find fulfillment in nurturing and raising children. Children are often an insurance policy for old age. Progeny provide parents with some form of immortality, through the genetic material, values,

---

[107] Satisfying condition (2) of Non-Identity Theodicy may be challenging for the theist committed to theological determinism. But she is not without options. She will have to argue either that there is a morally significant sense in which someone can be *offered* a great eternal life even if they are determined to reject that offer, or that God ensures that even those who are determined to reject him nevertheless have lives that are worth living overall, or that ultimately no one will reject God, or that condition (2) should be weakened so that not every person needs to be offered a great life in order for Non-Identity Theodicy to be successful.

[108] Cf. n. 107, this chapter.

and ideas that parents pass on to their children and which survive in their children and grandchildren after the parents themselves are dead.[109]

All the more so, then, given divine capabilities for pure motivations, can God be motivated by love in aiming for specific being-types.

Moreover, the virtuous nature of this motivation does not rely on the being-type aimed for being better than other being-types the parents could have created. The parents also could have acted virtuously had they chosen to breed a type of dog they had a special affection for rather than procreating a human person. Likewise, I believe my parents could have acted out of a virtuous love for my type even if they had the option of procreating a genetically enhanced super-baby in my stead. What is important ethically is that the parents recognize what is valuable in the type they aim for and act out of a desire and determination to love whichever individual of that type they ultimately produce.

Analogously, so long as God has control enough to aim for specific types of beings,[110] then even without deterministic or Molinist control God can be motivated in creating by a desire to love the unspecified individuals of one or more being-types, irrespective of whether those being-types are better or worse than other being-types God could have created. Because God remains motivated by grace, he can similarly resist the previously discussed charges of irrationality, selfishness, and lack of appropriate regret.

I take it that, if there is a God, human persons are *among* the being-types he has aimed for in creating and sustaining the universe. The remaining question is whether evil comparable to the evil of the actual world is necessary for us to be the type of being we are. Condition (3) of Non-Identity Theodicy is only satisfied if a universe prone to *horrendous evil* is a necessary condition of producing beings of our type. I believe that it is. Two questions will help fill out this proposal:

Firstly, under what descriptions might God be motivated by a desire to love beings of our type?

Secondly, are *horrendous evils* necessary for us to be the type of being we are under those descriptions?

---

[109] David Benatar, "Why It Is Better Never to Come into Existence," *American Philosophical Quarterly* 34 (1997), 351.

[110] I take it that most religious traditions that attribute to God the power to create universes and perform miracles will be happy to attribute to him a level of control sufficient for directing the unfolding of history to include certain being-types. I further assume that the theist committed to modern evolutionary theory can make this attribution for the reason Plantinga cites: "The scientific theory of evolution just as such is entirely compatible with the thought that God has guided and orchestrated the course of evolution, planned and directed it, in such a way as to achieve the ends he intends. Perhaps he causes the right mutations to arise at the right time; perhaps he preserves certain populations from extinction; perhaps he is active in many other ways" (Alvin Plantinga, *Where the Conflict Really Lies: Science, Religion, and Naturalism* (Oxford: Oxford University Press, 2011), 308).

I'll consider these in order.

If the motivation behind God's creation of our being-type were merely a desire to have some animals or others as such, it could not aid the justification of *horrendous evil*. I'm prepared to grant that God could have produced some possible animals without *horrors*. The divine end of animals thinly described, therefore, cannot entail the actuality of *horrendous evil*.

But there is reason to think God would love our being-type (and probably also the being-types of some non-human animals) under thicker descriptions. There is a particularity to the best forms of love. It is one thing to be loved as an instance of a generic type. It is quite another to be loved for the details of who you are, for the features, idiosyncrasies, even eccentricities particular to you. According to the first version of Non-Identity Theodicy presented, it is the particular love of individual persons and their detailed life histories that does justificatory work. On this alternative, second form of Non-Identity Theodicy, it is a more general love for a being-type that does the justificatory work. But insofar as it is in God's tendency to love with particularity—and ultimately to love with full particularity each individual who is created—I find it plausible that God's love for beings of our type is significantly more particular than a mere love for animals, or sentient beings, or rational beings, as such.

To what might God's love for beings of our type be particular? A good starting point might be to consider what we value in ourselves. Good lovers seek to help their beloveds to see and appreciate what is loveable in them. If God as an ideal lover created us out of love for our being-type, it is plausible that he would create us with an inclination to value in ourselves what it is that he values in us. I therefore suggest that, if God exists, identifying descriptions under which we value our type can take us some way toward identifying descriptions under which our type is valued by God.

Prominent theories of personal identity are a natural starting point for homing in on the descriptions under which we value individuals of our type. After briefly considering three of these, I'll suggest that similar descriptions also plausibly home in on what we—and perhaps God—value about our type.

Broadly construed, three of the most prominent theories of personal identity are psychological, biological, and narrative theories, reflecting the fact that what human persons value about themselves as individuals are—among other things— their psychological states such as memories, beliefs, intentions, desires, hopes, and faith, the biological organisms that they are continuous with, and the integrated stories running through their lives.

This valuing lines up well with the descriptions under which good parents are prone to love their children. Good parents come to love their offspring as psychologically continuous beings with characteristic psychological dispositions. A parent might value his child's joyful disposition and her tendency to be empathetic, her ability to see the glass half full and her faith that great success is right around the corner. Often a good parent will even value psychological features of his child that he would not be inclined to consider valuable in other contexts, for instance an endearing stubbornness that he cannot help but smile at.

Valuing children under psychological descriptions such as these is often closely related to valuing them under particular narrative descriptions. A parent may value not merely the stubbornness of the child, but that the child is stubborn *like her mother*. A parent may value not only the child's joyful disposition, but that her joy gave the parent hope when he was mourning the loss of his parents, not only the child's courage, but the courage she showed when having her appendix out, not only the child's memories, but also the memories that they share. Good parents love their children relative to ongoing narratives, both narratives particular to their child's life and broader narratives such as family histories. This is reflected in the fact that good parents are typically concerned with their children being better-off than they were in addition to their being well-off in some objective sense.

Thirdly, biology is relevant to admirable parental love. Good parents love their offspring prior to their having any psychological states. They love them when they are mere fetuses in the womb, and they would continue to love them at the end of life even if they wound up in permanent comatose states. This can be understood by recognizing that several of the narratives important to human relationship have key biological components. The shared narrative of biological birth, for instance, is important to the relationship between parent and child. If that biological history is missing, it can make it harder for that relationship to develop.

Additionally, the biology relevant to love for a child extends much further back than the time of the child's conception. Biological lineage is relevant to parental love. That someone is your biological descendant serves as good reason to love him.[111] It matters that I not only look like my dad and have shared experiences with him, but that we are part of the same family tree. I may look more like other people and have more shared experiences with them, but that doesn't make them family. Relatedly, an important part of loving someone is honoring their ancestors and their descendants. My affection for the troublemaking kid down the street has much to do with the fact that he is my good friend's son.[112]

Do these descriptive categories—biological, psychological, and narrative—carry over to what is important to us about our being-type? I believe they do.

Firstly, we value the human race for its psychological make-up. We value our ability to love, and all the more so for its vulnerability and for our ability to choose love in opposition to hate. We value our experience of pleasure and even pain, so much that I suspect many people would choose the ability to feel pain alone over

---

[111] Note that none of this implies that parents have more reason to love a biological child than an adopted child. I find it very plausible that reasons for love do not always aggregate in this way.

[112] There is a point of connection here with the God of the Bible, who is depicted as having a special affection for Abram's race, Abraham's offspring, the children of Israel, and David's line.

an inability to feel both pain and pleasure. We value our ability to be courageous, and all the more so for the extent of our fears and our proneness to cowardice. We value our ability to empathize with one another when courage turns to despair. We value how we appreciate art, and how we practice philosophy. We value the psychological states accompanying physical touch. We value the psychological states of those with various disabilities—the simple delights of children with Downs, for instance. We value our psychological proneness to effervescence in large groups and to hope against the evidence. None of this implies that we think we are psychologically *better* than other possible being-types. Irrespective of such comparisons, the value we place and see in the psychological dispositions of *our* type helps explain why many of us would prefer the continued existence of our own type to that of other types, even if those other types were better in some objective sense.

Secondly, we value our type biologically. We value the biological process by which we come to be, evidenced by the fact that—despite the substantial pain and other sacrifices involved—many women choose to procreate multiple times, even in places where adoption is a viable option, and many prefer natural birth over cesarean delivery. We also value our biological heritage, evidenced both by the pride—sometimes good and sometimes bad—that we take in our ethnicity and by our tendency, since Darwin, to categorize species according to their evolving lineages. As human families are delineated primarily by biological relations rather than by proximity, physical likeness, or social compatibility, so species tend to be delineated by unique biological ancestries rather than by genetic, developmental, behavioral, or ecological similarities. This reflects the importance we place on biology not only at the level of valuing individual human persons but also at the level of valuing the human race as a being-type.

Finally, and perhaps most clearly, we value our being-type for its narrative, as evidenced by the tendency of all human cultures to set up manifold structures and practices for the remembrance and commemoration of events, objects, and individuals important to the history of our race.

We value ourselves according to psychological, biological, and narrative descriptions, both as individuals and as a being-type, and our valuing of these aspects of humanity is some evidence for God's valuing of them. Insofar as a loving God would create us with a tendency to value in ourselves what he values in us, I take these to be three descriptions under which it is plausible that God, if he exists, desired our being-type in creating and sustaining the universe we inhabit.[113]

The remaining question is whether *horrors* are necessary for us to be the being-type that we are under each of these descriptions. I claim that they are. It strains

---

[113] This is a suggestion supported by theological traditions. The Hebrew Bible, for instance, can be understood as an unfolding narrative of psychologically-based divine–human relationship developed along biological lineages.

the imagination to think of what human psychology would be like if we lived in a world without *horrendous evils*. Part of what it is to be us is to be the fragile beings that we are, vulnerable to violation and destruction. So much of our meaning-making systems—what we value, desire, participate and invest in—depends on our living in an environment prone to *horrendous evil*. Resultantly, so much of our psyche is dominated by denying, worrying about, preventing, responding to, and dealing with *horrors* that any beings born into and maturing in a *horror*-free world would be radically psychologically different from us.

One might object that an omnipotent God could get mental states qualitatively identical to ours by creating a suitable virtual world for either immaterial beings or brains-in-vats. It's unclear to me that such a world would be any less *horrendous* than the actual world. But it might be claimed that the possibility of this virtual world shows that at least some of the *horrendous evil* of the actual world— any that entails material destruction, for instance—is not necessary for God to get our being-type under its psychological description.

Perhaps. But, firstly, this would require God being willing to get beings of our psychological type by a large-scale deception about the nature of our existence. It's reasonable to suspect this is at odds with the love for our type that motivated God to create us in the first place. Moreover, and perhaps more importantly, a large-scale deception of this sort would involve God getting our psychological type at the expense of getting our narrative type. Insofar as God creates out of love for us on all three of these descriptions, this is further reason for thinking God would not aim for our psychological type through large-scale deception.

If God were aiming for our being-type under a narrative description, that narrative would have to include stories of destruction that involved more than just our mental states. In addition to stories of false motives and bad decisions that have been at the root of many of the major turns in human history, it would have to include external destruction such as natural disasters, human diseases, and wars.[114] This is not to say that God loves these aspects of the human narrative; he may regret and even hate them. Rather, God loves beings of our type, and being our type is deeply interwoven with the narrative of human history. No narrative that did not include many of the sorts of things that would be the key features of any good documentary on the human race could plausibly be considered the narrative of our being-type.

Finally, are *horrors* necessary for us to be the type of being we are under a biological description? Technically, perhaps not. Human persons seem uniquely capable (among earthly creatures) of perpetrating and suffering some of the worst forms of actual evil. Only human persons have been capable of sex trafficking children, for instance, or of feeling prolonged hatred toward oneself. *Horrors* as

---

[114] This does not entail that God created a universe that would inevitably produce these forms of external destruction. See n. 127, this chapter, for further discussion of this point.

I have defined them entail the existence of persons who suffer. Thus, any processes or events that helped produce and hence preceded our biological type could not have included suffering that is conditional on the concurrent existence of our type. Moreover, with the resources of omnipotence, God could have miraculously protected our biological type from *horrors* once we came to exist. Therefore, it may be within the power of God both to produce and to sustain beings of our biological type without allowing *horrendous evil*.

However, once again, this would be to get our being-type under one description at the expense of the other two. Perhaps such persons would be the same species in a biological sense, but if they were continuously supernaturally protected from *horrors* from the commencement of our species, they would not share the psychology or narrative of our being-type.

Moreover, even if *horrors* are not necessary for our biological-type to exist, plausibly the natural processes out of which *horrors* emerge are. Our biological lineage and makeup would not look nearly the same without our world having had the natural threats to survival that it has had, without the laws of thermodynamics having underlain physical systems as they have. John Polkinghorne frames this recognition in evolutionary terms, appreciating that "[e]xactly the same biochemical processes that enable some cells to mutate and produce new forms of life—in other words, the very engine that has driven the stupendous four billion year history of life on Earth—these same processes will inevitably allow other cells to mutate and become malignant."[115]

Maybe God could have eradicated the biological processes underlying human existence once human persons came to exist, but there is good reason to think he would not have. Many parents value pregnancy intensely. Part of their love for their children is valuing the processes and events out of which their children came to be. If parents didn't value pregnancy, for example, if they considered it purely a burden, then that shows a lack in them. Likewise, the natural processes that God cares about in caring for us may be much richer than we are apt to assume, and God's love of us and his love of us in natural creation may not be so separable. Part of God's love for our type would be valuing the natural world out of which we came, and this is additional reason to think he would be resistant to discarding major features of that world as soon as human life had commenced.[116]

---

[115] John Polkinghorne, "Understanding the Universe," *Annals of the New York Academy of Sciences* 950 (2001), 181.

[116] This point may resonate especially strongly with those who affirm an evolutionary approach to speciation. Even if being-types are identified primarily as static essences created *ex nihilo*—as was more common prior to Darwin's influence—it is plausible to suppose that love for our being-type will be deeply intertwined with appreciation for the natural environment that sustains us and that we were designed to function within. But if being-type is more strongly connected to the biological lineage out of which a being-type came to be—as contemporary evolutionary speciation suggests—then appreciating the *horror*-prone processes of our natural world may be even more intimately linked with what it is for God to love beings of our type.

## Philosophical Precursors

This link between the laws of nature guiding our natural environment and the existence of our being-type connects with an important line of thought in modern theodicy that I have not yet discussed—namely, the idea that God's choice of the actual world was somehow significantly related to his choice of regular laws of nature.

Leibniz, like his contemporary Nicolas Malebranche, argues that God would be committed to simple laws since these best display his intelligence as creator.[117] God is concerned not only with the happiness of human persons but "that nature preserves the utmost order and beauty." Resultantly, "there is no reason to suppose that God, for the sake of some lessening of moral evil, would reverse the whole order of nature…[I]t would by no means follow that the interest of a certain number of men would prevail over the consideration of a general disorder diffused through an infinite number of creatures."[118] To the suggestion that God should protect human persons by consistent supernatural intervention, Leibniz replies that "[n]othing would be less rational than these perpetual miracles."[119] Miraculous intervention would be avoided by God unless hugely outweighing goods were at stake. In a similar vein, van Inwagen writes with sympathy of the view that "*any* degree of irregularity in a world is a defect, a sort of unlovely jury-rigging of things that is altogether unworthy of the power and wisdom of God."[120]

Van Inwagen therefore entertains a response to the problem of *horrendous evil* based on the thought that it was not possible for God to create a universe containing both regular laws of nature and higher-level sentient creatures without there being suffering morally equivalent to or greater than the suffering we observe. That is, perhaps every world containing both higher-level sentient creatures and less suffering than the actual world is "a world in which the laws of nature fail in some massive way."[121]

As ancestors in this thought, van Inwagen could look to Schleiermacher and F. R. Tennant, both of whom assumed the inevitability of suffering for intelligent beings embodied in a natural law-governed world. However, van Inwagen is right, I believe, to be "inclined to say that the mere avoidance of massive irregularity

---

[117] Leibniz writes, "If God chose what would not be the best absolutely and in all, that would be a greater evil than all the individual evils which he could prevent by this means. This wrong choice would destroy his wisdom and his goodness" (Gottfried Wilhelm Leibniz, *Theodicy: Essays on the Goodness of God, the Freedom of Man and the Origin of Evil*, (New York: Cosimo, Inc., 2009), 201 (Section,129.XIV)).

[118] Leibniz, *Theodicy*, 188–9 (Section 118.III).

[119] Leibniz, *Theodicy*, 193 (Section 120.V). Leibniz affirms this point in several places, for example when he writes later in the same work that "God cannot establish a system ill-connected and full of dissonances" (202 (Section 130.XV)).

[120] Van Inwagen, *The Problem of Evil*, 120.        [121] Van Inwagen, *The Problem of Evil*, 114.

cannot be a sufficient justification for the actual sufferings of human beings."[122] If only a divine commitment to regularity were at stake, God would opt for irregularity and avert *horrors*.

Supplementing the emphasis on law-regularity, then, one might speculate that the suffering of this world is necessary not just for intelligent, embodied life to exist in a regularly law-governed universe, but for such life to exist *at all*. Austin Farrer makes a move in this vicinity when he writes,

> Poor limping world, why does not your kind creator pull the thorn out of your paw? ... But what sort of thorn is this? And if it were pulled out, how much of the paw would remain? How much, indeed, of the creation? What would a physical universe be like, from which all mutual interference of systems was eliminated? It would be no physical universe at all. It would not be like an animal relieved of pain by the extraction of a thorn. It would be like an animal rendered incapable of pain by the removal of its nervous system; that is to say, of its animality. So the physical universe could be delivered from the mutual interference of its constituent systems, only by being deprived of its physicality.[123]

Though it's difficult to know exactly what Farrer has in mind, it seems that he takes regular laws of nature to be a necessary condition of any physical universe and to necessarily result in the suffering of any embodied sentient beings that come to exist. Much more is at stake here than mere law regularity. But I agree with Richard Swinburne that those who outright deny the possibility either of intelligent or of embodied, intelligent life in an evil-free, natural law-governed world do not tend to give rigorous arguments to show that this is not possible.[124] This is true of Farrer. The "So" in his final sentence is unearned.

A more recent example of a similar but less extreme move is found in Southgate, who deserves credit for at least acknowledging explicitly that he does not have any strong argument for the assumption he makes. Southgate holds that "the sort of universe we have, in which complexity emerges in a process governed by thermodynamic necessity and Darwinian natural selection, and therefore by death, pain, predation, and self-assertion, is the only sort of universe that could give rise to the range, beauty, complexity, and diversity of creatures the earth has produced."[125] Southgate refers to this as his "unprovable assumption," and is upfront in admitting that "[t]hough we cannot know [why God did not create a world without

---

[122] Van Inwagen, *The Problem of Evil*, 127. Van Inwagen is inclined to think that "the anti-irregularity defense satisfactorily explains the sufferings of sub-rational sentient animals" (Van Inwagen, *The Problem of Evil*, 127).

[123] Farrer, *Love Almighty and Ills Unlimited*, 51.

[124] Swinburne, *Providence and the Problem of Evil*, 43.

[125] Southgate, *The Groaning of Creation*, 29.

evil], a starting presumption must be that the formation of the sorts of life forms represented in the biosphere *required* an evolutionary process."[126]

What I have been suggesting in the previous sections of this chapter is that we *can* know that, on several descriptions, our sort of life form requires the biological processes of the actual world and the laws of nature that underpin them. The importance of law regularity—which can be traced back to Leibniz—is affirmed by Non-Identity Theodicy. But rather than being undermotivated as the primary moral justification of *horrendous* human suffering or lacking plausibility as a necessary condition of intelligent (or embodied, intelligent) life generally, it is shown necessary for God to aim for beings of our type and, *a fortiori*, for the individuals of our type who come to exist. Non-Identity Theodicy recommends justificatory goods on which the historically significant intuitions driving the concern for law-regularity can be appropriated.

## Conclusion

Non-Identity Theodicy suggests that God's reasons for allowing suffering are to be found neither in past human guilt nor in future human achievement, but rather in our present and enduring status as objects of divine love.

Moreover, I have argued that, even if non-Molinist human free will means God could not aim for specific individuals in creating and sustaining this universe, he nonetheless could aim for specific being-types, and that if there is a loving God we have some reason to think the descriptions under which *he* values our type would be correlated with the descriptions under which *we* value our type—among others, under psychological, biological, and narrative descriptions. For God to dispense with *horrors*, he would need to drastically change either the external natural processes that cause *horrors* or else our capacity to suffer *horrendously*. To do the latter would be to change our psychological make-up to such an extent that we would not plausibly remain the same psychological type. To do the former would also have drastic effects on our psychology, and in addition would either change our biological type or threaten God's ability to love us under our biological description. To do either would so radically alter the narrative of our race that God could not be said to be acting out of love for us under a narrative description of our type. That one day we may exist in an evil-free environment does not undermine these conclusions, because part of what it is to be of our type is to be headed for redemption in various respects.[127]

[126] Southgate, *The Groaning of Creation*, 47.
[127] Some theists may worry that God could not be aiming for our being-type, not because they believe things will be different in the end but because they believe things were different in the beginning. If humanity has fallen from some form of original righteousness, this could be taken to imply that, insofar as God aimed for a human being-type, he aimed for it under a pre-fall suffering-free

My conclusion, therefore, is that all three conditions of a successful Non-Identity Theodicy can be met even if non-Molinist human free will exists. If God creates out of a holistic love for beings of our type, we should expect his creation to have the *horror*-producing tendencies of the actual world. To borrow Marilyn Adams's words, one reason the universe includes *horrendous* suffering is "that God wanted to rejoice in human children, while vulnerability to participation in *horrors* is part of leading a merely human life."[128]

A final point can be made not as necessary for Non-Identity Theodicy but in support of it. Why would God create out of love for *horror*-sufferers rather than for some other type of being? Robert Adams has argued that if God acted out of grace, no answer to this question is necessary. In fact, any answer that implies God created those he did because they are *better* than others he could have created is in tension with the particularity of the purest forms of interpersonal love.

But an answer of a different sort is possible. Perhaps a partial reason why God would choose beings of our type is because choosing beings of our type fits well with other things God values.

Consider an analogy. It may be just as loving for a professional musician to fall in love with someone who can't sing in tune as with another professional musician. Still, you might find it less surprising to learn that a professional musician is dating someone musically talented than someone musically inept. It is less surprising because a musician's attraction to another musician fits well with the value he places on music and the valuing of music.

I have argued that a God of love would choose *out of love*, but it is also fitting for a God of love to choose *for love*. A choice for love would mean choosing a being-type capable of love. I suggest that love in its preeminent form includes meaning-makers being willing to risk their whole selves for one another. But this requires the possibility of *horrendous evil*, because *horrendous evil* is precisely for the life of a meaning-maker to be undermined. Dogs can risk their lives for one another, but they are not meaning-makers in a robust enough sense to be capable of mutually loving relationships. Angels (as Thomas Aquinas thinks of them)

---

description and not under the current description we have freely fallen into. But I think this conclusion is avoidable. Even if God did not desire for humanity to fall, one reason he could be taken to have *allowed* a fall and its consequences is because he desired to bring into existence and to love beings of our biological, psychological, and narrative description. God can love many different beings under many different descriptions. He could love the first human persons in their condition of original righteousness and subsequent human persons in their fallen condition.

I also take a fall of humanity to be reconcilable with the Molinist or deterministic version of Non-Identity Theodicy. A fall of humanity, as a significant event in history, would affect which individuals come to exist subsequently. God therefore could be taken to have allowed a fall in part in order to aim for specific individuals that he desired to create and love.

[128] Adams, *Horrendous Evils and the Goodness of God*, 163.

would be meaning-makers, but might not have it in their possibility of choice to risk their lives for others.[129]

Jeffrey Stout summarizes my claim well:

> Our circumstances would be fortunate indeed if they permitted us to act on the basis of benevolent concern for our loved ones without ever placing self-preservation or loving fellowship at risk. But if we are lucky in this respect, our lives cannot be ideally *salient* expressions of agape.[130]

Meaning-makers vulnerable to *horror* are best suited for the best sort of love. Given this, it is fitting to find that they would be created by a God interested in the best forms of love.

This is not to say that God's justification for creating out of love for *horror*-participants is any greater than the justification he would have for creating out of love for other being-types. Nor does it mean that we should expect God to create the being-type most prone to *horrors*, which would be one far more prone than we are. Whereas I am inclined to think one particularly valuable form of love requires lovers taking a real risk of their whole selves, it is less clear to me that the greatness of this love increases the greater that risk is. Moreover, even if this were the case, the badness of *horrors* gives God reason to limit the extent of them.

Given the fittingness of a divine choice *for love*, our being-type fits the bill. While this may not aid God's justification, it does give us greater reason to accept the plausibility of Non-Identity Theodicy. Insofar as the choice of *horror*-prone beings fits well with other things a God of love would value, this lessens the surprise that God would choose to create the universe we live in.

Robert Adams has argued that getting the individuals of the actual world requires the witting choice of a *horror*-prone world on the part of God. What I have now shown is that a similar witting choice is required for getting even the being-type to which those individuals belong, and that we have some reason to think creating our being-type is a fitting choice for a God of love. Both the choice for specific individuals and the choice for specific being-types are non-identity choices. The result is that some version of Non-Identity Theodicy is open to the theist regardless of her assumptions about free will.

I have argued that both versions of Non-Identity Theodicy can resist charges of divine character flaws by citing the motivation of love (either for specific individuals or for specific being-types) in creating. I have argued further that these theodicies are not implausible on other grounds. What's left is to consider in more

---

[129] Aquinas, *Summa Theologiae*, First Part, Question 62. Angels could lose their happiness according to Aquinas.

[130] Jeffrey Stout, "The Sacred Made Visible," the third of the 2007 Stone Lectures delivered at Princeton Theological Seminary.

detail whether anyone is wronged by being brought into existence in a manner described by Non-Identity Theodicy.

Focusing on the moral implications of the *horrendous* suggests that the answer to this question is not as straightforward as Robert Adams once assumed. According to Non-Identity Theodicy, God is in the precarious position of regularly causing or permitting *horrors*. I have argued that harm avoidance might plausibly justify this, but non-existence is not a harm. Moreover, I have argued that non-harm-averting goods in the form of pure benefits are not sufficient to morally justify *horror* causation or permission. For Non-Identity Theodicy to resist being morally impugned, then, it will have to claim that, among non-harm-averting goods, the good of being brought into existence and given a worthwhile human life is a good uniquely capable of justifying harm.

On the far other extreme stands Derek Parfit, who claims that the fact that one would not have existed had an action not been performed makes *no difference whatsoever* to the morality of that action. In the next chapter, I argue against Parfit that non-identity does make a moral difference, and I further argue that this difference may be significant enough to make Non-Identity Theodicy *structurally promising*.

# 7

# The Good of Life

## How Much Moral Difference Does Non-Identity Make?

Non-Identity Theodicy suggests that, in creating the universe, God is like a parent procreating. The parent is not just aiming to give her child any old good, but the good of life, and this good is importantly distinctive. One way it's distinctive is that the child wouldn't exist without it.

Likewise, the primary good proposed by Non-Identity Theodicy as morally justifying the divine policy of this-worldly evil allowance is the good of life for particular individuals. More precisely, the recommended justificatory good is that of each human person being brought into existence and offered a very worthwhile human life when they otherwise (that is, without the actual divine policy of evil allowance) would never have existed. (Hereafter, when I speak of "a worthwhile human life," I use it as a shorthand to denote this good.)

I have suggested that it is wrong to cause or permit *horrendous* suffering for pure benefit. Is it just as morally suspect to have a policy of *horror* causation or permission if the existence of those who suffer depends on it? The plausibility of Non-Identity Theodicy depends on a negative response. Robert Adams gives one. In fact, he claims that so long as those who suffer have lives worth living all things considered, God would be morally in the clear with respect to causing or permitting suffering that their existence depends on.

Derek Parfit takes the polar opposite position. In *Reasons and Persons*, Parfit considers the effects of present actions on future generations, and claims that the fact that someone would not have existed had some suffering not taken place makes *no difference at all* to the moral assessment of the agent who caused or permitted the suffering.[1] If Parfit is right about this *No-Difference View*, then there is nothing morally distinctive about the justificatory power of a worthwhile human life. Then Non-Identity Theodicy fares no better morally than Type A or Type B Theodicy.

---

[1] Because Parfit uses the term "moral" roughly as I use the term "ethical," he actually makes the more ambitious claim that non-identity makes no ethical difference whatsoever. I already argued against this last chapter when I showed that non-identity can have significant bearing on the intentions and therefore the character of those acting. These concerns are largely outside the scope of Parfit's consequentialism.

*Non-Identity Theodicy: A Grace-Based Response to the Problem of Evil*. Vince R. Vitale, Oxford University Press (2020).
© Vince R. Vitale.
DOI: 10.1093/oso/9780198864226.003.0007

Not far from this extreme stands Seana Shiffrin. While she does not commit herself to Parfit's *No-Difference View*, she claims that the good of a worthwhile human life typically has less justificatory power than that of pure benefits. If she is right, then even if depicting God in a non-identity scenario does *some* work toward maintaining the morality of God, it will not yield an endorsement of Adams's more ambitious claim that non-identity considerations make enough of a moral difference to acquit God of all charges that he has wronged human persons by creating them in a *horror*-prone world.

*Horrors* are so bad that any good that plausibly could be taken to justify their causation or permission would have to have very great justificatory force. If causing or permitting *horrors* for pure benefit is morally objectionable, and if the justificatory force of a worthwhile human life is in general less than that of pure benefits, as Shiffrin maintains, then Non-Identity Theodicy is *structurally unpromising*.

The argument of this chapter resists this conclusion in three steps. In the first section, I outline and raise some preliminary challenges to Parfit and Shiffrin's reasons for not thinking much of non-identity's claim to distinctive justificatory force. I then employ intuitions about the morality of procreation to make my strongest argument against Parfit and Shiffrin. I determine in this second section that the good of worthwhile human life has significantly greater justificatory force than pure benefits. In the third and final section, I argue that the good of *God-given* human life has even greater justificatory power. I conclude that it is reasonable to hold that the good of God-given human life is great enough to clear God of the charge that he has acted immorally in causing or permitting the *horrendous evils* of the actual world.

## Preliminary Challenges to Parfit and Shiffrin

### Parfit's *No-Difference View*

I here question Parfit's reasoning for the claim that non-identity makes no moral difference. As evidence in support of the *No-Difference View*,[2] Parfit offers the case of *The Medical Programmes*:

> There are two rare conditions, J and K, which cannot be detected without special tests. If a pregnant woman has Condition J, this will cause the child she is carrying to have a certain handicap. A simple treatment would prevent this effect. If a woman has Condition K when she conceives a child, this will cause the child to have the same particular handicap. Condition K cannot be treated, but always disappears within two months. Suppose next that we have planned two medical

---

[2] Parfit, *Reasons and Persons*, 363, 367.

programmes, but there are funds for only one; so one must be cancelled. In the first programme, millions of women would be tested during pregnancy. Those found to have Condition J would be treated. In the second programme, millions of women would be tested when they intend to try to become pregnant. Those found to have Condition K would be warned to postpone conception for at least two months, after which this incurable condition will have disappeared. Suppose finally that we can predict that these two programmes would achieve results in as many cases. If there is Pregnancy Testing, 1,000 children a year will be born normal rather than handicapped. If there is Preconception Testing, there will each year be born 1,000 normal children rather than 1,000, different, handi-capped children.[3]

If Pregnancy Testing is canceled, but not if Preconception Testing is canceled, the people who will live with the disability could have been cured. Parfit thinks this difference makes no moral difference; he judges the two programs equally worth-while. Even clearer, he thinks, is that if non-identity does make a moral differ-ence, it must be only a very slight difference. As evidence favoring this judgment, he cites his intuitions that if Preconception Testing would achieve results in even just a few more cases, he would judge it to be the better program,[4] and likewise if the disability being avoided by Preconception Testing were even very minimally worse than the disability being avoided by Pregnancy Testing, this would be enough to convince him to cancel Pregnancy Testing.

I am inclined to think that if this example seems to tell in favor of a no-or-marginal-difference view, that is only due to one or more of three problems with the example. Firstly, the example concerns fetuses, and many people are—con-sciously or not—inclined not to include fetuses as full members of the moral community. Parfit resists this objection. He says that in morally evaluating the programs,

> we need have no view about the moral status of a foetus. We can suppose that it would take a year before either kind of testing could begin. When we choose between the two programmes, none of the children has yet been conceived. And all those who are conceived will become adults. We are therefore considering effects, not on present foetuses, but on future people.[5]

But the relevant variable is not whether we are considering effects on present fetuses or future people but rather whether the future people who will exist would have existed had we chosen differently. Parfit assumes that Preconception Testing, though not Pregnancy Testing, bears on which persons will exist in the future.

---

[3] Parfit, *Reasons and Persons*, 367.   [4] Parfit, *Reasons and Persons*, 369.
[5] Parfit, *Reasons and Persons*, 367–8.

But many people will be inclined to think that either program will have this effect because, even if they judge the details of conception to be necessary for personal identity, they do not accept that these details are sufficient. For many evaluating Parfit's example, it will seem plausible that what happens to a fetus in the early stages of pregnancy partially determines the identity of the human person that fetus will become.

Secondly, even if *metaphysical* identity is fully determined at conception, the curing of a significant disease in a fetus would so radically change the details and the meaning of the ensuing life that it would not clearly be rational for the uncured person to wish he had been cured as a fetus at any time that he is capable of considering the question, nor would a fetus ever have the forward-looking perspective to judge himself self-interested in alternative lives. Plausibly, lives that diverge due to significant harm in a fetal state do not bear the *self-interest relation* to one another, and a rational self-interest also seems importantly relevant to morally evaluating one's life alternatives.

We should conclude, therefore, not that non-identity makes no moral difference in *The Medical Programmes* cases, but rather that both cases are cases either of non-identity or of something importantly similar to non-identity, and, as such, identical moral evaluations of them is not significant evidence favoring a no-or-marginal-difference view.

And Parfit's use of *The Medical Programmes* is questionable on a third count as well. The only reason suggested for why the medical establishment would not test all of the mothers in question is cost efficiency, and this reason is neither emphasized nor filled out in such a way that inclines the reader to see it as a significant reason. We may be inclined to think the medical establishment is running a frivolous risk if it cancels *either* program.

Something similar is true of other examples Parfit discusses in relation to his no-difference intuition as well. For instance, he suggests that excessive depletion or the mishandling of radioactive waste would be equally morally objectionable regardless of whether these actions affected the identities of future persons. But even more clearly here than in *The Medical Programmes*, the agents in question are presented as running frivolous risks. The fact that no potentially justifying reason for their actions is suggested or implied acts to obscure our intuitions about the moral significance of non-identity for at least three reasons.

Firstly, the agents are not presented as being aware that their actions will affect who will come to exist in the future. From a subjective perspective, then, the agents' actions would be just as bad regardless of whether those actions affect procreation history. Given *this* no-difference, it is easy to confuse our subjective moral evaluations of the agents in question for evaluations of whether and to what extent those harmed by the agents' actions have been wronged.

Secondly, in cases of serious and completely ungrounded harm, it does not clearly follow from there being more reasons to judge that an agent has acted wrongly that the one wronged has been wronged more severely. Consider what has become known as "happy slapping," where someone approaches a stranger in public and slaps them across the face, just for the rush of it. If I saw this happen, I would judge that the person slapped had been seriously wronged, and the groundlessness of the harm inclines me to judge that the victim would be just as (or very nearly as) wronged whether he had received one slap or three. Similarly, it seems reasonable to judge non-identity cases of frivolous and grievous harm risk no less bad for the fact that they are cases of non-identity.

Thirdly, perhaps even clearer than the claim that ungrounded harm such as "happy slapping" resists summative moral assessment is that it resists summative emotional reaction. I am confident that if I saw a "happy slapping" taking place, I would immediately become nearly as angry as I am capable of being. As such, additional slaps would add little if anything to my already very strong emotional reaction. Because some of Parfit's cases share with cases of "happy slapping" its most infuriating quality of complete moral groundlessness, I am inclined to think our imagined emotional reaction to the cases Parfit describes will be minimally if at all affected by non-identity, *even if* non-identity makes a significant moral difference in those cases. Here we have *another* no-difference that could easily be mistaken for the no *moral* difference Parfit suggests.

The cases Parfit uses to motivate his *No-Difference View* don't do a good enough job isolating our intuitions about non-identity to be reliable for his purpose. And even Parfit—despite claiming that those who exist in the future will have no stronger claim against the policy-decision regardless of which program is cancelled[6]—admits that he needs to make one qualification in order for this to hold true:

> If we decide to cancel Pregnancy Testing, those who are later born handicapped might know that, if we had made a different decision, they would have been cured. Such knowledge might make their handicap harder to bear. We should therefore assume that, though it is not deliberately concealed, these people would not know this fact. With this detail added, I judge the two programmes to be equally worthwhile.[7]

Parfit never discusses *why* such knowledge might make disabilities harder to bear for those who will exist if Pregnancy Testing is canceled. If we assume with Parfit that personal identity (in the morally relevant sense) is fully determined at conception, I think the answer is because they have had a right violated that the others have not—namely, the right not to have surrogate decision makers choose

---

[6] Parfit, *Reasons and Persons*, 369: "[W]e ought to choose to cure this group only if they have a stronger claim to be cured. And they do not have a stronger claim."
[7] Parfit, *Reasons and Persons*, 368.

poorly with respect to their alternatives for them. They have something to be upset about that the others don't because they could have been harmed less. This is why their disability would be harder to bear, and this is why they would have a stronger claim against canceling Pregnancy Testing than their counterparts would against canceling Preconception Testing.

Even with respect to *The Medical Programmes* as Parfit presents the case, it is plausible to conclude that non-identity makes at least some moral difference. But even were I wrong about this, there is a more fundamental reason for resisting at the outset any attempt to draw conclusions for Non-Identity Theodicy based on Parfit's reasoning to the *No-Difference View*.

Parfit's discussion of the *No-Difference View* is included in a chapter explicitly focused on beneficence, conceived as "our *general* moral reason to benefit other people, and to protect them from harm."[8] But according to Non-Identity Theodicy, the reasons for God's creative acts are not beneficence restricted in this way. Non-Identity Theodicy suggests that God acts as a lover of particular individuals, and further that a lover can have morally significant reasons for acting, in virtue of being a lover, that are over and above reasons of beneficence and that can lead him rightly to act in ways other than those that impartially maximize general value.

The moral question Parfit poses in *The Medical Programmes* is posed from the perspective of a government official, and bureaucrats should not prejudice their policy decisions based on love for particular individuals. But the God of Non-Identity Theodicy is not a bureaucrat, and his decisions—including decisions about which type of universe to create and which types of evil to allow—are largely based on love for particular individuals and being-types.

When the decision-making perspective of *The Medical Programmes* is changed from that of a bureaucrat to that of pregnant woman who loves the child growing within her, I doubt the mother will affirm Parfit's decision to flip a coin. Nor should she. Her love for her child gives her a morally serious reason to prefer to cancel Preconception Testing. Likewise, Non-Identity Theodicy suggests that it is from the parental perspective—in this case the perspective of a divine parent—that non-identity makes a moral difference.

I have suggested that it is plausible to suppose that non-identity can make a moral difference, even in beneficence-restricted cases, and that there is further reason to suppose that it can make a moral difference once this restriction is lifted. How great a difference non-identity can make will depend, in part, on the value and justificatory power of the good of a worthwhile human life, and how great a difference it makes for Non-Identity Theodicy will depend on the value

---

[8] Parfit, *Reasons and Persons*, 371 (italics mine).

and justificatory power of a *God-given* human life. The coming sections consider these issues.


## Shiffrin and the Limited Good of Human Life

The claim that non-identity significantly morally favors those who cause harm in non-identity situations is in some tension with literature in the ethics of procreation. Seana Shiffrin, for instance, while willing to concede against Parfit that non-identity is morally relevant, claims that any difference made by it is minimal.

She reasons firstly that "[t]here is a substantial asymmetry between the moral significance of harm delivered to avoid substantial, greater harms, and harms delivered to bestow pure benefits"[9] and that harming for non-harm-averting goods is typically "much harder to justify."[10] She further reasons that being caused to exist with a life worth living all things considered is at best a non-harm-averting good: "While causing a person to exist may benefit that person, it does not save the potential person from any harm, much less from greater harm."[11] Causing to exist cannot be a case of harm aversion for the one caused to exist because she wouldn't exist otherwise to be harmed. I follow Shiffrin this far.

But Shiffrin next claims that, *ceteris paribus*, the good of coming to exist with a human life worth living does *even less* justificatory work than pure benefits, for at least three reasons. I will firstly consider Shiffrin's reasons for thinking less of the justificatory force of worthwhile human life before offering counter-reasons for thinking more of it.

Shiffrin's first reason for thinking less of the justificatory force of coming to exist with a worthwhile human life is that "the condition bestowed is one that cannot be escaped without very high costs (suicide is often a physically, emotionally, and morally excruciating option)."[12] Even if you wind up never wanting to escape life, nevertheless coming to exist puts you in a position that is dangerous—as life always is—and that is costly to escape from if danger is realized. Many pure benefits might be thought less prone to harm than this.[13]

Secondly, Shiffrin suggests that "[i]n most cases, the absence of a pure benefit is experienced by a person or ... otherwise makes a difference in the content of his

---

[9] Shiffrin, "Wrongful Life, Procreative Responsibility, and the Significance of Harm," 126.
[10] Shiffrin, "Wrongful Life...," 127.    [11] Shiffrin, "Wrongful Life...," 134.
[12] Shiffrin, "Wrongful Life...," 133.
[13] Shiffrin may be concerned that coming to exist not only "puts" you into this position but *forces* you into it, and that the position is therefore not only dangerous but oppressive. She might claim that our autonomy is being violated in being procreated because life brings with it both dangers and obligations that we did not consent to. Because I am inclined to think that God's roles as creator and sustainer give him even much greater rights to make decisions on our behalf than parents have to make decisions on their children's behalf, I have framed the problem of evil primarily as a problem about harm-done rather than about autonomy-violated. I continue this focus in my treatment of Shiffrin.

life. This difference plays a significant explanatory role in the strength of the moral impetus to bestow pure benefits."[14] But if whatever good accompanies existence is not conferred, "the nonexistent person will not experience its absence; further, she has no life that will go worse."[15] Shiffrin draws the following conclusion:

> If the failure to impart them will have no influence on a life, benefits do not generate the same sort of moral reasons as those that compel us to avert and prevent harm that will affect a person. And they do not even generate the same reasons as are produced by pure benefits that would *improve* an ongoing life... The fact that the "harm" or absence of benefit represented by not procreating will not affect an existent person or her life in progress renders the benefit bestowed by creation far less morally significant.[16]

Thirdly, "The harms suffered [by being caused to exist with a life worth living] may be very severe."[17] In fact, given that the harm of death comes to all who come to exist, I think we can say that the harms suffered *will* be very severe.

## An Alternative Appraisal of the Good of Human Life

Shiffrin exclusively considers reasons for thinking *less* of the justificatory force of the good of a worthwhile human life than of pure benefits, but there are also objective, counterfactual, and subjective reasons for thinking more of it. This section has the modest aim of complicating Shiffrin's analysis by suggesting some *prima facie* reasons against her low appraisal of the good of worthwhile human life. Next section—the most significant for the argument of this chapter—draws on intuitions about the morality of procreation to more definitively arbitrate between Shiffrin's reasons and the counter-reasons presented here.

Shiffrin rightfully points out that very significant harms accompany even worthwhile human life, but a worthwhile human life also includes all of that life's benefits, harm averting and pure. This is one *prima facie* reason for thinking that the life taken as a whole is *objectively* more valuable than any component benefit within that life.

Moreover, particular benefits within a life can be more valuable for how they are related to other benefits in that life. Having one's eyesight enhanced is a pure benefit even if one never goes on to fulfill one's dream to be an astronaut. But if enhanced eyesight does allow for the realization of this dream, its value as a pure

---

[14] Shiffrin, "Wrongful Life...," 134.    [15] Shiffrin, "Wrongful Life...," 134.
[16] Shiffrin, "Wrongful Life...," 135.    [17] Shiffrin, "Wrongful Life...," 133.

benefit is much greater. Similarly, the value of the pure benefit of being given a dog for my fifteenth birthday is enhanced by the fifteen years of meaningful interactions I have now had with my dog. This is reason to think that the sum value of a worthwhile life's benefits considered as components of an entire life is greater than their sum value under the thinner descriptions that they tend to derive their justificatory force from in everyday decisions of whether to harm for benefit.

There is some *prima facie* reason for judging a worthwhile human life to be objectively more valuable than typical pure benefits both for including all of the benefits contained in that life and for including them under potentially value-enhancing descriptions.

Some further endorse the objective value of worthwhile human life by claiming that being alive as a human has significant intrinsic value—value independent of the quality of life. Some think this intrinsic value is so great as to justify the moral prohibition of abortion and euthanasia no matter how terrible the quality of life will be or has become. Perhaps the intuition that human life has significant intrinsic value is being expressed when people say, under even very bad circumstances, that they are "just glad to be alive."

Richard Swinburne highlights the intrinsic value of human life by reflecting on the following thought experiment:

Suppose that, throughout your life, you have available a machine by pressing a button on which you can become unconscious during the periods of pain, mental agony, and even boredom. Pressing the button will make you unconscious for an hour or two, during which you behave as though you were conscious, and after becoming conscious again you know what happened in the meantime. If when you become conscious again, you do not like what you then find yourself experiencing, you can go on pressing the button until you find your life more to your liking. Periods eliminated will not be replaced, and so pressing the button will shorten your conscious life, for as much or as little as you choose. How many of us would press the button for long? Not many, I suggest, would press the button very often. And that brings out that most of us value simply existing as conscious beings, whatever (within limits) life throws at us. We 'value' it, in the sense that we recognize it as objectively good for us.[18]

I think Swinburne overstates his case. Much addictive behavior such as binge drinking and mindless TV watching seem to be among the many ways that people do tend to "press the button very often." And I suspect most of us are happy that our bodies are wired to automatically "press the button" by losing consciousness in times of severe pain, grief, and fright. However, the more limited claim that not

[18] Swinburne, *Providence and the Problem of Evil*, 240.

pressing the button very often could be an admirable practice seems to me somewhat more plausible, and that not pressing the button even when our quality of life is poor could express a respect for the intrinsic value of life is one reasonable explanation for this intuition.

If unadorned human life has some intrinsic value, this would be value accrued by causing someone to exist though not by bestowing a pure benefit to one already existing (and hence already a recipient of the intrinsic value of being alive). Therefore, this would be another *prima facie* reason for weighting the objective value of a worthwhile human life over that of pure benefits.

In addition to some *prima facie* reasons to favor the objective value of worthwhile human life, there may also be some *prima facie* reasons for thinking that a worthwhile human life fares better than pure benefits when measured by counterfactual comparison. Shiffrin suggests that coming to exist with a life worth living cannot be a counterfactual comparative good for the one who comes to exist because one cannot be *better-off* existing than not existing. If one were *better-off* existing with a worthwhile human life than not existing, then it would seem to follow that she would be *worse off* not existing. But John Broome among many others reminds us that there can be no such comparison because one of the terms of the comparison is missing. Broome writes that "if she had never lived at all, there would have been no her for it to be worse for, so it could not have been worse for her."[19] Nonexistence is not a state one can be in, and so not a state that can be worse for one.

However, even granting Shiffrin this point,[20] there may be other ethically relevant ways of making a counterfactual comparison that favor the good of a worthwhile human life over pure benefits. We could compare, for instance, the value that accrues to some actual person in the actual world with the value that accrues to him in some possible world in which he never comes to exist. Nils Holtug recommends assigning "zero" as the value for a person of a life in which no positive or negative values befall her. He takes this to show that "there are cases in which it is the absence of certain (positive) properties that makes an ascription of zero value correct."[21] By the same reasoning, he then suggests we can assign zero value for an actual person to her non-existence. Both are assigned

---

[19] John Broome, "Goodness Is Reducible to Betterness: The Evil of Death Is the Value of Life," in *The Good and the Economical: Ethical Choices in Economics and Management*, ed. Peter Koslowski and Yuichi Shionoya (Berlin: Springer-Verlag, 1993), 77; quoted in Nils Holtug, "On the Value of Coming into Existence," *The Journal of Ethics* 5 (2001), 370. Derek Parfit makes the same point: "Causing someone to exist is a special case because the alternative would not have been worse for this person. We may admit that, for this reason, causing someone to exist cannot be *better* for this person" (Parfit, *Reasons and Persons*, 489; quoted in Holtug, "On the Value of Coming into Existence," 370).

[20] For an argument against Shiffrin on this point, see Holtug, "On the Value of Coming into Existence." Holtug argues that it can be better or worse to come into existence than never to exist for the person who comes to exist.

[21] Holtug, "On the Value of Coming into Existence," 381–2.

zero value because in both cases no positive or negative values would accrue to the specified person.[22]

If Holtug's ascription of zero value to nonexistence can be defended, then this would be a comparative reason to favor the good of coming to exist with a life worth living over typical pure benefits. One measure of a pure benefit is the percentage value difference for a person in worlds with and without that benefit. Even without knowing how much money someone has, if you can triple his money, that is in general a greater comparative benefit than doubling it. Quadrupling is better still, and so on. On this measure, a pure benefit that takes a life from zero value on balance to positive value on balance would be the limiting case of a comparatively great pure benefit. If the value of zero can be defensibly ascribed to nonexistence, then the good of coming to exist with a life worth living would share this comparative greatness even if not the status of a benefit.

Even if it is incoherent to claim that one who comes to exist with a life worth living is *better-off* for existing, there may nonetheless be ethical comparisons in the vicinity that favor the good of worthwhile human existence over both nonexistence and typical human pure benefits.

Finally, there are some *prima facie* reasons for thinking the good of a worthwhile human life tops pure benefits from the *subjective* point of view. This is important because loving creators are concerned not only with the objective and comparative value of their creatures' existence but also for those they create to appreciate enough of that value to see their lives as goods for them.

That we tend to consider life a great good comes out in various turns of phrase. When we say "you saved my life," we generally mean more than just, "you averted my death." It's not just that someone saved us from something bad but that they retained for us a particularly great good—life itself. We recognize something similar in "you gave me my life back" and in "I owe you my life," which often have the sense of "you gave me (or I owe you) the greatest gift possible."

Swinburne confirms this subjective assessment. He notes that "[v]ery few humans indeed commit suicide, although almost all of them could do so quite easily." He concedes that "some of them do not do so because of obligations to others;" to this I would add that some do not do so because of their biological instincts to privilege their own survival or out of fear about what might come next. But, nevertheless, I find it plausible with Swinburne that

> many others do not commit suicide because they want (i.e., desire) to go on living, even when life is unexciting or painful. One reason why they so desire is that they think that—unwilling though they often are to admit it, when badly depressed—the good outweighs the bad…The other reason why they desire to

---

[22] Holtug, "On the Value of Coming into Existence," 381.

go on living is that, even if they think that at present the bad outweighs the good, they live in hope of better times. Thereby they express their belief that a life good as a whole over time would be worth having even if its present state is on balance bad.[23]

People remain glad that they were born and desire to go on living because they judge that probably their human life will be worthwhile all things considered and that a worthwhile human life is a great good. For these reasons, in part, the vast majority of human persons share the belief that a human life is worth living despite even huge disadvantages.

Some faced with *horrendous* suffering even express this belief, whereas I have suggested that, in contrast, very few of us believe that pure benefits would be worth having if *horrendous* suffering were their cost. This suggests that from the point of view of self-interest, worthwhile human life is significantly privileged over pure benefits.

Considerations such as these lead Joel Feinberg to question whether nonexistence is "ever rationally preferable to a severely encumbered existence." Like Swinburne, he takes the widespread human tendency to "cling to life at all costs,"[24] even when great suffering accompanies such clinging, to reflect the fact that our considered subjective appraisal of our human lives is very high.

Shiffrin suggests that the value of a worthwhile life for its subject is diminished because life "cannot be escaped without very high costs (suicide is often a physically, emotionally, and morally excruciating option)."[25] What she doesn't consider, however, is that one important reason suicide is such an excruciating option is precisely because we're rarely sure it's what we want, and one reason we're rarely sure it's what we want is because there is such a strong and widespread belief that human life is a great good.

Moreover, if Swinburne is right to claim that we are apt to undervalue the good of human life due to our undervaluing of the good of being of use and our short-term and short-distance thinking about the ways in which our lives are of use to others,[26] then this is reason to think that the objective value of life is even greater than our current subjective appraisal of it, and that—on plausible theistic assumptions about the afterlife—this additional objective value will ultimately and eternally be appropriated by many into a still greater subjective appraisal of life.

While nothing in this section makes a decisive case for favoring the good of a worthwhile human life over pure benefits, it complicates Shiffrin's evaluation. While Shiffrin has usefully called attention to three *prima facie* reasons to be wary

---

[23] Swinburne, *Providence and the Problem of Evil*, 241.
[24] Joel Feinberg, "Wrongful Life and the Counterfactual Element in Harming," 159.
[25] Shiffrin, "Wrongful Life…," 133.
[26] Swinburne, *Providence and the Problem of Evil*, 244–5. I discuss these claims of Swinburne in more detail in Chapter 3.

of justifying harm by the good of coming to exist with a life worth living, there are also some *prima facie* reasons commending the justificatory potential of this good.

## The Morality of Procreation

Reflecting on the morality of procreation can help arbitrate between these reasons, and suggests that the good of a worthwhile human life in fact has far greater justificatory power than typical pure benefits.

There is a strong and widely cross-cultural sentiment that the giving of human life is a good thing and that people ought to be grateful to their parents for giving them life. But if the good of coming to exist with a human life worth living has the heavily depleted justificatory force that Shiffrin contends it does, this threatens to undermine this common sense appraisal of the morality of procreation. In general, harming seriously for pure benefit without consent is wrong. If Shiffrin is correct that the good of coming to exist with a human life worth living is still "far less morally significant" than other non-harm-averting goods, then this threatens to morally impugn human procreators even in the most fortunate cases of procreation.

Shiffrin takes her reflections to recommend an approach to parental liability that "would permit liability assessments for significant burdens associated with being created—even in cases in which the life is worth living and in which those responsible for creating did not have, nor should they have had, special knowledge that the child's life would feature unusual or substantial burdens."[27] Shiffrin is careful to say that she is "not advancing the claim that procreation is all-things-considered wrong,"[28] but I am doubtful that Shiffrin can maintain her other claims while plausibly denying a strong anti-procreation conclusion. Even very significant pure benefits seem helpless to justify even moderate harm, let alone certain death. If a worthwhile human life really has less justificatory force than pure benefits, it's hard to see how it could justify the severe harms inevitably accompanying any human life.

Some of Shiffrin's own examples attest to this difficulty, for instance a far-fetched case she details in which one is harmed as a result of being purely benefited all things considered:

Imagine a well-off character (Wealthy) who lives on an island. He is anxious for a project (whether because of boredom, self-interest, benevolence, or some combination of these). He decides to bestow some of his wealth upon his

---

[27] Shiffrin, "Wrongful Life…," 119. Reaffirming the point, "Does the argument waged so far imply that *all* children may have causes of action? *In theory*, the answer is yes" (141).
[28] Shiffrin, "Wrongful Life…," 139.

neighbors from an adjacent island. His neighbors are comfortably off, with more than an ample stock of resources. Still they would be (purely) benefited by an influx of monetary wealth. Unfortunately, due to historical tensions between the islands' governments, Wealthy and his agents are not permitted to visit the neighboring island. They are also precluded (either by law or by physical circumstances) from communicating with the island's people. To implement his project, then, he crafts a hundred cubes of gold bullion, each worth $5 million. (The windy islands lack paper currency.) He flies his plane over the island and drops the cubes near passers-by. He takes care to avoid hitting people, but he knows there is an element of risk in his activity and that someone may get hurt. Everyone is a little stunned when this million-dollar manna lands at their feet. Most are delighted. One person (Unlucky), though, is hit by the falling cube. The impact breaks his arm. Had the cube missed him, it would have landed at someone else's feet.[29]

Shiffrin says she is inclined to believe that Wealthy acts immorally in implementing his project.[30] I agree. This judgment becomes even clearer if we stipulate that Lucky *knew* one of his bullions would injure Unlucky and that in fact it would break *both* of Unlucky's arms. But if Wealthy has here acted immorally, and if all cases of procreation cause far more serious harm for a "far less morally significant" good (than the very significant pure benefit of five million dollars), then a strong anti-procreation conclusion seems warranted. If coming to exist typically has far less moral force than pure benefits, how could it justify a course of action that causes far greater harms than could be justified by even very great pure benefits?

Several of the key players in the ethics of procreation literature—a surprising number, to my mind—join Shiffrin in implying that procreation is permissible far less of the time than most people's intuitions suggest. David Benatar, for instance, reasons that "[b]ecause there is nothing bad about never coming into existence, but there is something bad about coming into existence, all things considered non-existence is preferable."[31] He suggests that "perhaps existence is so bad that it *is* wrong to have children"[32] and that the voluntary extinction of the human race would be a supererogatory or even heroic course of action.[33]

My diagnosis of this anti-natalist literature is that it counterintuitively narrows the scope of permissible procreation as a result of underappreciating the justificatory force of the good of worthwhile human life. This underappreciation is

[29] Shiffrin, "Wrongful Life...," 127.    [30] Shiffrin, "Wrongful Life...," 129.
[31] Benatar, "Why It Is Better Never to Come into Existence," 349.
[32] Benatar, "Why It Is Better Never to Come into Existence," 351.
[33] Benatar, "Why It Is Better Never to Come into Existence," 354. See also Benatar's more recent book-length treatment of these issues in *Better Never to Have Been: The Harm of Coming into Existence* (Oxford: Oxford University Press, 2006).

unsurprising for a couple of reasons. For one, in many non-identity cases, non-identity has no or minimal effect on our ethical assessment of the agents in question. In examples of excessive depletion, for instance, even if non-identity diminishes the extent to which those brought into existence generations later are wronged, it is unlikely that the depleters took this into account when deciding to act. Generally, excessive depleters act not out of a desire to benefit those who wouldn't exist otherwise, but out of the same selfishness that would have motivated depletion if it had no effect on who would come to exist.

Another reason we tend to underappreciate the justificatory force of worthwhile human life is that in cases of human procreation, parents tend to block out considerations of the harm they will cause in procreating and to focus almost exclusively on the good things they hope to give to their children. By not facing the moral costs of procreative harm, we fail to recognize how great the moral upside of procreation must be for it to be morally permissible.

But if, like me, you think procreation is morally permissible in favorable circumstances, you have reason to weight the reasons favoring the justificatory force of the good of worthwhile human life over the reasons detracting from it. You have reason to think that the good of worthwhile human life is *more* morally significant than typical pure benefits, indeed significant enough to justify the inevitable suffering and ultimate death accompanying even the best of lives. It is hard to think of non-harm-averting goods that justify causing a person to suffer death. But if procreation is not uncommonly permissible, the good of being born into a worthwhile human life is such a good. And even if you judge the morality of procreation a difficult case due to the harm that it occasions, this too suggests that the good of a worthwhile human life has distinctive justificatory force, for if its justificatory force were no greater than typical pure benefits, procreation would be clearly immoral.

What makes the good of worthwhile human life uniquely capable of justifying harm? We would not exist without it. If parents had the option, *ceteris paribus*, of having their very same children without them suffering severely and ultimately dying, and didn't take it, this would call into serious question the morality of their procreative act. Against both Parfit and Shiffrin, that the one who suffers as a result of a given action would not exist had that action not been performed can have a very significant effect on the morality of bringing human persons into existence.[34]

---

[34] That the good of worthwhile human life has this marked justificatory power also helps to make sense of the intuition that wrongful-life lawsuits are only morally compelling in exceptional circumstances. Feinberg expresses a concern that if we admit that children are harmed by being brought into existence by their parents, "that could have the unfortunate consequence of legitimizing wrongful life suits for such harmful states as illegitimacy, ugliness, below average intelligence, and the like, all of which are 'harmful conditions' but which, since all are rationally preferable to nonexistence, are not harms on balance...Minor harms could be awarded relatively minor but appropriate compensation, and the courts would be flooded with plaintiffs airing fancied 'grievances' against their parents for

## The Good of *God-Given* Human Life Has Even Greater Justificatory Power

### The *God-Given* Good of Human Life

The plausibility of the justification offered by Non-Identity Theodicy is aided by an analogy between divine creation and human procreation. In both cases, we have creators choosing to bring beings into existence when they know those beings will suffer significantly. Human parents who voluntarily have children do something that they know will result in serious suffering, because serious suffering accompanies even the most fortunate of human lives. Even more than that, they procreate knowing full well that one day their children will suffer death. Arguably, death (or the dying process) is one of the worst evils. Despite this, most people believe that voluntary human procreation is not uncommonly morally permissible. This raises the question, how does human procreation fare with respect to the conditions of morally acceptable creation recommended by Non-Identity Theodicy? In other words, is human procreation a non-identity case (1)? Do human procreators offer a great life to their children (2)? Are human procreators virtuously motivated in creating by a desire to love their future children (3)? If human procreation is morally justified despite faring worse with respect to these conditions, that favors the morality of divine creation.

Procreation matches divine creation in meeting condition (1) of Non-Identity Theodicy. If my parents had chosen not to procreate, I never would have existed. Procreation does not fare as well as divine creation with respect to justificatory condition (2). The best human procreators can offer to a new child is a probably worthwhile life. Only God can offer to each person an eternity in which any evil endured will be infinitely outweighed. Moreover, God has greater resources to see to it that we will welcome even our earthly careers in the end, even if *horrors* were their cost. From the perspective of eternity, we will be able to appreciate, for instance, the full extent to which our lives were of use, even of use to God. Perhaps such appreciation will even be commenced, as Julian of Norwich suggests, with words of divine gratitude: "Thank you for your suffering…"[35]

This is a very significant advantage. Because I don't think morally permissible procreation relies on certain theistic beliefs about the afterlife, I believe that the

---

providing them with disadvantageous environments or poor genetic inheritances" (Feinberg, "Wrongful Life and the Counterfactual Element in Harming," 173). Feinberg's solution is to deny that anything that does not harm on balance is a harm in the morally relevant sense (a position I have argued against in Chapter 2). My alternative solution is to argue that worthwhile human existence is particularly capable of justifying harm.

[35] Julian of Norwich, *Revelations of Divine Love*, trans. Clifton Wolters (London: Penguin Books, 1966), 85; quoted in Adams, *Horrendous Evils and the Goodness of God*, 162.

good of a merely natural human existence—limited in its duration, with the risks of misery that accompany it, and with death as its bad end—is often sufficient for justifying human procreation. With omniscience and omnipotence, God is capable of offering to each person a life such that physical death is not the end it appears to be, and such that all but the earliest fraction of human life will be spent in great happiness and fulfillment. God is in a more favorable position than human procreators with respect to condition (2) both for the afterlife only he can give and for the burden of final death only he can take away.

Finally, in addition to amplifying the objective and subjective value of the good of human life, these theistic assumptions about a great afterlife diminish the comparative value of earthly pure benefits. If we are headed for an exceedingly great eternal life all things considered, then the proportional value-difference between lives with and without pure benefits is diminished (or even made infinitesimal). If *horrors* are merely the price for first row heavenly seats, many of us will happily sit in the balcony. Any view of God is great enough. This is further reason to doubt that many of the pure benefits suggested by Type A and B Theodicies have a plausible claim to divine *horror* justification.

This leaves us with how human procreation fares with respect to condition (3). Again, it fares not nearly as well as divine creation. One's reasons for acting are relevant to the morality of one's action. If a concern for my good is not a significant reason why you harmed me, I may have a rightful grievance against you even if the results of your harming me happen to be good for me all things considered, and even if the good that results for me would have justified the harm had a desire for its realization been one of your primary reasons for acting. This would be the case, for instance, if you threw me to the ground in unprovoked anger, but in doing so happened to move my body out of the path of a bus that otherwise would have hit me. The closer a concern for the good of the one harmed is to being a motivationally sufficient reason for a harming action, the better the position the harmer is in with respect to justifying that action.

In divine creation as described by Non-Identity Theodicy, one of God's primary reasons for creating is a loving desire for the good of the specific persons who will come to exist. But even in morally favorable cases of human procreation, the reasons human persons have for procreating are complex, and a concern for the good of the one who will come to exist is not always central. Indeed, many times parents don't initially intend to procreate at all, procreation being a side effect of physical desire or relationship bonding. Even when they do, it is generally very difficult to judge to what extent the good of worthwhile human life is given for the good of those who will come to live it and to what extent for other reasons. Sometimes human persons procreate for selfish reasons, and a concern for the good of the one who will come to exist is absent altogether, or considered only as an afterthought. Even in more morally favorable cases, David Benatar recognizes (as previously discussed) that parental motivations for procreating are often at least partly self-serving: to "satisfy biological desires," to "find fulfillment," to ensure "an insurance policy for old age" and an influence beyond the grave.[36] Just because these reasons have an aspect of self-concern does not make them selfish or bad. Nevertheless, one has a more plausible claim to harm being justified the more the good of the one who suffers the harm was taken into account. That the good of those whom God harms is always significant with respect to divine reasons for harming gives God a significant moral advantage over human pro-creators when it comes to the motivations for giving the gift of life.

To conclude, as great of a good as the morality of procreation suggests worth-while human life is, *God-given* human life is greater still because God is in a much more favorable moral position than even the most fortunate of human procreators, at both the beginning and the end of human life. Consequently, God as a divine creator fares better than human procreators with respect to both condition (2) and condition (3) of Non-Identity Theodicy.

## The Payoff for Non-Identity Theodicy

I have argued that the good of worthwhile human life has greater justificatory force than pure benefits, and that the justificatory force of *God-given* human life is superior still. Is it enough to justify *horror* causation or permission? This is a difficult question to answer, but reflecting again on the morality of procreation gives us some reason to answer affirmatively.

If I am right that human procreation is not uncommonly morally permissible, then the good of (the mere probability of) a worthwhile natural human life is sufficient to justify causing death. Death itself may be a *horror*. Marilyn Adams suggests that it is:

> Confronting death compels the confession [that] no human being escapes [hor-rendous evil] in the end!...It is our vocation to *personalize* the material...Death degrades by halting and reversing the process, by *depersonalizing* the mater-ial...Death proves that there is not enough to us to maintain integrity, to hold body and soul together. It therefore *prima facie* defeats our efforts...It is in our nature and calling as human beings to strive against the forces that would undo us, and it is in our nature surely to lose. Death mocks our personal preten-sions...If death is a horror, and death is natural to human being, then to be human is to be headed for horror.[37]

---

[36] David Benatar, "Why It Is Better Never to Come into Existence," *American Philosophical Quarterly* 34.3 (1997), 351.

[37] Adams, *Christ and Horrors*, 208–9.

But even if death (or the dying process) is not always *horrendous*, it often is, and even when it is not, it tends to approach the *horrendous*. If the much more limited good of probably worthwhile natural human life is sufficient to justify a harm akin to *horror* even when as human procreators we cannot ensure that any life given will be a good for the one who lives it, then I find it reasonable to think that the good of God-given human life—with its substantial moral advantages at both the beginning and end of life—is sufficient for justifying causing or permitting *horrors*.

Someone might object that a morally relevant distinction favoring human pro-creation over divine creation is that human persons are not responsible for the reproductive system within which they procreate, and that it may be unfair to expect human persons to renounce their natural functions. However, even if being stuck with a certain frame makes acts of human procreation more under-standable, I doubt this diminishes human responsibility so far as to account for the extent of the moral freedom to procreate that many find strongly intuitive. For most of us, the frame we inherit makes lying, cheating, stealing, and a host of other bad acts come just as naturally as procreation, perhaps now even more nat-urally in places of readily available contraception. Just as our natural inclinations to such acts do little to diminish their immorality, our natural tendency to pro-create cannot morally excuse us from the harm resulting from procreation.

Moreover, God may be working with a similar frame. It is consonant with Non-Identity Theodicy that God's desire to create the actual world inhabitants is as strong or stronger than any human desires resulting in procreation, and Non-Identity Theodicy suggests that it is a necessary truth that creating those inhabit-ants would result in profound suffering. The divine case is then much like the human procreation case with the exception that God has significant moral advantages at both the beginning of human life (where he can create out of pure motivations) and the end of human life (where he can offer an eternity of fulfill-ment beyond the grave).

A second objection claims that *horrors* are so bad that they swallow up any reasons for allowing them, and therefore that non-identity, even if it aids the jus-tification of harm generally, does not do so where harm is *horrendous*. This objec-tion takes its cue from the idea that reasons for and against actions are not always additive. For example, when we think of two cases—one where a person is *hor-rendously* tortured for no perceivable benefit and another where the same torture occurs so that the torturer can get directions required in order not to break a promise to meet someone for tennis—it is reasonable, if controversial, to think the badness of the torturer's action in these two cases is equal, and that there is just as much overall moral reason not to torture in either case. What my reflec-tions on the morality of procreation suggest, however, is that the good of earthly human life is not trivial with respect to death in the way a promise to play tennis is with respect to *horrendous* torture. If so, it is reasonable to assume that the infinitely greater God-given good of human life is not trivial in this way with respect to *horrors*.

Even so, one might object that human procreation per se is not the appropriate analogy, that divine creation of this evil-prone universe is more like a parent intentionally conceiving a child with a *horrendous* genetic disease than like a normal case of procreation. However, there are a number of reasons to be morally suspicious of this sort of abnormal procreation that don't easily transfer to its divine analogue. Parents' desire to aim for a disease-affected child may reflect questionable motives for bringing a child into existence, and therefore may call into further question their fulfillment of condition (3). The parents may be using the child as a means to an end—say fame, or the chance to play hero (cf. Plantinga's Type A Theodicy), or fulfilling some other psychological or financial need of theirs—rather than valuing the child for her own sake. This concern about an immoral instrumentalism helps explain why many would have a similar aversion to the intentional conception of children with Down syndrome, despite the fact that children with this disorder arguably suffer no more on average than normal children.[38]

Moreover, in cases of intentionally conceiving a child with a genetic disease that causes great suffering, the parents may have good reason to doubt that the child's natural life will be worthwhile for her all things considered; that is, they may have less reason to be confident that they can meet condition (2). With God, though, we need not have concerns about suspect motivations, and, furthermore, we can be confident that he can offer even those born into *horrendous* suffering eternal lives that will be tremendous goods to them all things considered.[39]

In sum, human procreation fairs significantly worse than divine creation with respect to Non-Identity Theodicy's proposed conditions for the morally acceptable creation of beings vulnerable to significant suffering. If you think human procreation is in general morally permissible, all the more so should you think divine creation of our universe is permissible. Conversely, if you think God has acted immorally by creating human persons into an environment that produces suffering, then you have even more reason to think that human parents who

---

[38] Likewise, a concern about an immoral instrumentalism may help explain why some have intuitions that it is more plausibly morally permissible to intentionally procreate in a particularly dangerous part of the world than to intentionally procreate a deaf child, even if it is probable that the deaf child will suffer less overall than the child born in dangerous circumstances. The most common ways of imagining the details of such cases may leave the parents who procreate a deaf child more prone to a charge of immoral instrumentalism.

[39] A third reason that someone might be morally suspicious of the intentional conception of a child with a genetic disorder is if they take human beings to have a moral obligation to respect God's purposes for human life by not engineering human life in certain ways. Again, God is not vulnerable to this objection, for he has no creator to whom he is obligated. For further discussion of this point, see Adams, "Must God Create the Best?," 330–2.

procreate voluntarily are acting immorally, and therefore that many people would be justified in bringing wrongful-life lawsuits against their parents. If the more limited good of natural human life is sufficient to justify the serious human suffering and death that accompanies human procreation, then the far greater good of God-given human life—with its moral advantages at life's beginning and end—can reasonably be judged sufficient for justifying divine permission of actual evils.

## Divine Liability

Even if God doesn't wrong human persons, this does not mean he isn't liable for the harm he causes them. If I justifiably steal twenty dollars from someone because it was not possible to ask for permission and the money was necessary to avert some significant harm, I should not be blamed for my action, but nonetheless I probably owe someone twenty bucks. Similarly, if I borrow something and it breaks through no fault of my own while in my care, I have not done anything morally wrong, but I am liable to compensate for the damaged goods.

However, that God may be liable for some of the harm he causes or permits does not obviously tell against his ethical perfection. In fact, willingly accepting liability, when done for others' good, is sometimes a courageous and particularly praiseworthy act. Say you have to decide whether your unconscious friend should have a surgery that will improve his eyesight but will require some significant and painful rehabilitation. There is only a narrow time frame in which the surgery can be performed and so you don't have the option of waiting for him to regain consciousness. You reflect on the fact that your friend always had the dream to be an astronaut, but was recently barred from fulfilling that dream due to his average eyesight. You can either do nothing, in which case his eyesight will remain average but you will not accrue any liability, or you can opt for the surgery. But if you opt for the surgery and your friend, when he comes to, says that he regrets your decision, that he is particularly pain averse and would not have wanted the surgery, then—even if you know that eventually your friend will come not to regret your decision—you have some responsibility to compensate him. You at least would be obligated to offer to make some sacrifices in order to support him through the rehabilitation that awaits him as a result of your surrogate decision. In this situation, despite the liability risk, I think choosing the surgery and accepting the liability could be a courageous and praiseworthy act.

I suggest that pursuant to Non-Identity Theodicy, God has made a similarly difficult choice. God has not opted for clean hands, but even if that makes him liable for much of the harm that ensues, he is willing to accept liability by making sure things turn out well in the end and even by—on some theistic assumptions—living a human life and suffering a *horrendous* human death in order to be in solidarity with those whose suffering he is responsible for.[40] Affirming divine liability in this way allows one to offer morally justifying reasons for divine actions while paying respect to those who shake their fists at God.

## Conclusion

In Chapter 6, I noted that Robert Adams is inclined to think God does not wrong those he creates by harms that their existence depends on, so long as their lives will be worthwhile all things considered. In Chapters 2–4, I argued that pure benefits are not sufficient to justify *horrors*. For worthwhile human life to justify them, therefore, it must be a good of greater justificatory purchase.

Shiffrin suggests the opposite, that the good of worthwhile human life has even less justificatory force than pure benefits. I countered Shiffrin firstly with some preliminary reasons for thinking more of the justificatory force of the good of worthwhile human life, and then with a more definitive argument made from intuitions about the morality of procreation. In particular, I highlighted that parents who procreate knowing their children will suffer serious harms and ultimately death fare significantly better morally than agents who cause serious harm leading only to pure benefit. Moreover, I suggested that God is in a better moral position than even the most fortunate human procreators in several respects. Therefore, I am sympathetic to Adams's initial assumption. To the extent that God's allowance of *horrors* can be considered a non-identity choice, I find it reasonable to suppose that he does not wrong those he creates by that allowance. Conjoining this with the plausibility and character assessments of Chapter 6, I suggest that Non-Identity Theodicy is promising with respect to all three evaluative dimensions I have been considering.

We are not in an ideal epistemic position to determine whether the conclusion that Non-Identity Theodicy justifies God morally is not only reasonable but true. This may depend on just how great life can be for us all things considered. Many of those with religious faith and a belief in the afterlife suggest that we are apt to vastly underestimate this good.[41] I hope they are correct.

---

[40] Here I am intrigued by Friedrich Nietzsche's contention, written in reference to the ancient Greeks: "Thus do the gods justify the life of man: they themselves live it—the only satisfactory theodicy!" (*The Birth of Tragedy and the Case of Wagner*, trans. Walter Kaufmann (New York: Vintage Books, 1967), Chapter III, 43).

[41] I am reminded of 1 Corinthians 2:9: "'What no eye has seen, what no ear has heard, and what no human mind has conceived'—the things God has prepared for those who love him."

# 8

# Conclusion

## Distinctive Features of Non-Identity Theodicy

Newton's three laws are an excellent approximation for macroscopic objects interacting in everyday conditions. However, they are inappropriate for use in certain circumstances, most notably at very small scales and very high speeds. In philosophy as well as in science, extreme values have a tendency to resist standard approaches.

It is for this reason, in part, that the categories of the sacred and the horrendous have had wide and lasting influence in anthropology, sociology, and continental philosophy. As of yet, however, these categories have had little serious or sustained treatment in analytic philosophy.

Marilyn Adams's work has begun to address this lack in the contemporary analytic discussion of the problem of evil. When this discussion was revived in the second half of the twentieth century, the category of the horrendous was conceptually underdeveloped and, as a result, beyond the horizons of most of those considering problems of evil. Positions like the following endorsed by Roderick Chisholm were readily assumed: "Epicurus said that if God is able but unwilling to *prevent* evil, then he is malevolent. But if the evil in the world is defeated and contained in a larger whole that is absolutely good, one should rather say that, if God had been able but unwilling to *create* such evil, then he would have been malevolent."[1] Adams has helpfully complicated matters by highlighting the justificatory asymmetry between *horrendous* and non-*horrendous evil*. Even if maximizing overall value or aiming for greater goods are *usually* safe ways to stay within the bounds of moral permissibility, *horrendous evils* resist such comparative justifications; *horrors* pose distinctive challenges for the moral justification of harm.

Adams's complication exposes the dubiousness of the assumption—readily assumed by almost all philosophers of religion, theist and non-theist alike[2]—that the logical problem of evil has been solved. Adams reloads the logical problem by

---

[1] Chisholm, "The Defeat of Good and Evil," *Proceedings and Addresses of the American Philosophical Association* 42 (1969), 37.

[2] William Hasker, for instance, writes, "It is widely held that the logical problem of evil, which alleges an inconsistency between the existence of evil and that of an omnipotent and morally perfect God, has been solved" (William Hasker, "D.Z. Phillips' Problems with Evil and with God," *International Journal for Philosophy of Religion* 61 (2007), 151).

*Non-Identity Theodicy: A Grace-Based Response to the Problem of Evil.* Vince R. Vitale, Oxford University Press (2020). © Vince R. Vitale.
DOI: 10.1093/oso/9780198864226.003.0008

questioning the assumption of Leibniz, Chisholm, Pike, Plantinga, and others that God is morally in the clear so long as he has made the best he can. Sober reflection on *horrendous evils* commends the judgment that "it is far from obvious that a perfectly good God would accept them as the price of"[3] maximizing overall value.

The ethical framework and casuistry of Part I was designed to highlight this and other misemphases in contemporary theodicy. I used Cases A and B to highlight the distinctive moral constraints on *horror* production and to draw the conclusion that Types A and B Theodicy—theodicy which seeks justification by pure benefit—is *structurally unpromising* with respect to *horrors*.

Along the way, I diagnosed several more specific misemphases. Firstly, there is an overemphasis in theodicy on the moral distinction between causing and permitting. Even bracketing deep skepticism about this distinction in contemporary moral philosophy, reflection on a variety of examples shows that whatever moral difference this distinction might make in normal circumstances, it makes little at best where *horrendous harm* seeks purely beneficial justification. Moreover, the conceptual space between the related concepts of doing and allowing is markedly diminished when the agent under consideration is a divine being who is at every moment *doing* what it takes to sustain all things. Secondly, some of the theodicy literature overestimates the moral significance of caretaker rights, which are not of the right sort to justify *horrendous harm*. Thirdly, as alluded to above, there is a questionable focus on general and generic goods which manifests itself in a prioritizing of worlds over human persons, *generic* human persons over *individual* human persons, and all-things-considered benefit over more specific interests such as the aversion of serious harm.

Out of this final overemphasis comes an under-emphasis on considerations of character over and above any considerations of moral obligations in the analysis of ethical perfection. The need for character-based evaluation is italicized because the causation or permission of *horrendous harm* calls into question the harmer's love for those who are harmed. Also underappreciated is the justificatory asymmetry between pure and harm-averting benefits which looms increasingly large in the ethics of procreation literature but is largely unacknowledged in contemporary theodicy.

I found *prima facie structural promise* in the proposed blame-shift and harm aversion of Theodicy Types C and D, but further consideration of High Fall Theodicy in Chapter 5 showed these theodicies to be structurally vulnerable and otherwise implausible. These theodicy Types are wrought with their own misemphases. They overestimate the extent to which human persons can bear primary

---

[3] Adams, *Horrendous Evils and the Goodness of God*, 30.

responsibility for *horrendous evils* and the extent to which the responsibility of new intervening agents shifts responsibility away from the system creator.

Questioning these aspects of High Fall Theodicy exposes a related misdiagnosis, namely that moral evil—evil for which non-divine agents are among those morally responsible—is more easily accounted for by theodicy than natural evil—evil for which no non-divine agents are morally responsible. High Fall Theodicies attempt to collapse the category of natural evil into the category of moral evil, and cite human free will as curbing the justificatory demand placed on moral evil. But if we were set up for *horrors* and the badness of *horrors* necessarily outstrips human capacity to bear primary responsibility for them, then any conceptual collapse will be in the reverse. *Horrendous* moral evils join natural evils in their resistance to finding plausible candidates for primary moral responsibility in non-divine agents.

In Part II, I introduced and defended Non-Identity Theodicy. Non-Identity Theodicy shares with Type A Theodicy the belief that ultimate responsibility must remain with God. God is too powerful, knowledgeable, and resourceful for theodicy to find its success in minimizing the causal impact of divine agency. Non-Identity Theodicy also shares Type D Theodicy's aversion to seeking justification in *pure* benefits. Type D Theodicy proposes the natural alternative justification of *harm-averting* benefits. But Non-Identity Theodicy falls outside the taxonomy I constructed in Part I by seeking justification in the goods of human persons themselves rather than in benefits of any sort, in the very objects of divine love rather than in the bettering of those objects.

Unlike most theodicies, Non-Identity Theodicy does not suggest that evil and suffering (or the possibility of evil and suffering) allows those who exist to live more valuable or more meaningful lives than the lives they would have lived without evil and suffering. Rather, it suggests that without evil and suffering those who exist could not have lived at all. The primary justificatory good proposed by Non-Identity Theodicy is not some benefit to life, but life itself; it is not some form of human existence, but human persons in their own right. Human persons are thereby treated not as means to something else but as ends in themselves.

In this way, Non-Identity Theodicy suggests that considerations of personal identity have intriguing and almost completely unappreciated bearing on theodicy. Considerations of personal identity both motivate God to create this universe (the universe in which he can get the specific community of persons—or the specific types of beings—he is moved to love) and counter the reasons against doing so (because the good of a worthwhile human life has unique justificatory force).

This new emphasis corrects for several of the misemphases I have been enumerating. For instance, Non-Identity Theodicy eschews contemporary theodicy's focus on greater and generic goods and instead focuses its attention on particular

228 NON-IDENTITY THEODICY

goods in the forms of particular individuals, relationships, and being-types loved for their own sakes. In the same breath, it pays tribute to the ethical importance of character by conceiving of God first and foremost not as a creator of goods but as a lover of persons.

Moreover, a non-identity approach to theodicy surfaces additional lopsidedness in contemporary theodicy, perhaps the most significant aspect of which being an overemphasis on free will. All of the theodicies considered in this project have relied heavily on libertarian free will, either as essential to the goods for which evil is allowed by God or to shift blame for evil away from God. For Hick, God creates human persons at an epistemic distance from himself so that they will have the "genuine freedom" either "to acknowledge and worship God" or "to doubt the reality of God." Human persons are thereby positioned to attain the great good of "coming freely to know and love their Maker."[4] Likewise, the exercise of meaningful free will and our being of use in creating opportunities for others to exercise meaningful free will are at the heart of Swinburne's theodicy. Libertarian sins in need of atonement take center stage for Plantinga. Van Inwagen and Stump attempt to shift blame by suggesting that God cannot ensure the great goods of free love or willed union, respectively, with human persons without risking that those persons will use their free will to rebel and cause suffering.

Swinburne seems to speak on behalf of many contemporary theodicists in suggesting that "[i]t would...be very difficult to construct a satisfactory theodicy which did not rely on the doctrine of human free will"[5] and that "[t]he central core of any theodicy must...be the 'free-will defence.'"[6] William Hasker is in agreement: "Theological determinism is emphatically rejected, not least because of the difficulty—the insuperable difficulty, as I believe—it creates for any attempt to deal constructively with the problem of evil."[7] And Eleonore Stump adds her affirmation: "Christians who reject a belief in free will...will also reject any attempt at a solution to the problem of evil."[8]

Non-Identity Theodicy is distinct in being available to the theist regardless of her assumptions about the existence and nature of free will. In Chapter 6, I advanced two versions of Non-identity Theodicy—one in which God aims for specific individuals and one in which he aims more broadly for individuals of a specific being-type. The first of these versions not only does not rely on libertarian free will but—due to the level of control necessary for God to aim for individual persons—fits most naturally in a deterministic framework. If this approach to theodicy has anywhere near the promise I have suggested it has, this calls into serious question the widespread supposed wedlock of theodicy with libertarianism.

---

[4] Hick, "An Irenaean Theodicy" (2001), 43.
[5] Swinburne, *Providence and the Problem of Evil*, 241.
[6] Richard Swinburne, *Is There a God?*, revised edition (Oxford: Oxford University Press, 2010), 86.
[7] William Hasker, *The Triumph of God over Evil*, 93.      [8] Stump, "The Problem of Evil," 398.

This loosing of theodicy from libertarian free will also guards against over-emphasis in the form of extreme anthropocentrism. As Robert Adams suggests, "The perspective of omniscience must be less bound to the human than ours, and the creator of a universe of which humanity occupies so small a part may be presumed interested in other things in it besides us."[9] Unlike free-will-based theodicies, Non-Identity Theodicy can, without theoretical complication, spread its net of divine interest as widely as it likes. Whereas plausibly only human persons (among earthly beings) have the sort of significant libertarian free will that takes central place in most theodicies, fairly narrow origin constraints on identity are as plausible for stars, mountains, plants, and animals as they are for human persons.

Animal suffering, therefore, including any pre-human animal suffering, can be accounted for not only by the particular human persons it allows to exist, but also by the particular animals God desires to exist. Returning to the three conditions of Non-Identity Theodicy, animal suffering affects which human persons come to exist (condition (1)), but it also affects which animals come to exist. Even if there is a special form of love God can share with human persons as free beings (condition (3)), God nevertheless has affection for animals and creates them out of a desire to appreciate and bestow value upon them.

It is a disputed point among Christians and other theists whether the animals that exist in the present age will partake in an afterlife, but it is plausibly within the vast resources of omnipotence for God to give each animal a life worth living (or even very worth living) on the whole (condition (2)). One may object that some animals perish from starvation or other forms of suffering very early in life. However, even the short lives of these animals will have an effect on the movement of matter and therefore, over time, on which humans come to exist. Perhaps it is a great good *for an animal* if that animal is used by God for his purpose of bringing human persons into existence. But if some animals have earthly lives that are not worth living, God can ensure that they exist after death in a long enough and good enough state for condition (2) to be satisfied.

This suggests that with no more than slight amendments, the three conditions of Non-Identity Theodicy can account plausibly for animal suffering. If you believe that animals can enjoy an afterlife, then the conditions of Non-Identity Theodicy can account for animal suffering even without making reference to human persons (or any other non-divine beings, such as angels). This may be attractive to anyone concerned for animals to be treated as ends in themselves (as opposed to mere means to benefit others) in the context of theodicy.

I have judged Non-Identity Theodicy to be the most promising of the contemporary theodicies I have considered. I therefore commend it to further consideration. Though perhaps it is worth noting, in closing, that Non-Identity Theodicy

---

[9]  Adams, *Finite and Infinite Goods*, 148.

is available to the theist regardless of her appraisal of most other theodicies. Moreover, my rejection of Types A, B, C, and D Theodicy is not a dismissal of many of the insights contained therein. Even if the goods cited in these theodicies cannot play the primary justificatory role they have been assigned, many of the resources of these theodicies can be re-appropriated to Non-Identity Theodicy as partial supplementary justifications.[10]

Something similar is true of many complex decisions. To note just one of countless examples, parents may take into consideration the desire of their children for another sibling when deciding whether to adopt a child. Their current children's desire would not in most cases be sufficient justification for adopting, but it could very well be one of a number of reasons for adopting that taken together are sufficient.

Non-Identity Theodicy suggests that the goodness of God can be defended because God creates and sustains the universe out of a desire to love and offer eternal life to people who otherwise could not have existed. But perhaps it is also true, as some versions of free-will-based theodicies suggest, that God permits rather than causes suffering and that God has greater moral reason not to cause suffering than not to permit it. Or perhaps greater-goods theodicists are correct that God only allows evil to occur when it serves greater goods such as the opportunity to freely form our character and to be of help to others.

More specifically, Hick is surely right that the sort of soul-making possible in a world like ours is a very good thing. Swinburne is surely right that we are apt to be ignorant of many and much of the webs of meaning that our lives contribute to, and therefore to underestimate and undervalue the good of being of use. I believe Plantinga is right that atonement is a great good, and perhaps he is right that atonement is more fitting in a world of serious sin and suffering. Stump and van Inwagen are right that at least sometimes *horrendous* suffering can humble us and incline us to seek contiguity with God, and perhaps Marilyn Adams is right that God has resources to imbue even *horrendous* suffering with personal meaning in the end.[11]

More good reasons for performing an action generally make it more likely that one has morally sufficient reason for performing that action. If you think the reasons proffered by Non-Identity Theodicy are sufficient to justify God's allowance of suffering, then the cumulative reason provided by multiple theodicies may provide God with overdetermined justification. If you think the reasons recommended by Non-Identity Theodicy are morally significant but not sufficient, they may nevertheless contribute to a successful cumulative case theodicy.

---

[10] Swinburne makes a similar recognition when he writes that "[b]ad states often serve many good purposes, none of which by itself may give God enough reason for allowing the bad state to occur but together they may do so" (*Providence and the Problem of Evil*, 162). See also 238.

[11] It can be debated whether Marilyn Adams has a theodicy because she attempts to offer only partial rather than sufficient reasons why God allows the evil he allows.

Thinking that no individual theodicy is sufficient to maintain the goodness of God in the face of evil and suffering is not sufficient to defeat the project of theodicy, for it would not be at all surprising if an infinitely wise and omniscient God had more than one reason for a decision as complex and significant as which universe to create and sustain.

I argued in Chapter 7 that typical cases of voluntary procreation only have a claim to moral permissibility because they are cases of non-identity—that is, because the person who comes to exist would not have existed otherwise. Nevertheless, the better the life you can give to the one you procreate, the less controversial the morality of the procreation. Likewise, the resources of contemporary theodicy can be re-appropriated as supplementing divine justification even if they are not the sufficient justifications they are often posited to be. Even if only the good of God-given human life has a plausible claim to being sufficiently justificatory as a theodicy for a *horror*-ridden world, the better that life is, the more plausible its claim. Incorporated in this way into Non-Identity Theodicy, the goods posited by other theodicies as benefits act as additional reasons in support of Non-Identity Theodicy's main contention—that the good of a God-given human life has superlative value and justificatory force.[12]

This contention finds its closest analogy in human procreation, where many parents give the gift of life despite knowing full well that even the most fortunate of human lives will include serious suffering. I have suggested that sustained reflection on this analogy yields the following conclusion: If you think it would be in principle evil to create people into a world that you know will produce serious suffering in their lives, you not only will need to call God evil; you also will need to call evil anyone who decides to have a child.

Non-Identity Theodicy suggests that the problem of evil may be too quick to hold God to a standard we don't hold ourselves to. A good parent is not the one who never allows suffering in a child's life; a good parent—whether human or divine—is the one who creates children out of love, who is committed to suffering alongside those children, and who is willing to make whatever personal sacrifices necessary to ensure that one day suffering can be overcome.

---

[12] Although there is not space to discuss this further in this book, considerations of non-identity can also challenge objections to theism in the forms of divine hiddenness and divine favoritism. If those to whom God seems hidden or to whom God has revealed himself less clearly than to others would not have existed had they not been born into the epistemic conditions they were in fact born into, then this raises questions about whether—so long as their lives are worth living overall—they have been treated unfairly or unlovingly by being born as such.

# Bibliography

Adams, Marilyn McCord. "Horrendous Evils and the Goodness of God." *Proceedings of the Aristotelian Society*, supplementary vol. 63 (1989): 297–310. Reprinted in *Philosophy of Religion: The Big Questions*, edited by Eleonore Stump and Michael J. Murray, 250–7. Oxford: Blackwell Publishers Ltd, 1999.

Adams, Marilyn McCord. "Love of Learning, Reality of God." In *God and the Philosophers: The Reconciliation of Faith and Reason*, edited by Thomas V. Morris, 137–61. Oxford: Oxford University Press, 1994.

Adams, Marilyn McCord. *Horrendous Evils and the Goodness of God*. Ithaca and London: Cornell University Press, 1999.

Adams, Marilyn McCord. Afterword to *Encountering Evil*, edited by Stephen T. Davis, 191–203. Louisville and London: John Knox Press, 2001.

Adams, Marilyn McCord. *Christ and Horrors: The Coherence of Christology*. Cambridge: Cambridge University Press, 2006.

Adams, Marilyn McCord, and Robert Merrihew Adams, eds. *The Problem of Evil*. Oxford: Oxford University Press, 1990.

Adams, Robert Merrihew. "Must God Create the Best?" *The Philosophical Review* 81.3 (1972): 317–32. Reprinted in Robert Merrihew Adams, *The Virtue of Faith and Other Essays in Philosophical Theology*, 51–64. Oxford: Oxford University Press, 1987.

Adams, Robert Merrihew. "Theories of Actuality." *Noûs* 8 (1974): 211–31.

Adams, Robert Merrihew. "Primitive Thisness and Primitive Identity." *Journal of Philosophy* 76 (1979): 5–26.

Adams, Robert Merrihew. "Actualism and Thisness." *Synthese* 49 (1981): 3–41.

Adams, Robert Merrihew. "Existence, Self-Interest, and the Problem of Evil." In *The Virtue of Faith and Other Essays in Philosophical Theology*, 65–76. Oxford: Oxford University Press, 1987.

Adams, Robert Merrihew. *The Virtue of Faith and Other Essays in Philosophical Theology*. Oxford: Oxford University Press, 1987.

Adams, Robert Merrihew. "Should Ethics Be More Impersonal? A Critical Notice of Derek Parfit, *Reasons and Persons*." *The Philosophical Review* 98.4 (1989): 439–84.

Adams, Robert Merrihew. "Middle Knowledge and the Problem of Evil." In *The Problem of Evil*, edited by Marilyn McCord Adams and Robert Merrihew Adams, 110–25. Oxford: Oxford University Press, 1990.

Adams, Robert Merrihew. *Finite and Infinite Goods*. Oxford: Oxford University Press, 2002.

Adams, Robert Merrihew. "Love and the Problem of Evil." *Philosophia* 34.3 (2006): 243–51.

Anscombe, G. E. M. "Modern Moral Philosophy." *Philosophy* 33.124 (1958): 1–19.

Augustine. *De Genesi ad litteram*. New York: Paulist Press, 1982.

Augustine. *De libero arbitrio*. In *On the Free Choice of the Will, on Grace and Free Choice, and Other Writings*, translated and edited by Peter King. Cambridge: Cambridge University Press, 2010.

Benatar, David. "Why It Is Better Never to Come into Existence." *American Philosophical Quarterly* 34.3 (1997): 345–55.

Benatar, David. *Better Never to Have Been: The Harm of Coming into Existence*. Oxford: Oxford University Press, 2006.

Black, Max. "The Identity of Indiscernibles." *Mind* 61 (1952): 153–64.

Boër, Steven E. "The Irrelevance of the Free Will Defence." *Analysis* 38.2 (1978): 110–12.

Broome, John. "Goodness Is Reducible to Betterness: The Evil of Death Is the Value of Life." In *The Good and the Economical: Ethical Choices in Economics and Management*, edited by Peter Koslowski and Yuichi Shionoya, 70–84. Berlin: Springer-Verlag, 1993.

Chisholm, Roderick M. "The Defeat of Good and Evil." *Proceedings and Addresses of the American Philosophical Association* 42 (1969): 21–38. Reprinted in revised form in *The Problem of Evil*, edited by Marilyn McCord Adams and Robert Merrihew Adams, 53–68. New York: Oxford University Press, 1990.

Davis, Stephen T. "Critique of Hick's 'An Irenaean Theodicy.'" In *Encountering Evil*, edited by Stephen T. Davis, 58–61. Edinburgh: John Knox Press, 1981.

Davis, Stephen T., ed. *Encountering Evil: Live Options in Theodicy.* Edinburgh: John Knox Press, 1981.

Davis, Stephen T., ed. *Encountering Evil.* New edition. Louisville and London: John Knox Press, 2001.

Draper, Paul. "Pain and Pleasure: An Evidential Problem for Theists." In *The Evidential Argument From Evil*, edited by Daniel Howard-Snyder, 12–29. Bloomington and Indianapolis: Indiana University Press, 1996.

Dworkin, Ronald. *Life's Dominion: An Argument About Abortion, Euthanasia, and Individual Freedom.* New York: Knopf, 1993.

Farrer, Austin. *Love Almighty and Ills Unlimited.* London: Collins, 1966.

Feinberg, Joel. *Harm to Others.* New York: Oxford University Press, 1984.

Feinberg, Joel. "Wrongful Life and the Counterfactual Element in Harming." *Social Philosophy and Policy* 4.1 (1986): 145–78. Reprinted in Joel Feinberg, *Freedom and Fulfillment: Philosophical Essays*, 3–37. Princeton: Princeton University Press, 1992.

Forbes, Graeme. *The Metaphysics of Possibility.* Oxford: Oxford University Press, 1985.

Freddoso, Alfred. J. "Comment on Van Inwagen's 'The Place of Chance in a World Sustained by God.'" Unpublished work. (Notre Dame, 1987). Accessed August 23, 2011. http://www.nd.edu/~afreddos/papers/chance.htm.

Gale, Richard. "R. M. Adams's Theodicy of Grace." *Philo: A Journal of Philosophy* 1 (1998): 36–44.

Goodwin, Brian. *How the Leopard Changed Its Spots: The Evolution of Complexity.* Princeton: Princeton University Press, 2001.

Gunkel, Hermann. *Genesis.* Macon, Georgia: Mercer University Press, 1997.

Hallo, William W. and K. Lawson Younger (eds.), *The Context of Scripture: Canonical Compositions from the Biblical World*, vol. 1. Leiden and New York: Brill, 1997.

Hanser, Matthew. "Harming Future People." *Philosophy and Public Affairs* 19.1 (1990): 47–70.

Hanser, Matthew. "The Metaphysics of Harm." *Philosophy and Phenomenological Research* 77.2 (2008): 421–50.

Harman, Elizabeth. "Can We Harm and Benefit in Creating?" *Philosophical Perspectives* 18, *Ethics* (2004): 89–113.

Hasker, William. *Providence, Evil and the Openness of God.* London: Routledge, 2004.

Hasker, William. "D. Z. Phillips' Problems with Evil and with God." *International Journal for Philosophy of Religion* 61.3 (2007): 151–60.

Hasker, William. *The Triumph of God Over Evil: Theodicy for a World of Suffering.* Downers Grove, Illinois: IVP Academic, 2008.

Hick, John. *Evil and the God of Love.* 2nd ed. London and Basingstoke: The Macmillan Press, 1977.

Hick, John. "An Irenaean Theodicy." In *Encountering Evil*, edited by Stephen T. Davis, 39–52. Edinburgh: John Knox Press, 1981.

Hitchcock, Christopher. "Three Concepts of Causation." *Philosophy Compass* 2.3 (2007): 508–16.

Holtug, Nils. "On the Value of Coming into Existence." *The Journal of Ethics* 5.4 (2001): 361–84.

Howard-Snyder, Daniel, ed. *The Evidential Argument from Evil*. Bloomington: Indiana University Press, 1996.

Howard-Snyder, Daniel. Introduction to *The Evidential Argument from Evil*, edited by Daniel Howard-Snyder, xi–xx. Bloomington and Indianapolis: Indiana University Press, 1996.

Howard-Snyder, Frances and Daniel. Review of *God, Knowledge and Mystery: Essays in Philosophical Theology*, by Peter van Inwagen. *Faith and Philosophy* 16.1 (1999): 126–34.

Hudson, Hud. *The Fall and Hypertime*. Oxford: Oxford University Press, 2014.

Julian of Norwich. *Revelations of Divine Love*. Translated by Clifton Wolters. London: Penguin Books, 1966.

Kahane, Guy. "History and Persons." *Philosophy and Phenomenological Research* 99.1 (2019): 162–87.

Kavka, Gregory S. "The Paradox of Future Individuals." *Philosophy and Public Affairs* 11.2 (1982): 93–112.

Kelly, John Norman Davidson. *Early Christian Doctrines*, 5th ed. London and New York: Continuum, 1977.

Leftow, Brian. "No best world: creaturely freedom." *Religious Studies* 41.3 (2005): 269–85.

Leftow, Brian. "No best world: moral luck." *Religious Studies* 41.2 (2005): 165–81.

Leibniz, Gottfried Wilhelm. "The Confessions of a Philosopher." In *G.W. Leibniz, Confessio philosophi: Papers Concerning the Problem of Evil, 1671–1678*, edited by Robert C. Sleigh Jr., 26–109. New Haven and London: Yale University Press, 2005.

Leibniz, Gottfried Wilhelm. *Theodicy: Essays on the Goodness of God, the Freedom of Man and the Origin of Evil*. New York: Cosimo, Inc., 2009.

Lennon, Thomas M. and Michael Hickson, "Pierre Bayle." *The Stanford Encyclopedia of Philosophy* (Spring 2009 Edition). Accessed August 23, 2011. http://plato.stanford.edu/entries/bayle/.

Lewis, David. "Divine Evil." (Published posthumously with Philip Kitcher.) In *Philosophers Without Gods: Meditations on Atheism and the Secular Life*, edited by Louis M. Antony, 231–42. Oxford, Oxford University Press, 2007.

Lovejoy, Arthur O., *The Great Chain of Being*. Cambridge, Massachusetts and London: Harvard University Press, 1936.

Mackie, J. L. "Evil and Omnipotence." In *The Problem of Evil*, edited by Marilyn McCord Adams and Robert Merrihew Adams, 25–37. New York: Oxford University Press, 1990.

Mawson, Tim. "The Problem of Evil and Moral Indifference." *Religious Studies* 35.3 (1999): 323–45.

Murray, Michael J. *Nature Red in Tooth and Claw: Theism and the Problem of Animal Suffering*. Oxford: Oxford University Press, 2008.

Nietzsche, Friedrich, and Walter Kaufmann. *The Birth of Tragedy and the Case of Wagner*. New York: Vintage Books, 1967.

Oderberg, David. *Real Essentialism*. New York: Routledge, 2007.

Parfit, Derek. "Future Generations: Further Problems." *Philosophy and Public Affairs* 11.2 (1982): 113–72.

Parfit, Derek. "Comments." *Ethics* 96.4 (1986): 832–72.

Parfit, Derek. *Reasons and Persons*. Oxford: Oxford University Press, 1991.

Peacocke, Arthur. *Theology for a Scientific Age: Being and Becoming—Natural, Divine and Human*, enlarged ed. London: SCM Press Ltd, 1993.

Pike, Nelson. "Hume on Evil." In *The Problem of Evil*, edited by Marilyn McCord Adams and Robert Merrihew Adams, 38–52. New York: Oxford University Press, 1990.

Plantinga, Alvin. *God, Freedom, and Evil*. New York: Harper and Row, 1974.

Plantinga, Alvin. *The Nature of Necessity*. Oxford: Clarendon Press, 1974.

Plantinga, Alvin. "Self-Profile." In *Alvin Plantinga*, edited by James E. Tomberlin and Peter van Inwagen, 3–97. Dordrecht, Holland: D. Reidel Publishing, 1985.

Plantinga, Alvin. "Epistemic Probability and Evil." In *The Evidential Argument from Evil*, edited by Daniel Howard-Snyder, 69–96. Bloomington: Indiana University Press, 1996.

Plantinga, Alvin. "Supralapsarianism, or 'O Felix Culpa.'" In *Christian Faith and the Problem of Evil*, edited by Peter van Inwagen, 1–25. Grand Rapids: Wm. B. Eerdmans Publishing Co, 2004.

Plantinga, Alvin. *Where the Conflict Really Lies: Science, Religion, and Naturalism*. Oxford: Oxford University Press, 2011.

Plantinga, Alvin. "Historical Adam: One Possible Scenario." *Think Christian* (blog). Accessed February 14, 2013. http://thinkchristian.reframemedia.com/historical-adam-one-possible-scenario.

Polkinghorne, John. "Understanding the Universe." *Annals of the New York Academy of Sciences* 950 (2001): 175–82.

*Protocol Additional to the Geneva Conventions of 12 August 1949. Protocol I*, Art. 86.2. (1977).

Pruss, Alexander and Joshua Rasmussen. *Necessary Existence*. Oxford: Oxford University Press, 2018.

Quine, W. V. "Worlds Away." *The Journal of Philosophy* 73.22 (1976): 859–63.

Quinn, Warren S. "Actions, Intentions, and Consequences: the Doctrine of Doing and Allowing." *The Philosophical Review* 98.3 (1989): 287–312.

Quinn, Warren S. "Actions, Intentions, and Consequences: the Doctrine of Double Effect." *Philosophy and Public Affairs* 18.4 (1989): 334–51.

Rescher, Nicholas. *Luck: The Brilliant Randomness of Everyday Life*. New York: Farrar, Straus and Giroux, 1995.

Rowe, William L. "The Problem of Evil and Some Varieties of Atheism." *American Philosophical Quarterly* 16.4 (1979): 335–41. Reprinted in *The Problem of Evil*, edited by Marilyn McCord Adams and Robert Merrihew Adams, 126–37. New York: Oxford University Press, 1990.

Rowe, William L. "Ruminations about Evil." *Philosophical Perspectives* 5 (1991): 69–88.

Rowe, William L. "Friendly Atheism, Skeptical Theism, and the Problem of Evil." *International Journal for Philosophy of Religion* 59.2 (2006): 79–92.

Shiffrin, Seana Valentine. "Wrongful Life, Procreative Responsibility, and the Significance of Harm." *Legal Theory* 5 (1999): 117–48.

Shiffrin, Seana Valentine. "Harm and Its Moral Significance." *Legal Theory* 18.3 (2012): 357–98.

Smith, Quentin. "An Atheological Argument from Evil Natural Laws." *International Journal for Philosophy of Religion* 29.3 (1991): 159–74.

Sontag, Frederick. "Critique of Hick's 'An Irenaean Theodicy.'" In *Encountering Evil*, edited by Stephen T. Davis, 55–8. Edinburgh: John Knox Press, 1981.

Southgate, Christopher. *The Groaning of Creation: God, Evolution, and the Problem of Evil*. Louisville: Westminster John Knox Press, 2008.

Statman, Daniel. Introduction to *Moral Luck*, edited by Daniel Statman, 1–34. Albany: State University of New York Press, 1993.

Stocker, Michael. "The Schizophrenia of Modern Ethical Theories." *The Journal of Philosophy* 73.14, On Motives and Morals (1976): 453–66.

Stout, Jeffrey. "The Sacred Made Visible." The third lecture in "A Light That Shines in the Darkness: Evil, Egotism, and the Sacred in Film," Stone Lectures, Princeton Theological Seminary, 2007.

Stump, Eleonore. "Knowledge, Freedom and the Problem of Evil." *International Journal for Philosophy of Religion.* 14.1 (1983): 49–58.

Stump, Eleonore. "The Problem of Evil." *Faith and Philosophy* 2.4 (1985): 392–423.

Stump, Eleonore. "Suffering for Redemption: A Reply to Smith." *Faith and Philosophy* 2.4 (1985): 430–5.

Stump, Eleonore. "Sanctification, Hardening of the Heart, and Frankfurt's Concept of Free Will." *The Journal of Philosophy* 85.8 (1988): 395–420.

Stump, Eleonore. "The Mirror of Evil." In *God and the Philosophers: The Reconciliation of Faith and Reason,* edited by Thomas V. Morris, 235–47. Oxford: Oxford University Press, 1994.

Stump, Eleonore. "Saadya Gaon and the Problem of Evil." *Faith and Philosophy* 14.4 (1997): 523–49.

Stump, Eleonore. *Aquinas.* London: Routledge, 2003.

Stump, Eleonore. *Wandering in Darkness: Narrative and the Problem of Suffering.* Oxford: Oxford University Press, 2010.

Swinburne, Richard. *Responsibility and Atonement.* Oxford: Oxford University Press, 1989.

Swinburne, Richard. *The Existence of God.* 2d ed. Oxford: Oxford University Press, 1991.

Swinburne, Richard. "Some Major Strands of Theodicy." In *The Evidential Argument From Evil,* edited by Daniel Howard-Snyder, 30–48. Bloomington and Indianapolis: Indiana University Press, 1996.

Swinburne, Richard. *Providence and the Problem of Evil.* Oxford: Oxford University Press, 1998.

Tennant, Frederick Robert. *The Origin and Propagation of Sin.* 2d ed. Cambridge: Cambridge University Press, 1906.

*Universal Declaration of Human Rights.* Geneva: United Nations, Department of Public Information, 2007. Accessed August 25, 2011. http://www.un.org/en/documents/udhr/. First adopted by the United Nations General Assembly on December 10, 1948.

Van Inwagen, Peter. "The Possibility of Resurrection." *International Journal for Philosophy of Religion* 9.2 (1978): 114–21.

Van Inwagen, Peter. "The Place of Chance in a World Sustained by God." In *Divine and Human Action: Essays in the Metaphysics of Theism,* edited by Thomas V. Morris, 211–35. Ithaca: Cornell University Press, 1988. Reprinted in Peter van Inwagen, *God, Knowledge, and Mystery: Essays in Philosophical Theology,* 42–65. Ithaca: Cornell University Press, 1995.

Van Inwagen, Peter. "Genesis and Evolution." In *God, Knowledge, and Mystery: Essays in Philosophical Theology,* 128–62. Ithaca: Cornell University Press, 1995. Reprinted from *Reasoned Faith,* edited by Eleonore Stump, 93–127. Ithaca: Cornell University Press, 1993.

Van Inwagen, Peter. "Doubts About Darwinism." In *Darwinism: Science or Philosophy?,* edited by Jon Buell and Virginia Hearn, 177–91. Richardson, TX: Foundation for Thought and Ethics, 1994.

Van Inwagen, Peter. "The Magnitude, Duration, and Distribution of Evil: A Theodicy." *Philosophical Topics* 16.2 (1988): 161–87. Reprinted in Peter van Inwagen, *God, Knowledge and Mystery: Essays in Philosophical Theology,* 96–122. Ithaca: Cornell University Press, 1995.

Van Inwagen, Peter. "Non Est Hick." In *The Rationality of Belief and the Plurality of Faith: Essays in Honor of William P. Alston*, edited by Thomas D. Senor, 216–41. Ithaca: Cornell University Press, 1995. Reprinted in Peter van Inwagen, *God, Knowledge and Mystery: Essays in Philosophical Theology*. Ithaca: Cornell University Press, 1995.

Van Inwagen, Peter. "The Problem of Evil, the Problem of Air, and the Problem of Silence." *Philosophical Perspectives* 5, Philosophy of Religion, (1991): 135–65. Reprinted in Peter van Inwagen, *God, Knowledge, and Mystery: Essays in Philosophical Theology*, 66–95. Ithaca and London: Cornell University Press, 1995.

Van Inwagen, Peter. "The Argument from Evil." In *Christian Faith and the Problem of Evil*, edited by Peter van Inwagen, 55–73. Grand Rapids: Wm. B. Eerdmans Publishing Co, 2004.

Van Inwagen, Peter. "The Problem of Evil." In *The Oxford Handbook of Philosophy of Religion*, edited by William Wainwright, 188–219. Oxford: Oxford University Press, 2005.

Van Inwagen, Peter. *The Problem of Evil*. Oxford: Oxford University Press, 2006.

Vitale, Vince. Review of *Wandering in Darkness: Narrative and the Problem of Suffering*, by Eleonore Stump. *Mind* 122.488 (2013): 1193–201.

Vitale, Vince. "Non-Identity Theodicy." *Philosophia Christi* 19.2 (2017): 269–90.

Ward, Keith. *God, Faith, and the New Millenium: Christian Belief in an Age of Science*. Oxford: Oneworld Publications, 1998.

Ward, Keith. *Religion and Human Nature*. Oxford: Oxford University Press, 1998.

Weil, Simone. "The Love of God and Affliction." In Simone Weil, *On Science, Necessity, and the Love of God*, edited by Richard Rees, 170–98. London: Oxford University Press, 1968.

Weil, Simone. "The Cross." In Simone Weil, *Gravity and Grace*, edited by Gustave Thibon, 87–91. London and New York: Routledge, 2002.

Westermann, Claus. *Genesis 1–11: A Continental Commentary*. Minneapolis: Fortress Press, 1994.

Williams, Bernard. *Moral Luck*. Cambridge: Cambridge University Press, 1981.

Williams, Norman Powell. *The Ideas of the Fall and of Original Sin*. New York: Longmans, Green and Co. Ltd., 1927.

Woodward, James. "The Non-Identity Problem." *Ethics* 96.4 (1986): 804–31.

Woodward, James. "Reply to Parfit." *Ethics* 97.4 (1987): 800–16.

Wykstra, Stephen J. "The Humean Obstacle to Evidential Arguments from Suffering: On Avoiding the Evils of 'Appearance.'" *International Journal for Philosophy of Religion* 16.2 (1984): 73–93. Reprinted in *The Problem of Evil*, edited by Marilyn McCord Adams and Robert Merrihew Adams, 138–60. Oxford: Oxford University Press, 1990.

Wynn, Mark. *God and Goodness: A Natural Theological Perspective*. London: Routledge, 1999.

# Index

The manufacturer's authorised representative in the EU for product
safety is Oxford University Press España S.A. of El Parque Empresarial
San Fernando de Henares, Avenida de Castilla, 2 - 28830 Madrid
(www.oup.es/en or product.safety@oup.com). OUP España S.A. also acts
as importer into Spain of products made by the manufacturer.
Printed and bound by CPI Group (UK) Ltd, Croydon, CR0 4YY

22/01/2025

01824116-0004